Vene
Civilis

by

Will Black

First published 2018
by Frontline Noir, an imprint of Books Noir

Text copyright © 2018 Will Black

Print edition ISBN: 978 1 904684 72 5

A CIP record for this book is available from the British Library

1 2 3 4 5 6 7 8 9 10

Typeset in Garamond by Park Productions

*This book is dedicated to my grandmother,
whose 16th birthday was ruined
by Hitler, and to my sister.*

Contents

Introduction   vii

Chapter 1 – Paradoxes of 'civilisation'   1

Chapter 2 – Scientific racism, evolutionism
    and savage theories   19

Chapter 3 – Voyeurs, radicals, spies and the
    war on freedom   27

Chapter 4 – Attempts at liberation: Part 1   46

Chapter 5 – Attempts at liberation: Part 2   56

Chapter 6 – Globalisation, neoliberalism
    and predation   73

Chapter 7 – When the veneer is torn away   104

Chapter 8 – When the veneer erodes in a
    key strategic centre   120

Chapter 9 – From far-right to 'alt-right'   155

Chapter 10 – Paradoxes of technology   205

Conclusion   243

References   265
Also by Will Black   268

Introduction

Growing up in a time of exciting technical and creative innovation, with huge breakthroughs in the capacities of computers, music, film, comedy and – it seemed – politics, there was a sense of an evolution to a brighter and better world. However, though games got better, the world got brighter, music got more intense and comedy got better at puncturing the pomposity of disastrous politicians, there was always the lurking sense of dread that it could all unravel – that the progress of our age could be torn away and we could fall back to an age of darkness. Brutal and barren times before even black and white television.

One particular memory I have that relates to the name of this book and troubling concerns I have had lurking beneath the surface, like a dark swirling current, occurred in an otherwise idyllic week with my sister and grandparents. My grandparents had moved from London to the Essex coast and my sister and I used to stay for some of each of our school holidays. In the summer, we would go to the beach, visit piers, go skating, venture into a hall of mirrors, gamble away 2p pieces in amusement arcades and take part in a myriad of other fun things – exciting but essentially safe things.

One day, however, when I was maybe six or seven, we were in Southend. Not far from the longest pier in the world, flashing lights of the arcades and fair rides, we saw something that took us a long way from the excitement of the era. The ship was called the Golden Hind and outside the replica galleon was a man secured to a table, with a massive swinging blade above him going back and forth in a terrifying arc. The perception was that the blade was lowering as I'm pretty sure there was blood on his chest or head from where the blade had apparently already begun to cut his skin.

I remember my sister and I being both scared and captivated by this awful predicament, even though we understood that the man was just a dummy. The man and the blade on the pendulum represented just the introduction to a torture chamber inside the ship. Perhaps the relative dinginess within the ship in contrast to the bright sunny seaside world outside amplified the sense of doom and feeling of being transformed to an earlier age where it was acceptable to attach people to tables and lower blades onto them.

Other torture chamber 'wonders', taking us underneath the veneer of that bright day and glittering time, included thumbscrews, a contraption that sticks a nail through someone's tongue and a 'lead boot' into which molten metal would be poured to cook somebody's foot. The models all looked suitably anguished and I can remember sharing some of their anguish in the pit of my stomach.

I should say though that, like most children, we were fascinated by the torture ship and my grandparents were certainly by no means sadistic. I expect we asked many times to go on the ship before it was allowed. At the time, it felt as though the artefacts were from a time that would never come again. However, from time to time, I worried that something could happen that would tear away our bright world and allow the sort of people who poured molten metal onto feet or tortured others with massive blades to rule.

Overall though, the trajectory seemed bright. Yes, there were wars, but these seemed remote and a remnant of the past. In Britain, we had a television programme called *Tomorrow's World*, which each week gave us glimpses of a life we fully expected to live in, full of innovation, fun and ease. With every development in music a different section of the youth could finally feel that their time had come, and with each exciting new film director it seemed, for a while, that someone was finally showing us a world we recognised and wanted to live in.

When, as children, we looked at photos from what seemed like long ago, even 15 or 20 years ago, the clothes and hairstyles looked funny. Those people in the past simply didn't get things, they were strange semi-evolved creatures – almost like cavemen. The world hadn't quite got there yet when those primitive pictures were taken. The past was a world of simple people with ridiculous clothes, serious expressions and little or no grasp of the modern realities I was immersed in. These were not modern people.

I could understand how these black and white or sepia people were necessary to have enabled us in the *real* world of now to exist, but they and their concerns were almost as remote as the man in the glass case facing the pendulum blade. The still world of the past, where things don't change as often as the pop charts, troubled me almost as much as the torture ship came to do. A world of relentless stagnation and tradition was not as gory as a descending blade, but the olden days did seem tortuously slow and mundane. They didn't represent where I wanted to be. I was part of the age of rapid change, where there were new adventures all the time, and I felt sorry for the people of the past.

Nevertheless, this simplistic perception of a world progressing as though up a shiny silver escalator in an ever-transforming department store sometimes flickered for me and was challenged – as was no doubt the case for most readers. For example, in the classic old 20th century sci-fi film *The Matrix*, 'reality' wobbled from time to time. Once you had seen it, it became hard to ignore.

With pesky intrusions such as recessions, terrorist attacks, murder sprees, elections of people who seemed idiotic and horrible turns in music and fashion, my linear evolutionist model of progress was shaken. As I became a bit older, the perception that all that was good could be violently swept away grew and grew. Not only were there nuclear missiles apparently aiming at all our heads, but it did appear that eras of torture and tyrants were not as far behind us as I had imagined. I enjoyed the life I was in enough to realise that it was vulnerable and the veneer of civilisation was a lot thinner than I would have liked. Perhaps the value I placed on progress made any threat to it seem more apocalyptic.

To complicate matters, as we lunged towards more and more vivid futures, grabbing at each new development, people were constantly banging on about the past – misty-eyed old people talking about eras when you could leave your front door open and gangsters were men of honour, or even older people who seemed to cherish a time when bombs rained from the skies as you sat in freezing outside toilets, having eaten just bread and dripping all week.

Though I felt nostalgic about places I'd been, video games I'd played or music I'd heard when I was small, I found nostalgic people tedious and troubling. It may be that life was grey for almost all of the past, as old films and photos suggested, but it wasn't grey *now* and I didn't want to be dragged back into their grey world, where even wars were drab. With so many developments all around that had pushed the world to levels that, I hoped, could never be undone by the forces of darkness or greyness, nostalgia seemed like it belonged in the past.

My remembered thoughts on this are clearly full of problems. For one thing, the perceptions I describe are those of a child and teenager living in a time of rapid and exciting technical evolution, blinded to stark realities by the wonders materialising perpetually before my eyes. The simplistic linear model set out above is also problematic because the 'world' had not been pushed to levels that could never be undone. Much of the world was a long way off having clean water or accessible medicine, let alone brand new video games to play every week.

Furthermore, it was not merely the case that much of the world lacked the exciting products that gave me and others the illusion of progress. In fact, our illusion was enabled by other people being trampled underfoot, just as it is now. I lived in an impoverished part of an impoverished region, but my life was full of riches beyond the reach of most children in the world.

Perhaps as we look at the poverty and technical deprivation of certain other societies, and 'their' wars and oppression, our desire to 'progress', differentiate ourselves from them with consumption and gain a foothold to a level that cannot be destroyed is heightened – as though we can use our advantages and buy ourselves distance from the 'primitive' 'other' and 'their' savage conflicts and chaos. If we just buy enough things – and the right things – and do the right things (as though performing some ritual), we can keep going up that ever-brighter evolutionary escalator. It is an arrogant and dangerous illusion but an alluring one.

It is very easy, in a complex world full of complicated organisations, networks, systems and ever-shifting cultures, to distance ourselves from chaos and conflict that seems remote – especially when, through our consumption, including our education and political decisions, we can conceptualise those immersed in conflict and chaos as essentially different from us. But if we do what William Burroughs suggested in *The Naked Lunch* and look at what is on the end of our forks – and consider the impact of our consumption of *everything* – we have to acknowledge that 'they' are not primitive. In fact, there is no 'they', just different people affected in different ways by global and historical circumstances, just as our relative wealth has come from global and historic circumstances.

Wars, conflicts and terror being fought elsewhere, and chaos and extreme poverty experienced elsewhere, do not happen in a vacuum. We are all in the same global 'shop' of consumption and decisions. Anyone willing to consider how what they consume came to be, where the resources to make it came from – and why they want it – must come to the realisation that there is no 'primitive' and 'sophisticate', but an endless struggle for food, power, objects, experiences and life. It is not eternal Christmas, nor is there a never-ending pot of porridge. Resources are finite but unfortunately expectations and greed are not.

We have all seen and can think of numerous examples of where the veneer of our 'civilisation' cracks and something we would rather avoid crashes or slithers into our 'sophisticated' world, as though we are at a glitzy ball and some aggressive drunk smashes their way through the door, hurls champagne bottles around and vomits in the chocolate fountain. This would probably kill the mood, but largely because the mood was an illusion. The glitz was never anything but contrived, and the sense of safety inside was dependent on hyper-vigilant security staff keeping the dangerous and volatile outside world outside.

For those of us interested in getting to the heart of reality, if there is such a thing, we could argue that the interloper popped the pomposity and brought a healthy dose of reality into the tedious glitz and controlled raucousness. On the one hand, the invader represents the chaos and danger of the outside world, but they are also an unwelcome surreal reflection of the contrived hedonism within. In booze-soiled clothes, with violent ranting and wild abandon, they take the drunken party to its final conclusion. They could even be described as the embodiment of the party, albeit in a shadowy form from which many would rather distance themselves.

In this book, I draw on different examples of where the veneer of civilisation has been broken and something 'savage' appears to have got in. I say "appears to have got in" as my suggestion is that savagery and chaos were always here. It wasn't so much that savagery from outside got in and spoiled the party, but that a fresh perspective from outside revealed what was true all along. The party (or society), however sophisticated it may have looked, was always brimming with 'savage' things such as greed, oppression, territoriality, conflict, violence and primal passions. These things do not make us bad, they just make us human. It is when we do not take responsibility for them and instead project them on an imagined 'other' who we construct as inferior that we can lose some of our humanity.

Chapter 1 – Paradoxes of 'civilisation'

We humans have a pretty muddled relationship with notions of civilisation, savagery, stability, safety and freedom. Consequently, we can have fears that are really quite extreme considering the actual risk, and at the same time be blissfully trusting of things that are a great threat to our world. The things that make us anxious are often things that could ultimately help build a better society, while things – and views – that give us comfort can be our enemies without us realising.

Another confusing and often paradoxical issue is our relationship with history. When people imagine civilisation breaking down, they often imagine a brutal world where food is scarce and we have to fight to survive – something between what they imagine 'cavemen' to be like and a *Mad Max* film. But if we consider that contemporary hunter-gatherer people regard the incursion of Western industry, working practices, technologies and ideologies into their worlds as savage and destructive, the picture switches. We can look at things differently. Their party is being invaded by dangerous interlopers.

Amazonian tribes threatened by dam projects – which flood their lands, increase deforestation and reduce biodiversity – naturally see invasion as savage. This is an extreme, though important, contemporary example to illustrate a point. A vast range of examples can be drawn on from around the world where societies rich in tradition and relatively stable have felt that sudden or rapid change, from outside or within, was a threat to their ways of life.

Those of us lucky enough to still have grandparents or who have elderly parents will probably hear stories relating to this each time we visit, whether featuring technologies, immigrants or any other apparent threat to the 'way things were'. These fears and perceptions are certainly not unique to older people, and it would not be fair to imply that older people uniformly lack enthusiasm for change. These sorts of fears are widely distributed, and are exploited and aggravated by far-right and nativist movements. As we have seen in recent years, these sorts of movements use as a selling point discourses about making countries how they were, taking back control or regaining a supposed 'golden age'.

Ideas of civilisation breaking down are therefore not just about fantasies of having to fend for ourselves outside, cooking on fires and running around forests, deserts or decaying cities killing one another. More prevalent are concerns about our ways of life changing, our identities being threatened and our history being eroded.

The paradox is that those driving the changes, whether by means of technologies, new ideologies or physical movement, do not generally view themselves as breaking down civilisation but actually building it up. Just as one person's meat is another person's poison, one person's progress is another person's doom. And for the innovator or visionary, the traditionalist's conservatism is a dangerous stubbornness that will keep us in the dark ages.

For those struggling with change, a sense of safety and security is provided by what they have known. For the progressive, a sense of well-being comes from change – especially change that they can shape. This all boils down to issues of power and authority – who can be trusted to drive society – and, frequently, generation gaps.

It is not always the case, however, that it is the older generation pulling back to traditional values. As we have seen in certain Islamist movements, younger generations can impose moral conservatism. There is a further paradox in cults such as Daesh ('ISIS') in that they regard those who do not adhere to their rigid ideologies as degenerate and a threat, while most people regard chopping off heads as the antithesis to civilisation. Similarly, Nazis regarded others (such as Jews and gypsies) as a threat to the 'civilisation' they sought to build, while for most people the Nazis represented a threat to civilisation.

Ultra-conservative movements driven by younger generations, such as Daesh, notwithstanding, it is more commonly the case that children and young people are, quite unfairly, associated with a savagery, impulsivity or irrationality that must to tamed by the forces of civilisation. Rather than regarding children as open-minded and full of wonder, there has often been a tendency to view them as dangerous and requiring intense – and sometimes violent – control.

Whether regarding them as vessels of original sin or bubbling cauldrons of unpredictable impulses at odds with society, dominant religious and influential social theories have treated children with suspicion.

In the study of any society, it is extremely valuable to consider how they treat and view children. This reveals a great deal about the ideologies, priorities, fears and aspirations of that society. In relation to this examination of civilisation and perceived threats to it, consideration of childhood has particular relevance. Not only have psychology, psychiatry, sociology and criminology focused a great deal on children and young people, but numerous stories about, and for, children relate to problems with civilisation itself. Some notable examples will be discussed.

The Austrian neurologist, psychiatrist and philosopher Sigmund Freud's book *Civilization and its Discontents* (1930) had a radical message and a profound impact on societies. Although he is not as widely read or respected as he was in the 20th century, his ideas continue to influence everything from child rearing practices, education, healthcare, marketing, political focus groups and the arts. I certainly do not agree with all his theories, but would not throw the baby out with the bathwater as some of his perspectives have helped thought and societies progress.

Freud is primarily known for being the founding father of psychoanalysis, a form of therapy which assumes that different forces operate with each of our minds, much of which happens outside conscious awareness. Freudian psychoanalysis sets out to understand and to encourage the patient to understand these different forces, exploring how early experiences impact upon the current functioning and mental health of the individual.

Though Freud certainly contributed original concepts and managed to move complex ideas into popular discourse, it is important to note that he was by no means the first to recognise different forces within individual minds, the unconscious or the importance of childhood experiences on future health and functioning. From Shakespeare, poets, creators of fairy tales and Greek philosophers, to tribal healers who go into a trance, it is clear that people thought about the dynamics of the mind long before Freud, just as people noticed the actions of gravity long before Isaac Newton outlined his observations and theories.

Viewing early childhood experience as a key factor in the development of personality, maladaptive behaviours and relationships, Freud was very much focused on childhood in both his theories and therapy. Rather than view infants as empty boxes or blank slates, he recognised that they have certain inherent drives which can put them at odds with civilisation and its socialising forces. These drives, according to Freud, can be sexual or destructive.

Just as Christian churches saddled children with the notion of original sin, Freud suggested that even very young children have dark and dangerous impulses that need to be curbed – both by society and by a moralistic and authoritarian component of the psyche called the 'super-ego'. Conversely, the 'id' (or 'it' in English) is the unconscious, impulsive drive within all of our minds which seeks immediate gratification. Freud also described this as the 'pleasure principle'. Between the extremes of the moralistic and controlling super-ego and the hedonistic and impulsive id, the rational aspect of our minds has been defined as the 'ego'.

In *Civilization and its Discontents* (initially titled *The Uneasiness in Civilization*), Freud discusses the apparently universal and enduring struggle between the individual, with the drive towards pleasure and freedom, and societies, which moralise, control and push towards conformity. In the book, Freud goes beyond psychodynamics within the individual to anthropological and sociological speculation, suggesting that laws and other social institutions are created to curtail human drives which would be damaging to society.

According to Freud, civilisations must restrict drive to be able to function. He says that society hindering us from satisfying our desires leads to discontent among citizens. He goes further than the term discontent, suggesting that society frustrating our natural desires causes certain types of mental illness, termed neuroses.

As well as sexual desire, with which few people would quibble, and a drive towards life and creativity, Freud suggested that humans have a drive towards death, self-destruction and aggression. Interestingly, Freud refined his theories to include the death drive in the wake of World War One, in which two of his sons served. A

1920 publication, *Beyond the Pleasure Principle*, sheds light on this development in his thinking. His daughter Sophie died aged 27 of influenza, as he was working on the publication. He denied that this tragic event influenced the development of this theory.

It is interesting to note that certain behaviours that would, in Freud's time, have led to punishment by the moralising 'civilisation', are very common now and do not, in many parts of the world, lead to prosecution or even ostracisation. These include adultery and having numerous sexual partners. Dating lots of people and polyamorousness are quite common now and are not, I would contend, the biggest threats to civilisation. Equally, it is questionable that following every sexual desire or other pleasure-seeking impulse leads to ultimate satisfaction or protects us from psychological and emotional problems.

We now know that pleasure-seeking activities are rewarded by the actions of the neurotransmitter dopamine, and also that repeatedly doing things that get us that neurological reward often brings us diminished pleasure over time. Once the chemical reward is diminished, some people move on to other activities, while others perform the behaviour more and more to try to make up for a diminishing reward. A good example of this is cocaine use.

Interestingly, Freud was an early adopter of cocaine, preoccupied with its potential as a medicine for various ailments, and he became addicted to it. It is hard to say how much Freud's early addiction to cocaine helped shape his view that human beings' desire for pleasure is perpetually frustrated.

What we can say for certain is that all sorts of desires and cravings are easily satisfied now in environments where civilisation seems reasonably robust. However, we also know that there are settings, such as parts of South America, where civilisation *is* arguably coming apart at the seams *because* of cocaine. I would contend, though, that the lucrative, competitive and violent nature of the drug trade and corrupt officials threatens local societies more than the direct pharmacological effect of the drug. Underlying the lucrative drug trade is a poverty that makes the pull of that hazardous industry stronger.

Returning to Freud's suggestion that the repression of sexual desires leads to neurosis, compelling evidence suggests that, beyond the impact on the individual, this can be catastrophic for societies. Observing the rise of Nazism, a young doctor and Freudian psychoanalyst called Wilhelm Reich wrote a fascinating, brave and chilling book called *The Mass Psychology of Fascism* (1933). This not only had relevance for authoritarian movements of his time and helped inspire the sexual revolution of the 1960s, but is also pertinent for contemporary oppressive societies and brutal ideological movements.

Living in Berlin at the time of the release of the book, Dr Reich proposed that authoritarian movements such as fascism are a symptom of sexual repression. Using principles of psychoanalysis, Reich sought to explain why populations choose or permit authoritarian systems, even when these systems do not work to the benefit of people.

A member of the Communist Party of Germany (though expelled after the book was published), Reich proposed that Germans chose the far-right Nazi regime rather than communism because of a culture of sexual repression. He argued that children in the country brought up to suppress sexual desire had become adults made anxious not just by sex but also by other 'rebellious' impulses. A culture was therefore created that was fearful of sexuality and non-conformity. The authoritarian system is therefore enabled by this widespread anxiety, linked to imposed inhibition.

Explaining the impact of this culture of repression on individuals and society, Reich stated: "Suppression of the natural sexuality in the child, particularly of its genital sexuality, makes the child apprehensive, shy, obedient, afraid of authority, good and adjusted in the authoritarian sense; it paralyses the rebellious forces because any rebellion is laden with anxiety; it produces, by inhibiting sexual curiosity and sexual thinking in the child, a general inhibition of thinking and of critical faculties. In brief, the goal of sexual suppression is that of producing an individual who is adjusted to the authoritarian order and who will submit to it in spite of all misery and degradation."

Some readers will be thinking something like: "The above doesn't really make sense, as surely the emergence of fascism itself is a form of revolution.". However, Reich distinguished fascism from revolution, stating: "If, by being revolutionary, one means rational rebellion against intolerable social conditions, if, by being radical, one means 'going to the root of things', the rational will to improve them, then fascism is never revolutionary. True, it may have the aspect of revolutionary emotions. But one would not call that physician revolutionary who proceeds against a disease with violent cursing but the other who quietly, courageously and conscientiously studies and fights the causes of the disease. Fascist rebelliousness always occurs where fear of the truth turns a revolutionary emotion into illusions."

Unsurprisingly, the Nazis didn't take kindly to *The Mass Psychology of Fascism*. Hitler became Chancellor of Germany in January 1933 and Reich's book was released in September of that year. The Nazis banned the book, and Reich fled Germany. More than a decade later, a judge in the USA ordered the book and others by Reich to be burned.

Having coined the term 'orgone' to describe a universal life-force, he developed boxes to sit in called 'orgone accumulators', which he believed worked therapeutically. After some sensationalist reporting of Reich's bold claims, the US Food and Drug Administration deemed them a fraud and had his books destroyed. He was jailed in 1956 for contempt of court and died in prison the next year of heart failure.

Reich's era was one of dramatic cultural change, scientific development and technological evolution. Living in an era of extraordinary transformation, he was one of the most interesting and innovative people of that time. His orgone accumulators, in which Albert Einstein himself was interested enough to test over a period of several days, did not live up to Reich's hopes, and proved his undoing. His obsession with them also appears to be one symptom of a deterioration of his mental state. Nevertheless, Reich's ideas about sexual repression and vulnerability to authoritarian regimes still ring true today.

When we consider the actions and ideologies of groups such as ISIS and their misogyny and hostility towards homosexuality, this make a lot of sense when viewed from Reich's perspective. Even when we read reports of homosexuality amongst Daesh terrorists, despite the Jihadists murdering gay men, the model still fits. History has shown us repeatedly that the repression of others can be a response to unwelcome desires within oneself. We have seen it in Christian denominations and in ultra-conservative Islamist movements, to name but two examples.

From simple symbols to stories of monsters tearing at civilisation

Just as social science – and aggressive reactions to challenging ideas from social science – can tell us a lot about the tension between civilisation and threats (and imagined threats) to civilisation, stories tell us a great deal too. Tales written for or about children are not only among the most familiar to us but also represent an exceptional way to explore the theme of threats to our civilisations. Sometimes the threat is a strange monster from beyond the child's everyday world, sometimes they come from closer to home – and sometimes they, horrifyingly, emerge from within the self.

Tales, whether passed on through word of mouth, written in books or presented in films or plays, are one of the most important productions of our human world. They bind communities together, pass information down through the ages, entertain, inspire, educate and lay the foundations of other fruits of cultural evolution, including religion, politics and science. *Some* scientists might not like the idea and resent being classed alongside storytellers and religion as part of our ongoing cultural evolution. However, the truly rational approach is to recognise this lineage and learn to value it. The best scientists I know appreciate the eternal marriage between science and art, and the importance of imagination and symbolism in both.

The English for the Latin term 'Homo sapiens' is 'wise man', which, interestingly, is also the archaic meaning of the word 'wizard'. Homo sapiens are the last survivors of the genus of homo (human), which also included Neanderthals and several other extinct species of hominids. Other human species – sometimes called 'archaic humans' – lived alongside us until quite recently, evolutionarily speaking. Our ancestors were close enough biologically and geographically for there to have been inbreeding between Homo sapiens and other human groups. However, culturally, our ancestors distinguished themselves, and that appears to have made all the difference in the world.

The pivotal thing to distinguish Homo sapiens from the other humans, enabling us to thrive as they died out, was not our physical strength, as we were not the strongest, but our use of symbols. There is archaeological evidence of our ancestors' use and value of symbols, suggesting a capacity for abstract thought and creativity that archaic humans apparently lacked.

Arguably, the use of symbols is even more significant than harnessing fire, as it allows us to share meanings with others, hastening the evolution of language and leading to shared narratives which bind societies together – geographically and through time. Communities bound together with shared symbols and meanings have greater cohesion, even during migrations, and are more effective at cooperating, which gives them an edge over competitors. There is no compelling evidence that Homo sapiens physically killed off our archaic human neighbours. They appear instead to have outperformed them as thinkers, communicators and creators of meaning.

Using symbols will seem very easy to everyone reading this book, which is made up of familiar symbols. In fact, it would probably be hard to contemplate the world with no symbols as the mind is arguably constructed of symbols and held together by abstract associations.

Symbols, stories and the value we place on them got us to where we are as a species and also bound us with all those who have gone before. Symbols and the tales, myths and religions they enabled are as critical to the emergence and evolution of science as revelatory physical experiences, such as Isaac Newton having an apple fall on his head, which is, of course, a story – an intriguing and inspiring story, with an interesting history and significance for the history of science, but nonetheless a story.

Stories are absolutely core to our species and key to our survival and progress. They pass down warnings and insights, which can help those with the wisdom to value them to work through current problems, avoid pitfalls and create more narratives to help others. I would compare stories Homo sapiens have told each other to the pebbles Hansel and Gretel dropped to find their way from the forest after almost being enslaved and devoured, or to the thread Theseus used to find his way out of the labyrinth after defeating the dreaded Minotaur. In these particular readings of those stories, humanity is Hansel, Gretel and Theseus. Many more interpretations and valuable meanings can be found in these tales – which is the point. Reality is complex and dynamic, and good stories are multi-vocal.

Stories can also be the lure leading young heroes and heroines on dangerous adventures to hazardous and bewildering 'places' such as Neverland or Wonderland. Just as the songs of sirens can lure sailors to their deaths, alluring and manipulative political narratives can lure whole societies into catastrophe, as will be discussed. Stories can be empowering or treacherous, and both at once – just as life itself can be.

Just as there are a great many paradoxes in humanity's relationship with civilisation, there are in tales about our world collapsing, strange new worlds suddenly appearing and old worlds being transformed. The eyes of a child, which we can look through when we venture into these dark and confusing mythological journeys, are the perfect apparatus with which to view peculiar paradoxes relating to civilisation and chaos. These stories often explore risks to civilisations and threats of certain sorts of societies in palatable ways.

It is therefore valuable to compare and contrast some of the most well-known books about children. The *Harry Potter* series, by J.K. Rowling, is full of supernatural occurrences and some incredibly complicated twists and turns that keep readers of all ages gripped. *Lord of the Flies*, written by William Golding nine years after the end of World War Two, is quite different in style and approach, but both writers say a lot about the complex relationship between civilisation and forces that can challenge it.

If we look beneath the style of each to fundamental issues raised, they are both about the impact of destabilising and dangerous forces on civilisation. Importantly, in both cases, the forces that attack civilisation come from, or have been nurtured by, key institutions at the very core of that civilisation. Both are about the relationship between chaos and control – and both demonstrate how the need for control can ultimately be one of the most destructive forces and sources of chaos. This is something we have seen time and time again in history and is still painfully apparent in conflicts and political systems around the world.

At the age of 11, Harry Potter is taken from a neglectful middle-class suburban English household to a prestigious school of magic, which appears to be in the Scottish Highlands. The boys in *Lord of the Flies* are removed from their English boarding school environment during a nuclear war – about as intense as a break in the veneer of civilisation can be. As a result of a plane crash, which could in itself be regarded as a breakdown of civilisation, they end up on a tropical island. Left to their own devices, many of the boys quickly – sometimes fearfully and sometimes gleefully – degenerate from young 'gentlemen' to savagery and cruelty.

In some ways, Harry Potter's journey was in the opposite direction to that of the *Lord of the Flies* boys. His trajectory was from a hostile environment in which he was treated like a despised animal to an elite institution where he was nurtured. However, his escape from mistreatment to the palatial wonders of Hogwarts did not rescue him from the dark forces impinging on civilisation and jeopardising his personal safety. He just experienced vulnerability with much greater clarity, got to understand the history of his predicament and developed critical skills to defend against malice.

In both the *Harry Potter* books and *Lord of the Flies*, we see that the threats to civilisation do not come from 'primitive' 'savages' lurking in some jungle or desert. The dangers come from something rotten at the heart of the system and lurking within the minds and impulses of those nurtured by that civilisation.

In *Lord of the Flies* it ultimately seems to be the inherent nature of some of the boys, aged between six and 12, rather than the hostility of the habitat, that leads to their mini 'civilisation' violently breaking down. Soon after arriving on the island, a fear grew about what was believed to be a 'beast' lurking somewhere. However, it was the boys themselves, products of an 'elite' culture, who were the most savage and dangerous creatures on the island. Fear and confusion drove the violence, but so too did competitiveness and sadism.

The physical and social habitat to which Harry Potter is removed is civilising and nurturing, while also dangerous and unpredictable. In the same environment – and even within the same individuals – there is the glue to bind civilisation *and* the destructiveness and weaponry to tear it down. Locating the story in a magical environment helped Rowling to create a rich multi-coloured tapestry where 'good' and 'evil' are often hard to identify accurately. Running over several books, it is a much more convoluted story than *Lord of the Flies*, but both Golding and Rowling manage to conjure up complicated ideas about the relationship between humans and nature, and our own potential for decency and malice.

At the start of *Lord of the Flies*, the plane full of boys has crashed on the island and two boys explore the environment. One of the boys, Ralph, is dominant, adventurous and confident, while the other, known as Piggy, is overweight, seems more sensitive and suffers from asthma. Reminiscent of Peter Pan with his pan pipes, Ralph sounds a conch shell to draw the boys together. The boys elect Ralph as their leader, which causes tension with a rival boy called Jack, who is initially appeased by being given responsibility for some boys.

Over time, fear, conflict over division of labour (hunting or making shelter) and different ways of prioritising what is important takes its toll, with violence erupting quite quickly. Jack punches Piggy, causing his glasses to be broken, which could be seen as a breakdown of civilisation. In Golding's allegory, Piggy could be seen to represent scientific and intellectual progress while Jack appears to represent unbounded savagery and the desire for power. The glasses can be seen as a product of civilisation and, as Ralph realised that they could be used to make fire, a producer of civilisation.

The younger boys in particular become increasingly fearful of the beast, which one boy claims to have seen. Piggy, as the embodiment of rationality, responds to this by suggesting that the only fear is within the minds of people. The community further disintegrates as Jack becomes insistent on locating and fighting the 'beast', while Ralph and others, more concerned with building a habitable environment, disregard this activity. The hunter group quickly learns to relish the violence of their role, with one sadistic boy, Roger, needlessly torturing a sow and putting her head on a spear.

Another boy, Simon, discovers that the 'beast' is actually an illusion created by the presence of a dead airman hanging from a tree, and seeks to tell the others the secret. As the group dance and chant, led by Jack, while re-enacting a hunt, a bloodied Simon comes into their circle and is frenetically killed with spears.

In their frenzied state, the group believes the beast was upon them. To justify the killing, Jack tells the other boys that Simon was actually the beast in disguise. I find this extremely interesting, as given his and Roger's actions when free of the restraints of society, they are closer to the projected savagery of the mythical beast. It is often the case in our societies that the accused capacities of those maligned 'others' from outside are suspiciously identical to those of the power-hungry within, who thrive on conflict, fear and division. I will say more about this in a later chapter about the far-right.

Things rapidly degenerate further, with the boys getting into conflict over ownership of the fire, and of Piggy's glasses as the tool to create fire. Roger murders Piggy with a boulder and Jack stabs Ralph with a spear. Ralph gets away but is then hunted like an animal through the forest. After the hunters set fire to the forest to smoke him out, Ralph flees and runs into a naval officer on the beach. The surviving boys are rescued by a naval cruiser, apparently ceasing their savage war.

On one hand, *Lord of the Flies* suggests that, without external control of adults, children, however privileged their background, have the potential to degenerate into savagery. This view is certainly in line with Sigmund Freud's concerns in *Civilization and its Discontents* and an untold number of teachers, parents and playground supervisors through the centuries. However, there are deeper and even more troubling interpretations.

The children Golding describes represent humanity more generally, our species of dangerously volatile creatures, driven by base capacities such as jealousy, fear, competitiveness and sadism. Given the tendency of a great many people to follow dominant people, it does not take many truly sadistic and ruthless people to create hostile, damaging and cruel human cultures. This is a theme I explore in my last book, *Psychopathic Cultures and Toxic Empires*. I suggest that, because of the tendency for people to conform, those lacking conscience and who are manipulative can shape systems that are incredibly harmful to those both inside and outside them.

In *Lord of the Flies*, it only took one Jack and one Roger, who complemented one another in their respective savagery and sadism, to create an oppressive and murderous 'world'. To do so, however, required the support of those who were conformist, quick to violence when ordered or subdued by fear. This is a pattern we have seen in multiple different human cultures, on subtle levels to the most extreme, such as in Nazism.

Another thing that the emerging tribe described in the *Lord of the Flies* can suggest to us is that the microcosm is reflective of the bigger world outside. Writing soon after World War Two, where he served on a Royal Navy 'destroyer' ship, it is hardly surprising that Golding was concerned with the capacity for mankind to rapidly degenerate into brutality, cruelty and conflict and division and hate that can seem childlike at best – some would say completely insane and irrational. The brutal divided world quickly created by the children on the island was therefore a mirror of the adult world beyond, which had degenerated into nuclear war.

Another reality that we can see writ large in the microcosm of the children on the island is the competitive environment of boarding – and other – schools, as well as universities. These in turn are reflective of and help to create the cut-throat world of business and the adversarial cultures of politics, law and even some religions.

The more contemporary dystopian fantasy, *The Hunger Games*, not only has strong thematic links to *Lord of the Flies* but is also regarded by many as a metaphor for stark realities in our increasingly competitive world. In this 'world', a contrived environment is imposed on the most unfortunate in order to drive them into savagery for entertainment purposes, and also as an expression of totalitarian power over the masses.

This deliberate production of conflict and playing the most vulnerable off against one another takes things to a whole new level and reflects a cruelty within the 'elite' beyond the brutality the poorest are made to endure and express to survive. In *The Hunger Games*, the young endure most of the vulnerability and hardship, and this is often the same in the real world we find ourselves in. Though better educated than older generations, the young in Britain and many other societies bear the brunt of economic downturns and imposed austerity.

In any society over a period of time, there are always winners and losers, with distinct sections of society more likely than others to be neglected, left behind, demonised or even brutalised. Literature and film attempts to reflect this inequality of opportunity and victimisation, and the genre of dystopian literature is particularly good at this. However, to understand dystopia, we have to understand utopia, as they are inextricably linked.

A basic dictionary definition of utopia is "an imagined place or state of things in which everything is perfect". A glaring issue here is that 'perfection' depends on individual perspectives. Some people might desire a calm rustic environment where life is slower, but many of us would be so bored that this could seem like a prison. Alternatively, as in the case in *Lord of the Flies*, a desert island can quickly become a brutal hell because of human failings and dynamics.

There are few environments so wild or barren that humans cannot build communities. However, there are no environments so wonderful that humans cannot screw things up spectacularly. Breakdowns of civilisation are generally linked to human activity and not to something inherently sinister about the planet we are lucky enough to live on or other animals around us.

The term utopia was coined by the lawyer and philosopher Thomas More in the early 16th century but the concept goes back much further. The biblical Eden, for example, as well as heaven, are notable examples of utopias from mystical stories. Many utopias imagined since have been set in unspoiled habitats where there is peace, and society works fairly. Numerous attempts have also been made to establish small-scale communities based on such ideals. The term dystopia describes the dark side of utopia – the anti-utopia. Dark dystopian tales have, in recent centuries, become much more prevalent than optimistic utopian visions.

Just as in unequal and unjust societies there are many who are quite happy with their fortunate positions, one person's dystopia can be another person's utopia. As we know from the emergence of Nazism and other fascist regimes, some citizens accept and even relish totalitarianism. We still see many examples of groups of people wishing to see liberal systems and human rights overturned and extreme control imposed on citizens. The support for Donald Trump by white supremacists vehemently opposed to liberal values is one disturbing recent example. More will be said about Trump's rise to power and the dangers of populist politics.

Some apparent utopias in literature are futuristic and hedonistic, with robots doing much of the work, leaving humans free to seek pleasure. However, these often turn sour or are revealed to be inherently flawed, unfair, malicious or in some way sinister. Our ambivalence towards technology and cultural complexity is reflected by such stories.

Devices that save us work and give us more free time for leisure activities are attractive. Ironically, however, we have already reached the stage where devices like mobile phones and computers capitalise our time and reduce our sense of leisure. Many people reach for their mobile phones the moment they wake and immediately go onto social media.

This ability to engage with the world without even getting out of bed, challenge politicians and the media from our phones, and find out whatever we want to know immediately is an extraordinary thing. I have written elsewhere about the power of social media to weaken the influence of traditional media and expose wrongdoing. However, there are shortcomings in our technological age. As in many stories, our utopia is also our dystopia.

The *Harry Potter* series, like many fantasy stories, dystopian novels and fairy tales, puts a magical gloss on stark realities. The stories are set in the present era but the characters contend with supernatural powers rather than the unstoppable march of technology. However, just as dystopian stories about the future or those set on other planets are often about real world concerns, presented from a different vantage point, supernatural themes in stories can represent a sugar coating on an otherwise bitter pill.

If you strip away the sugary magic coating of the Harry Potter tales, you get a horrific story of an orphan whose parents were murdered by a malicious psychopath with Nazi-like ideologies. Harry is then begrudgingly 'looked after' by envious, dishonest and neglectful relatives who try to deny him his education. When he does go away to school, Harry learns about the horrific injustices that created his predicament and that of the wider world.

Like many students, Harry also learns – in both formal education and hard experience – about inequality, entitlement, snobbery and racial oppression. Racial oppression and supremacy is sugar coated in the books by the focus on 'muggles' and 'half-bloods'. In his journey towards adulthood, Harry encounters increasing violence and danger, becomes vengeful and is ultimately involved in a fatal fight to preserve the civilisation he values.

I am in no way criticising J.K. Rowling or other fantasy authors for either the sugar coating or the essential bitterness of the realities contained within the stories. I believe that the stories she communicates have important truths, just as there are important truths in older fairy tales. Also, if not for the sugar coating, Rowling almost certainly would not have been able to keep hundreds of millions of children and adults spellbound. However, it is certainly also the case that the underlying themes that many experience, of loss, injustice, neglect, fear, confusion, betrayal, vengefulness and conflict, would have connected on a fundamental level with readers and viewers of the films.

It seems likely that a great many people who read or were read *Harry Potter* had not heard the term 'dystopia' when plunging headlong into the dark and frightening world described by Rowling. Nevertheless, the stories fit the dystopian novel format well, as does *Lord of the Flies*. Just as dreams often present insights to us in an abstract way, dystopian stories present realities about society or possible future societies in a way that is easier to engage with.

If our dreams just told us our threats and shortcomings in a blunt and literal manner, we could lose vital rest, and sleep would be less appealing. Similarly, if authors of dystopian literature passed on their insights in a stark and non-fantastical way, their books would be less enjoyable.

Social science authors attempt to pass on concerns in a starker way and, unsurprisingly, such books are not as popular as dystopian fantasy. They are probably rarely, if ever, read to children at bed-time. In the next chapter, I talk about stories social science tells us about realities. I say 'realities' rather than 'reality' as the stories social scientists – and other observers — tell always represent a partial picture. In some cases, the narrative presented is a flawed or even dishonestly distorted picture.

Dystopian novels do not claim to present a literal or definitive picture, and more honest social scientists also acknowledge that their narratives are based on partial impressions of something so complex and dynamic that it is not feasible to claim to offer a definitive account.

Chapter 2 – Scientific racism, evolutionism and savage theories

Part of anthropology's history is shameful, and this shame, and a desire to make amends, has driven many of the good things it has done since. It is interesting to note, however, that the thing that anthropology has been ashamed of still seems acceptable to a good number of citizens, including powerful figures in politics and other areas of public life. I am referring to models concerning human evolution that enable what has been termed 'scientific racism'.

Scientific racism, or 'pseudo-scientific racism' as it is more accurate to call it, uses pseudo-scientific theories and techniques to justify ideas about 'racial' superiority or inferiority. It also includes the drive to classify people exhibiting particular observable traits and perceived psychological traits into distinctive categories or 'races'. I put 'racial' and 'race' in inverted commas as it is now acknowledged by experts that race is a cultural construct. We are a single species and variation has nothing to do with worth.

This tendency to classify human beings as though markedly distinct races, though seen as problematic by most anthropologists, psychologists and biologists nowadays, is quite common to the human experience, from folk notions differentiating one's tribe from others to notions of purity peddled by 'elites' wielding bits of physical anthropology, such as anthropometry (measuring people) and craniometry (measuring heads). This has also been apparent in the speculations of a range of philosophers, theologians and scientists going back through the centuries.

Given that many theorists in the 17th century and beyond had not seen a person from Africa or Asia – let alone known any socially – it is understandable, perhaps, that they often looked upon other human communities as different subspecies or even species. An early attempt to suggest that all human beings share a common descent was met with scorn by 17th century scientists. Robert

Boyle, an Irish chemist, physicist, natural philosopher and inventor, proposed that that all human communities, despite our diversity, come from the same source. Today, this completely uncontroversial idea is known as monogenism.

The opposite to monogenism is polygenism, the notion that each 'race' has a separate origin. Centuries before Darwin put the cat among the pigeons for proposing that we descended from (other) apes, 17th century debates about monogenism and polygenism related to religion rather than genes, and this continued for quite some time. In some origin stories a single human species is created, such as in Genesis, in which humanity descends from a single pair of ancestors. In others, a variety of human 'species' are made. This conception, whether pushed by native folk tales, organised religions, scientists or tyrants, opens the path to division and conflict.

In contrast to Robert Boyle, French nobleman and historian Henri de Boulainvilliers favoured polygenism as this enabled him to claim that the French could be divided into two distinct races. He claimed that the aristocratic 'French race' were descended from Germanic Franks, who were essentially a different species from the indigenous 'Gallo-Roman race'.

This supposed racial difference legitimised the domination of the Gauls by the Frankish aristocracy. As they were a superior 'race', they had every right to conquer and rule. He used a mixture of mythology and scientific notions to justify argument for racist oppression of the less powerful members of French society. Readers will note parallels between this justification and that which drove the genocidal Nazis centuries later.

Following on from Henri de Boulainvilliers, and born a few years after Boyle died, the French philosopher and writer Voltaire was also a vehement believer in polygenism. Though an advocate of freedom of speech and of religion, Voltaire was also disturbingly racist. Responding to the idea of monogenism, as suggested by the Bible, he wrote: "Our wise men have said that man was created in the image of God. Now here is a lovely image of the Divine Maker: a flat and black nose with little or hardly any intelligence."

Writing in 1767, around the same time Voltaire penned the outlined material, the Swedish medic, botanist and zoologist Carl

Linnaeus proposed classifying humans into five 'varieties' or species. Indigenous Americans were described as "Red, choleraic, righteous; black, straight, thick hair; stubborn, zealous, free; painting himself with red lines, and regulated by customs." Whereas, of white Europeans, he noted: "Abundant, long hair; blue eyes; gentle, acute, inventive; covered with close vestments; and regulated by customs." Asian people, he stated, were: "Yellow, melancholic, stiff; black hair, dark eyes; severe, haughty, greedy; covered with loose clothing; and regulated by opinions."

I will leave the reader to guess which huge variety of human communities were neatly clustered together by Linnaeus with these words: "Frizzled hair; silky skin, flat nose, tumid lips; females without shame; mammary glands give milk abundantly; crafty, sly, careless; anoints himself with grease; and regulated by will."

He also suggested a mythological human race called "the Monstrosus" split into subspecies including Homo feralis (feral man), Juvenis lupinus hessensis (Hessian wolf boy), Juvenis hannoveranus (Hannoverian boy), Puella campanica (wild girl of Champagne), the Patagonian giant and the dwarf of the Alps. In later work he talked of troglodytes and the satyr but also appears to have credited the mythological hydra and the phoenix as though human-like species.

We can be sure that if a white 'thinker' had collected such ludicrous narratives from an African or indigenous American at that time, this would have been used to reinforce the view that those 'races' are irrational, ignorant and inferior. Given how absurd much of the thinking of Carl Linnaeus will seem to most readers today, it will be shocking to many that his general classification system was still very influential two centuries later when pseudo-scientific racism had become very popular, and was routinely used to justify imperialism and all the violence, exploitation and oppression this entailed.

Britain's was by no means the only empire to colonise and exploit African countries and numerous other environments, but information from 'our' imperialist invasions shows quite clearly the tendency to regard other human communities as unevolved, savage and inferior. This is quite ironic as, within the British colonial system, mediocre white people could gain considerable power. They did not do so because of some innate superiority, but because they were part of a heavily armed exploitative system that I have, elsewhere, described as a psychopathic culture.

Even the mining magnate and prominent imperialist Cecil Rhodes was not someone who might immediately be picked out as a likely statesman. However, in a southern Africa dominated by colonial exploitation, this manipulative and callous white supremacist thrived, even serving as the prime minister of the Cape Colony, a British colony in present-day South Africa and Namibia.

Despite the obvious exploitation of colonised countries by Britain and other colonial powers, Rhodes genuinely felt that the 'British race' was innately superior to black Africans and other 'races'. As a result, he seems to have truly believed that the Empire was a positive thing for those communities invaded, despite evidence that it promoted inequality, oppression and brutality. He called other human communities, "despicable specimens of human beings". Though living from 1853 until 1902, with access to a comparatively modern Oxford education, Rhodes' views were no more enlightened than those of Voltaire and Linnaeus.

If it was the case that white people are innately superior to black people, it is strange that, with all the opportunities in the world, there was little evidence of substantial progress in the century or so between Linnaeus and Rhodes. Though there were some who were brave enough to reject orthodoxy, the Anglo-Saxon world continued to labour under the delusion that black people were fundamentally inferior to whites – as though a different species.

Given how flawed and simplistic this sort of thinking is, it is ironic that it was later used by Nazis to justify the genocide of Jews and gypsies and to attempt to build a 'master race'. It has also been used to justify slavery and systems of segregation. Pseudo-scientific racism is still used to dehumanise, segregate, oppress and victimise those of different ethnicities and backgrounds. From eugenics to genocide and 'class' systems, hierarchical ideas are inherent to these divisive and dangerous narratives.

If human beings can be categorised into racial categories based on superficial traits and external speculation about their psychology, then they can be ranked – in an equally pseudo-scientific and divisive way. The concept of evolution was misused to do so. Pointing out the erroneousness of the concept of evolutionism is not a dismissal of the Darwinian model of natural selection in nature. It is a dismissal of the idea that you can rank 'races' in terms of intelligence, ability or worth.

Racist evolutionists either misread or deliberately misrepresented Darwin's ideas, just as some people do today when using the concept of natural selection to justify extreme inequality and the dominance of the fortunate over the less so. Darwin's pivotal book *On the Origin of Species by Means of Natural Selection, or the Preservation of Favoured Races in the Struggle for Life*, first published in 1859, was about natural selection in nature. It certainly did not rank human communities in the way that those who misunderstand and misappropriate his ideas sometimes have.

Darwin's terminology 'favoured races' in the full title of *On the Origin of Species* is a very long way from the supremacist fantasies of Rhodes and others. Darwin was actually alluding to varieties of plant and animal life. From his later book, *The Descent of Man, and Selection in Relation to Sex* (1871), it is quite clear that Darwin did not view human communities as separate species but recognised that all have the same ancestry. Physical variation is the result of adaptation to different circumstances rather than evidence of different subspecies of humans.

Despite Darwin's prominence and the sophistication of his understanding, scientific racism trundled on dangerously, along with evolutionary polygenism. This continued through the 19th century and well into the 20th century. Sometimes this speculation included doomsday scenarios which now look like white supremacist fantasies.

For example, the German naturalist, physician and philosopher Ernst Haeckel claimed that humans could be divided into ten races, Caucasians being the 'highest', and the 'lower' races heading for extinction. He also found 'evidence' that negroes were descended from apes in his claim that they have stronger and more flexible toes than Caucasians. Haeckel died in 1919 and his explosive blend of scientific racism and ideas about German purity helped lay the foundations of Nazism.

With a life spanning exactly the same decades as Ernst Haeckel, the English anthropologist Edward Tylor shared a similar sort of evolutionist thinking. Tylor suggested that there were distinctive stages that each human society must pass through to become 'civilised'. The stages, he suggested, were 'savagery' and 'barbarism' prior to 'civilisation'. Of course, Western European culture, cherished by privileged white people at old universities, represented the pinnacle of civilisation, a summit to which those dark-skinned 'primitives' must slowly ascend.

The 'advanced' wealthy white man would, of course, be waiting patiently at the summit and not in the least be plundering the lands of the 'primitives' in the meantime or using their countries as strategic posts in white supremacist world domination.

Tylor's view that each society has the ability to evolve arguably makes him more progressive in his thinking that many in the scientific racism field who regarded non-whites as essentially inferior species. A pioneer of cultural anthropology, he recognised that culture transforms over time. However, given that Tylor lived until 1917, when 'civilised' white people were machine gunning one another to bits in World War One, it would have been a feat of denial to retain a simplistic evolutionist model until the very end of his life.

A key contribution of anthropology has been to demonstrate, in response to theories mentioned here, the erroneousness of racist ideologies and to show the value and wisdom of all human cultural groups. A key figure in this was Franz Boas, a German-born anthropologist and physicist whose pioneering work challenged scientific racism and the eugenics associated with it.

Boas has been described as the 'father of American anthropology' and his contribution has helped the discipline globally transcend models that hindered it. His work, and that of his successors, has also helped human society to rise above rigid ideas about 'race' in which people are arbitrarily ranked in a way that is not only destructive but also delusional.

Boas' concept of cultural relativism is key in the shift from evolutionist anthropology, favoured by class-obsessed 'elite' British social scientists. The model proposes that, rather than rank human cultures by comparing them against some imagined ideal (white and just like those who impose the model), it is critical to understand that all humans perceive reality through the lens of their own distinct cultural experience and this background drives distinctive behaviour.

By recognising that culture shapes how we view and engage with the world around us, it becomes possible to understand human groups in a much more complex and dynamic way, rather than force us into some pre-conceived pigeonhole based on superficial features. In doing so, it also opens the way to consider how historical factors like oppression, power and exploitation – as opposed to innate inferiority – led any human group to its particular predicament.

Boas' approach was therefore radical and rather threatening to those who preferred to imagine that certain human groups are essentially inferior and therefore deserving of hardship and oppression. We all, no doubt, know of people who prefer to cling to the pre-Boas way of thinking of human existence than engage with what we now know to be reality. There is some irony in this. Those clinging to an evolutionist model have some more evolving to do on a personal level to accept that they are now, many decades after Boas' breakthrough, being wantonly ignorant.

Just as Darwin did in his work, Boas worked meticulously to dispel the divisive narratives of the pseudo-Darwinian cultural evolutionists. Darwin did not suggest that human beings are *descended* from chimps and that chimpanzees would one day evolve into Homo sapiens. The point is that we are one of a number of Hominidae (apes) that have evolved to adapt to the world. It could actually be argued now, as we observe and contribute to ecological peril, that we have not adapted as well as other apes to live sustainably in the natural habitat.

By drawing on, developing and integrating the fields of physical anthropology, linguistics, archaeology and cultural anthropology, Boas revolutionised anthropology in the US and trained a new generation of practitioners. British anthropology, though making great strides in research methods, was not quick to emulate Boas' integrated approach. However, his relativist approach, which sunk scientific racism narratives, was generally adopted by British anthropologists – though not the pseudo-intellectual eugenicists who were very vocal in the early 20th century.

Proponents of eugenics were not so vocal after World War Two but, as many of us see on social media day after day, flawed ideals about the relative value of particular human groups and the disturbing desire to eradicate aspects of the 'other' have not gone away. It is both ironic and troubling that a narrative often peddled by white supremacists on social media concerns the completely spurious notion of 'white genocide'.

To follow the ideologies of genocidal fascists but to project that disturbed mindset onto others with different skin tones is a considerable feat of distortion. They often manage this mental contortionism by conflating Muslims with Islamist terrorists, as though the overwhelming majority of law-abiding peaceable Muslims (who it should be noted have a variety of skin tones, including white) are terrorist sleeper cells disguised as normal families.

The reality is that ultra-conservative Islamists who wish to attack democracy and community have much more in common with the far-right antagonists who *appear* to oppose them than with the vast majority of Muslims. More will be said later in this book about the roots and drivers of ultra-conservative Islamist terrorism and the drivers of far-right white supremacist and Islamophobic movements.

Chapter 3 – Voyeurs, radicals, spies and the war on freedom

Anthropology is not a subject that creates much excitement among the public, which is a great pity as it is *about* the public – not just those in distant places but *everywhere* in the world. The discipline has more to do if it would like to share its observations and insights with a broader range of people than a narrow tribe of 'insiders'. However, my experience is that people tend to find the subject fascinating once they become aware of its scope and stance in relation to dominant powers.

It is true that many anthropologists come from privileged backgrounds, but it is also true that they are rarely on the side of the establishment. Theirs is actually a rather radical discipline that tends to question and challenge dominant institutions and power structures. This could help to explain its lack of prominence in mainstream discourse, despite its popularity among university students in our age of multiculturalism and globalisation, in which identity is increasingly complex.

When researchers return 'from the field', whether they have been studying African legal systems, a new religious movement in California or adolescence in Samoa, scrutiny inevitably turns on the environment they have come from. There is nothing like spending time in a different culture to make you see the strangeness of your familiar social and political habitat. This is perhaps one of the key aspects of anthropology about which much of the public has not been made aware. If they realised that this strange tribe was so focused on questioning *our* systems and authorities, I suspect many more people would be interested.

There was a time when anthropology books were much more popular among general readers. Many drawing rooms held books with titles such as *The Sexual Lives of Savages* and *Coming of Age in Samoa* in the early 20th century. These are both excellent books and well worth reading, but their popularity after publication says something about the perceptions of the Western public of those deemed 'exotic' at best and, more commonly, 'savage'. There is a tendency to marvel at difference and sexuality, and to conceptualise those people studied as essentially different, as though a distinct species.

At a time when the British colonial system allowed privileged anthropologists opportunities to go and observe distant people and document their behaviours, the British drawing room reader was a voyeur by proxy – a bit like looking at wildlife from a great distance, through a telescope, with the 'expert' at your shoulder telling you what is going on. What was observed, however, was a partial insight into the communities observed, just as snippets of phone camera footage of zoo animals gives only partial insight into the capacities and social complexity of any species.

It is interesting to note that, as the British middle and upper classes were primarily reading books about the exotic 'other', full of words such as 'savage' and 'primitive', 'advanced' societies were between two world wars. Tens of millions of soldiers and civilians were killed, with more deaths on the horizon, yet the black faces on the front of coffee table books were the 'savages'. And, of course, the Germans were described as Huns, from the name of nomads that had moved into Europe from Asia, who were often described as 'savage'.

There is a tendency to project 'savagery' on others living in or from distant places, rather than recognising the shared capacities of *all* human beings. Awareness of commonality, let alone unity, has a lot of progress yet to make.

Greater political interest and investment in anthropology existed when fieldwork was of value to the establishment. During the British colonial era, for example, government had a lot to gain from anthropologists in the regions they were governing. However, there was a strong sense that, rather than being radical critics of colonial powers, the anthropologists of the time were representatives of the British establishment and upholders of imperialism. Once societies subdued by colonialism began to challenge those powers, the anthropologist suddenly looked suspiciously like a spy.

The suspicions of communities studied of the spy status of anthropologists have sometimes been justified. For example, Project Camelot was a clandestine US military 'counter-insurgency' operation that covered numerous countries, including several in Latin America. The project, which started in 1964, had the goal of enhancing the military's ability to anticipate and influence cultural shifts overseas. Anthropologists and other social scientists were used in the project and, once exposed, it had a detrimental impact on the profession of anthropology and hindered generations of researchers from undertaking fieldwork in certain places.

From the perspective of dominant governments, such as that of the USA, and of intelligence services such as the CIA, they are able to believe that they are actually supporting civilisation (and certainly their country's own interests) by monitoring, influencing, and sometimes destroying, social and political movements. However, from the perspective of local communities and political groups that do not conform to the US agenda, or that of other dominant powers, those interfering intelligence organisations and their agents are undermining society and progress.

Just as the British establishment installed regimes they thought they could control in 'their' former colonies as the British Empire declined, US powers frequently installed their own puppet presidents in the hope that this would protect US economic interests and ward off ideologies it found threatening. This has often back-fired – just as British meddling and manipulation has.

A notable example for Britain was Idi Amin, who was installed in Uganda and went on to commit terrible atrocities. The British powers decided that this illiterate narcissistic psychopath, trained by their military, would be a pliable leader who would serve British interests sometime after the country had gained independence. The British favoured him over President Milton Obote, who was deposed by a military coup led by Amin. Obote had been in the process of nationalising British businesses in Uganda when the coup took place. There is not compelling evidence, however, that the UK state directly supported the coup. Amin does appear to have been covertly supported by Israel though, most likely because of his potential to destabilise Islamic Sudan.

Idi Amin's rule and support from other regimes ultimately led to up to half a million people being killed by his tyrannical regime, out of a population of just 12 million. Many more fled the country amid his nativist attack on Asian Ugandans, who actually played critical roles in keeping the country functioning and fed.

Many people starved to death as a result of Amin's and his cronies' mismanagement of the country after farms were seized and businesses taken from Ugandan Asians, many of whom had lived and contributed there for generations. Even after Idi Amin's atrocities became well-known by the international community, the CIA continued to give military assistance to his regime.

The CIA has repeatedly been implicated in the installation of puppet governments to overthrow popular parties and stand in the way of political and economic change. Some of those put in place were dictators who were allowed to carry out all sorts of atrocities as long as US interests were protected. In some cases, the CIA has been linked to the assassination of popular political leaders before more pliable politicians were installed.

Those people who took up or believed Donald Trump's mantra, 'make America great again', *might* like to look into the depths the CIA and the US government routinely stooped to try to 'make America great'. I will include a selection in the next chapter to give readers a sense of this, but it would take a multivolume book to cover all that the CIA and other intelligence services have done to protect the interests of their own empires and undermine democratic decisions of which their paymasters disapproved.

To undermine political movements and groups overseas, when the CIA has decided that these represent a threat to US economic interests or resistance to complicity, the tried and tested approach seems to have been to find a local right-wing group to do its bidding. Often, the agency uses the military to action a coup. Whether supporting a right-wing group to take over from a recently elected government or using an authoritarian local military, this is clearly a very long way from the democratic principles that US politicians, as least on the surface and at home, supposedly cherish.

The CIA has been linked to all sorts of methods of weakening the democratically elected government of particular countries. These include creating smear stories about politicians, infiltrating parties to undermine them, using blackmail to weaken the party, vote-rigging, violence, torture and kidnapping. The 'sexier' sounding term they use is counter-insurgency – as though they are protecting civilisation and societies rather than attacking them.

As within the US, when politicians and the CIA want to smear critics or popular radical figures, those they wish to discredit and destroy have routinely been labelled communists. In such cases, the individual or group concerned is likely to be more left-wing than their destroyers, which is not hard considering the anti-democratic authoritarian approaches of the US agents and their hard-right local puppets. In reality, the 'dangerous' radicals the agency has sought to destroy were more likely to be local union leaders, liberal-minded politicians, academics or peasant groups seeking better working conditions.

These covert operations to undermine democracy appear to have been systematic, numerous and catastrophic. The Association for Responsible Dissent, which was established by CIA whistle-blower David MacMichael, estimated that by the late 1980s several million people had died as a result of such operations. As the British found with Idi Amin, US administrations have often discovered that the dictator they put in place was not ultimately as compliant as they had hoped and had become greedy.

Dictators have a tendency towards stubbornness and unpredictability, to put it mildly. Consequently, it sometimes takes a war or wars to get rid of them. This was the case with Saddam Hussein in Iraq and Manuel Noriega of Panama.

The CIA was created in 1947, along with the National Security Council, by then President Harry Truman. The legislation that created these organisations was the National Security Act, and the way this was devised made the CIA directly accountable to the president only, so it was shielded from democratic scrutiny. The following year, a 'covert-action' wing of the CIA was established, but this was given the less suspicious name of the 'Office of Policy Coordination'. The branch was concerned with propaganda, economic warfare, sabotage and subversion against states deemed hostile, and propping up groups abroad that were antagonistic towards the left.

These capacities of the CIA were put into action the very same year, with the undermining of the Italian election to prevent communists from being elected. Actions reportedly taken included broadcasting propaganda, vote-rigging, intimidation of and threats against communist political candidates.

Just as Project Camelot recruited social scientists, Operation Mockingbird, which started in the 1950s and continued formally until the late 1970s, recruited journalists and news organisations to become spies and propagandists. The CIA has admitted to this operation, which used more than two dozen news outlets and hundreds of journalists.

Organisations involved included The Washington Post, Hearst Newspapers, Reuters, Time, Newsweek, the Associated Press, ABC, NBC and CBS. As journalists routinely travel abroad and meet powerful people, these were valuable assets to the CIA. After the project was terminated in 1976, some relationships between the CIA and individual journalists were allowed to continue, but on a voluntary basis.

It should be pointed out that the CIA is certainly not the only intelligence service to recruit journalists as agents. The English broadcast journalist Jon Snow has revealed that he was approached in the mid-1970s by MI5, which offered him a monthly retainer to spy on left-wingers working in television. Snow, who was previously a student protester, which led to him being kicked out of Liverpool University, rejected their advance. It seems very unlikely that this young radical was the only one tapped up, given that the vast majority of British journalists are more compliant and right-wing than Jon Snow.

Numerous CIA operations in the 1950s were designed to take down unwelcome political administrations and undermine local democratic systems. These included overthrowing the Guatemalan president Jacob Arbenz in 1954 by means of a military coup. This appears to have been prompted by Arbenz seeking to nationalise the United Fruit Company, in which the then CIA director Allen Dulles happened to own shares. Arbenz, who had great influence across Latin America, was replaced by a succession of brutal right-wing dictators.

From the early 1950s the CIA attempted to overthrow the communist government in North Vietnam. A key part of this effort was attempting to use the US-compliant South Vietnam regime. These clumsy and ineffective attempts to intervene in Vietnam preceded the lengthy Vietnam War, which resulted in the deaths of millions of people and fundamentally altered the USA's self-perception.

Operation Phoenix, which ran from 1965 and 1972, was led by the CIA and involved US and Australian special forces. The operation was to support South Vietnamese agents to capture, interrogate, allegedly torture and kill people believed to be leaders of the National Liberation Front (dubbed the 'Viet Cong' by the US). According to the author and journalist Douglas Valentine, methods of torture included: "Gang rape, rape using eels, snakes, or hard objects, and rape followed by murder; electric shock rendered by attaching wires to the genitals or other sensitive parts of the body, like the tongue." (Blakely 2009).

As we might expect, Douglas Valentine's account, based on interviews with those involved, has been attacked by those who defend 'counter-insurgency' as an important part of such conflicts. However, in a 2008 book by Joe Allen and John Pilger, military intelligence officer K. Milton Osborne confirms the use of torture and gruesome murder, stating: "The use of the insertion of the 6-inch dowel into the canal of one of my detainee's ears, and the tapping through the brain until dead. The starvation to death, in a cage, of a Vietnamese woman who was suspected of being part of the local political education cadre in one of the local villages."

A number of other intelligence officers and special force operatives have given accounts of torture and murder carried out under the Phoenix programme. Accounts suggest that torture was carried out by South Vietnamese forces in conjunction with or under the supervision of the CIA and special forces.

Estimates vary but the number of suspected National Liberation Front supporters and operatives killed between 1965 and 1972 is certainly in the tens of thousands. These sorts of activities also appear to have gone on after 1972, when the heavily criticised operation was stopped. They appear to have continued, in one form or another, until the decisive capture of the South Vietnam capital of

Saigon in 1975 by the People's Army of Vietnam and the National Liberation Front of South Vietnam. It is hard to imagine that randomly abducting suspected communists, terrifying them and killing many of them and their kin, would have strengthened the position of the American invaders or convinced locals of the superiority of US ideologies.

Interconnected with the manipulations and war in neighbouring Vietnam, in Laos the CIA's attempt to destroy the left spanned from 1957 until 1973. Military coup after military coup by US puppets was followed by US-driven mercenary attacks on the Pathet Lao, a popular left-wing organisation. After this proved unsuccessful, the US relentlessly bombed the country. Between 1964 and 1973, the US dropped approximately two million tons of bombs on Laos, roughly the same as it dropped on Europe and Asia during World War Two. The USA also supported anti-communist forces in Laos as well as South Vietnamese incursions into the country.

Another failed US attempt to fight communist ideologies with violence, again involving the CIA, was the Bay of Pigs Invasion in Cuba. In that case the CIA used a paramilitary group made up of around 1,300 Cuban exiles called Brigade 2506, recruited from the Miami area. The botched invasion, which took place in 1961, was not only badly planned but the air support the US had promised to give the invaders was ineffective.

The hope had been that the invasion would trigger a popular uprising against the left-wing Cuban prime minister Fidel Castro. However, most of the attackers were captured, four US bombers were shot down and two US supply ships were sunk. Castro's position was ultimately strengthened, and the failure led to US president John F. Kennedy replacing the director of the CIA. This failure was a real blow to US pride and the prestige of the CIA. However, the same pattern of semi-covert attacks on other societies continued.

Also in 1961, the CIA was linked to the assassination of the brutal Dominican Republic dictator Rafael Trujillo, who US administrations had supported for more than 30 years. In that time, he imprisoned, tortured and murdered anyone who dared oppose him, and he remained the dictator of the country even when there were puppet leaders nominally in office.

The US powers seemed happy to turn a blind eye to the murderous regime, in which tens of thousands of citizens were killed, including thousands of Haitians massacred over the space of a week in 1937 after being deemed enemies of society. However, over time Trujillo's business interests grew large enough to compete with American interests. Two years later the democratically elected left-winger Juan Bosch, a writer and historian, was deposed by a military coup, only to be replaced by a repressive, right-wing junta.

The CIA has been implicated in two more regime changes that happened in 1961, in Ecuador and the Republic of Congo (as it was then known). In Ecuador the democratically elected president José Velasco was forced to resign by the military after refusing US instructions to break relations with Cuba and to clamp down on left-wingers in his country. Two years later a military coup removed the next president, Carlos Julio Arosemana, after he criticised the US government and refused to break links with Fidel Castro. A military junta took over and the forthcoming election was terminated.

In the Republic of Congo in 1961, the elected leader Patrice Lumumba was executed by a Belgian firing squad, and CIA documents have revealed plans to kill him. The Belgian and US authorities appear to have collaborated in Lumumba's destruction. For more than 100 years, Belgium and the USA had exerted considerable power over the Congo's destiny, and Patrice Lumumba was the first prime minister of the newly independent country.

Patrice Lumumba was not only considered a threat as a result of his focus on economic independence and realistic promises to improve living conditions of Congolese citizens, but he was also a champion of pan-African solidarity. In that era, with the fear that communism could spread like wildfire, the US government was alarmed by such movements, especially when there were valuable resources in a region. The execution of Lumumba led to years of turmoil in the country.

In Brazil in 1964, a military coup overthrew the elected government of left-winger João Goulart. He was ousted because his 'Basic Reforms Plan' was devised to take profits from large companies and nationalise oil reserves to improve the lives of the majority of Brazilians. Right-wing sectors of Brazil, including the military, organised demonstrations against the government and polices before the CIA-backed coup. US president Lyndon Johnson offered military support, including a US Navy fleet led by an aircraft carrier to support the coup.

After the coup, the military regime instigated policies that served the interests of the US establishment. The junta, which used death squads and secret police to hunt, interrogate, torture and murder those accused of being communists, was in power until 1985. The CIA has been implicated in the training of the junta's death squads.

In 1965 in Indonesia, a botched coup took place against the left-wing Sukarno government, which resulted in six generals being killed. The army and some religious organisations pinned the coup attempt on the Indonesian Communist Party and one of the surviving generals, Suharto, subsequently led an anti-communist purge, in which a vast number of civilians were massacred over a period of months. Estimates of the number of citizens killed range from half a million to three million. As well as alleged communists, the massacre targeted ethnic Chinese citizens. After seizing power from Sukarno, Suharto remained in power until 1998.

Sukarno has attracted the wrath of the US government for choosing to remain neutral in the Cold War. There is evidence, in the form of a 1962 CIA memo, of consensus between the US and UK governments that Sukarno should be "liquidated". Good evidence also exists of links between the US military and anti-communist Indonesian officers. The US military provided training, weapons and money to senior Indonesian military figures.

It has also been proved that the US embassy provided the Indonesian death squads with lists of alleged communists in the country, compiled by CIA and State Department officials. Commenting on the lists, Robert Martens, political officer at the US Embassy in Jakarta, said: "It really was a big help to the army. They probably killed a lot of people, and I probably have a lot of blood on my hands, but that's not all bad. There's a time when you have to strike hard at a decisive moment."

CIA plots to oust or kill Sukarno went back as far as the mid-1950s. In 1955, operatives plotted an assassination attempt, though Richard Nixon, who was vice-president at the time, objected to this. Two years later, President Eisenhower ordered the CIA to overthrow Sukarno's government and this was followed by a failed coup attempt in 1958. However, despite all the detailed facts and the clear desire to destroy Sukarno and communism within the country, the CIA has denied direct involvement in the 1965 purge. This is perhaps not surprising because many US voters could find such a large number of deaths being caused by *their* agents atrocious.

The CIA's involvement in Chile in the early 1970s was so significant that its ripples are still being felt today, including in the UK where a prime minister supported a murderous tyrant. In 1973, the CIA was involved in the overthrow of Salvador Allende, a democratically elected socialist leader. Allende was assassinated and replaced with General Augusto Pinochet, who went on to torture and kill several thousand citizens. Allende was inspired by Castro's Cuba, which he had visited before coming to power.

The CIA attempted to stop him coming to office and, once he was in power, the US president Nixon, as well as ordering the CIA to overthrow him, waged economic war on Chile. This included funding strikes in the country. Allende became president of Chile in 1970 and the country was visited by Fidel Castro the following year, much to the alarm of the US administration.

Before the CIA-backed coup, Chile had a strong history of political stability. While other South American countries struggled with oppressive juntas, Chile had a robust democratic system. By attacking the Chilean system, the CIA and the US administration attacked the capacity of South America to nurture more democratically elected left-leaning governments. As has often been the case, the 'land of the free' was attacking freedom itself – the profits of US interests and hard-right US political ideology taking precedence over democracy.

Allende was killed during the Pinochet-led coup on September 11, 1973, a date that would become synonymous decades later for attacks on the US. Despite denials at the time, there is good evidence that the US government, aided by the CIA, was directly responsible for the overthrow and death of Allende and the installation of the sadistic Pinochet. The evidence includes recorded phone calls between Nixon and Henry Kissinger, who was national security adviser before becoming Secretary of State.

Documents declassified during Bill Clinton's administration make clear the Nixon government's opposition to Allende being elected and that CIA operatives were located in Chile for the purpose of preventing or destroying a left-wing government. There were convoluted plots to stop him taking office and clear efforts to undermine his administration politically and economically and create a climate of unrest in the country. There is evidence that the Australian Secret Intelligence Service, at the CIA's request, was also involved in efforts to undermine the Allende government.

A CIA document released in 2000 entitled *CIA Activities in Chile* reveals that the US government supported the Pinochet junta after the coup. This is a junta that killed thousands of left-wingers and those accused of being so in the months after the coup, imprisoned 40,000 people as 'political enemies' and tortured tens of thousands of citizens. General Pinochet, a friend of UK prime minister Margaret Thatcher, managed, with support from his overseas allies, to cling to power until 1988.

During a 1998 visit to London, Pinochet was served an international arrest warrant and arrested on charges of multiple human rights violations. While held in house arrest in Surrey, fighting extradition to Spain, he was visited by Baroness Thatcher. During the televised visit, in 1999, Thatcher thanked Pinochet for "bringing democracy to Chile". By the time of the visit Thatcher was an extremely unpopular figure in the UK but the visit and her decision to speak against Pinochet's extradition to Spain brought her even lower in the public's estimation. When she finally died in 2013, her support for the murderous dictator was mentioned by many.

Despite a House of Lords ruling that Pinochet should have been extradited to face charges, the Home Secretary of the time, Jack Straw, overruled the decision on medical grounds. However, in 2004, a Chilean judge ruled him fit to stand trial and he was placed under house arrest. At the point of his death, in 2006, he faced approximately 300 charges, ranging from human rights atrocities, embezzlement and tax evasion.

In 1975, driven by public outrage about US intelligence activities and concerns about accountability, a committee was established to investigate. The Senate Select Committee to Study Governmental Operations with Respect to Intelligence Activities became known as the Church Committee as it was headed by Idaho Senator Frank Church. The committee not only focused on CIA abuses of power and alleged crimes but also on the National Security Agency (NSA) and Federal Bureau of Investigation (FBI).

A key factor in the establishment of the Committee was the Watergate scandal, in which communications of the Democrats were illegally intercepted. The Democratic National Committee headquarters at the Watergate building in Washington was broken into in 1972 by President Richard Nixon's team. The illegal activity was to gain political advantage and the Nixon team compounded their criminal conspiracy with attempted cover-ups. The intelligence services were used by Nixon and the CIA was even used to undermine a subsequent FBI investigation.

Overseas activities, such as sabotage and assassination and attempted assassination of political leaders, were also significant in the establishment of the Church Committee. Unfavourable press reports emerged in the early 1970s as well as revelations from intelligence service whistle-blowers. The committee investigated many of the atrocities mentioned here.

As a result of the committee, President Gerald Ford issued an Executive Order in 1976 designed to improve oversight of intelligence activities and ban the assassinations of foreign politicians. An Intelligence Oversight Board was established, tasked with reporting illegal activities to the attorney general and the president. In relation to political assassinations, the Executive Order stated: "No employee of the United States Government shall engage in, or conspire to engage in, political assassination."

Such was the concern about these politically motivated murders that President Jimmy Carter, who came to power in 1977, issued an Executive Order that reiterated the message, while also closing any potential loopholes. The 1978 Executive Order stated: "No person employed by or acting on behalf of the United States Government shall engage in, or conspire to engage in, assassination."

Despite efforts to clean up the CIA and make it more account-able, it continued as rather a law unto itself or politicians turned a blind eye to some of its skulduggery until something so big that could not be buried was exposed. It is difficult to accept that the most senior politicians were not aware of the CIA's actions as many of its excesses were connected to the US political classes' obsession with the 'red menace'.

In late 1979, the Soviets invaded Afghanistan and the CIA immediately backed with arms any group in the region that would fight Soviet troops. The CIA programme, called Operation Cyclone, channelled funds through Pakistan's intelligence service to the mujahideen fighting the Soviets for the USA. The amount the US government spent on training and funding forces to defeat the Soviets in Afghanistan was colossal, in excess of $20 billion. Backers in Saudi Arabia also supported the activity with substantial amounts of money.

While some CIA efforts to crush left-wing uprisings were against populist local movements with socialist ideologies, the battle in Afghanistan was closer to a proxy war between the US and Soviet Union – using local factions as mercenaries as well as groups from other states. As well as being an ideological war between the US and Russia, however, there were ideological aspects in relation to the Saudi backing and those actually doing the fighting

The war lasted nine years but the US's actions, through the CIA, had ramifications still being felt, from the 2001 US-led invasion of Afghanistan to the rise of far-right apocalyptic Islamists in many places around the world and prominent terror attacks.

The National Security Archive states that "the CIA played a significant role in asserting US influence in Afghanistan by fund-ing military operations designed to frustrate the Soviet invasion of that country." Given how destabilising and damaging these groups appear to be now, it will seem crazy to many readers to think that the US, via the CIA, used and armed the Jihadist mujahideen. It is indicative of how threatening the US establishment found the Soviets that this is exactly what happened. The war resulted in the deaths of up to two million civilians. Many more became refugees, seeking asylum in Pakistan and Iran.

The context to the Soviet invasion was that communists had taken power in Afghanistan the year before via a coup. Their leader, Nur Mohammad Taraki, attempted to introduce radical reforms which proved highly unpopular. However, the regime crushed dissent, thousands of people were arrested and tens of thousands of political prisoners executed. Nevertheless, the uprising continued, with armed militia rising up against government forces.

There was disarray and conflict within the government and, in September 1979, Taraki was assassinated on the orders of rival Hafizullah Amin, who had spent time in the US and may have been favoured, if not appointed, by the CIA. Conflict in the country continued to escalate after Amin became president and, in December 1979, the Soviet leader Leonid Brezhnev sent in troops, who staged another coup. Amin was killed and new president Babrak Karmal was installed.

In early 1980, the United Nations General Assembly passed a resolution condemning the Soviet intervention and there was widespread condemnation from politicians in Islamic nations. The US and Persian Gulf countries were key funders of counter-insurgency against the communist regime, with Afghan fighters being trained in Pakistan. The CIA appears to have worked with the Pakistani intelligence services to support Afghani guerrillas, who would no doubt be called terrorists today if fighting *against* US interests.

The mountainous landscape and climate of Afghanistan makes it difficult for state forces to tackle insurgents or for invading powers to win against knowledgeable and resilient Afghanis. British forces found this out to their horror before retreating from Kabul in 1842. In the Soviet-Afghan conflict, the mujahideen was successful by waging a guerrilla war, with small units scattered across most of the country. Just as US troops in Vietnam struggled against locals with expert knowledge of the environment, the Soviets struggled against guerrillas who were familiar with the mountains and climate.

As we have seen in Syria more recently with Russian airstrikes, the Soviets used aerial bombardment indiscriminately, killing both civilians and rebel forces. Villages were destroyed and millions of land mines were laid across the country, which were more likely to kill children than guerrillas.

The Soviet forces were increased as the 1980s progressed. but the guerrillas – and whoever was backing them – ultimately won. In 1987 the Soviet Union was entering a new era, led by Mikhail Gorbachev, who announced withdrawal of forces from Afghanistan. They were gone by early 1989. It is widely accepted that the Soviet Union's defeat in Afghanistan marked the decline of the USSR. Another way of putting this is that the Soviet invasion hastened the dissolution of the Soviet Union. As has been the case for many empires, it was a battle too far.

After the Soviet retreat, civil war in Afghanistan lasted for three years. The conflict between the Afghan army and the mujahideen resulted in approximately 400,000 Afghan civilians being killed in the period up to 1992. The impact of the civil war and the conflict that preceded it, however, has been and continues to be much greater than that.

I view the Afghan battle zone, created, occupied and supported by a myriad of parties, as a horrendous laboratory from which cultural viruses spread. Some of these continued to mutate and continue to destroy human communities and habitats. In my previous book, *Psychopathic Cultures and Toxic Empires*, I discuss how human groups of all sizes can express the characteristics associated with psychopathy. This can be seen in extreme forms when different factions fight over land, resources or control of populations. As we have seen in Afghanistan, the pathology can spread beyond borders and in all directions.

Some people would like to simplify things and link to Islam all the horror that has spread outwards from the Afghan theatre of war. However, the US, UK, Russia, other states and intelligence services must take some responsibility for the pathological systems they have incubated. Religion is not the only manifestation of ideology, and political ideologies can be just as dangerous, as can be the fundamental desire for power, which may or may not be dressed up in religious costumes or in political discourses about 'liberation'.

As well as local fighters, tens of thousands of militants had been brought into Afghanistan for the CIA-led anti-Soviet Jihad. After the Soviets withdrew and Western powers followed suit, a large number of these were left behind. These included members of a multinational militant Sunni Islamist organisation called Al-Qaeda.

The Arabic name Al-Qaeda can be translated to 'the basis' or 'the base'. This appears to refer to a computer database of thousands of mujahideen recruited and trained by the CIA to wage war on the Soviet forces. One notable person on the database was Osama bin Laden. After the retreat of the Russians and consequent diminished American interest, Al-Qaeda carried on with the violent Jihad, which the CIA had instigated, in Afghanistan, Pakistan and elsewhere.

Skills honed within CIA-funded training camps enabled many fighters to become accomplished military leaders and this helped them move easily into insurgency and terrorist cells in a variety of different and strategic places. These included Egypt, Algeria, Bosnia and Chechnya, where many notable atrocities have subsequently taken place.

In tandem with this physical process of highly trained militia spreading out geographically and gaining greater power, ideologies of extremism and resentment were being nurtured in the young. Many thousand Afghan children orphaned by the war who had ended up in Pakistan were taught at conservative madrassas.

As we have seen with Daesh (ISIS), the far-right leanings of some of those who passed through that process were even more pronounced that those of militia fighting for the USA against the Soviets. This can, to an extent, be explained by ultra-conservative religious education, but the experience of war and loss driven by foreign empires created fertile ground for the manipulations of teachers and preachers. And for young boys brought up with stories of Muslim heroes defeating the Soviet Empire, a worldwide caliphate seemed possible.

Above are some of the factors behind the spread of Jihad to other countries. In tandem with the spread of Jihadist groups we have seen the development of new far-right groups, such as the English Defence League (EDL) and Britain First in the UK and the resurgence of Nazi groups. Interestingly, Jihadist groups and Islamophobic and white supremacist movements share far-right ideologies. Arguably, these highly authoritarian movements, which many would characterise as fascist, support one another's existence by their ideological conflict and all have a damaging impact on societies.

There is tyranny, misogyny, homophobia and sadism on all sides of this ultra-conservative uprising, and a common desire to take away societies' freedom and social progress. Curiously, these motivations echo those seen in CIA atrocities described earlier, when democratic progress was met with carefully planned violence and devious manipulation.

There are many narratives about the September 11, 2001, attacks on the World Trade Center and the Pentagon. I am not going to go into the many conspiracy theories, which have been discussed widely in recent decades. It is not necessary to believe that the attacks were false flag operations initiated by US bodies to recognise that CIA and US government activities played a part in what happened. They did not fly the planes but they launched and nurtured the network that did commit those atrocities.

Without justifying terrorism and without having any respect for the motives or actions of Osama Bin Laden and his associates, the context set out above helps us to understand what happened and why. The attacks on these symbols of US power, not to mention citizens, represented an unintended yet real consequence of CIA funding and training of the mujahideen to do America's dirty work against the Soviet Union. Those Al-Qaeda figures involved with the September 11 attacks and the earlier 1993 World Trade Center bombing were inextricably linked to the CIA's Afghan Jihad.

There are many other examples of CIA efforts to alter the course of history of other countries I could give, and ways in which these have sometimes backfired on the agency and the US itself. However, the examples listed offer readers a clear idea of the concerns that have driven many of its activities and challenges it has had of controlling monsters it has created and nurtured.

An obsession with stopping nations becoming socialist states that potentially undermine US economic interests, has been the primary driver of violent conflicts, coups, assassination attempts and full-blown wars. It is extremely interesting that an economic model so often labelled unworkable by the US capitalist establishment should need so much money, aggression, deviousness and cruelty to undermine.

It should be clear by now to most people that ideas and ideologies cannot be bombed into oblivion or destroyed by assassinating popular political leaders. The best way to weaken ideas we do not like is to come up with and articulate better ideas. Bolstering our own old ideas with missiles and guns merely undermines the purity and integrity of the model we are advocating.

It is impossible to know how the world would be if the US had not spent trillions of dollars attacking socialist movements overseas. Although the use of militia in Afghanistan to tackle the 'red menace' may have brought the USSR to its knees, it also spawned the multiheaded beast of Jihadist warfare and terrorism with which we have been contending in the last couple of decades. A 19th century ideology about equality was attacked using everything the largest beneficiary of the capitalist system could throw at it. In doing so, we have seen brutal medieval religiosity spread, using the communication technology of capitalism as a means of propagation.

Chapter 4 – Attempts at liberation: Part 1

The previous chapter examined ways in which certain states and intelligence services undermined and attacked political and social movements that they, or their paymasters, found threatening. In this chapter the focus is on the other side of the coin – attempts by citizens to rise up and shake off systems experienced as oppressive. By focusing on uprisings that happened at distinct points in time, spanning different areas, we can appreciate the significance of context in uprisings and modes of suppression.

This chapter focuses on uprisings that happened towards the end of the 1960s and subsequent chapters concentrate on the chain of uprisings known as the Arab Spring or Arab Uprising.

The 1968 liberation and aftermath

Many factors led to 1968 being a flashpoint of radical activity in many locations in the world, sometimes followed by rather desperate authoritarian crackdowns. In the US, baby-boomers who emerged in teen movements in the late 1950s and early 1960s morphed into counter-cultural activists in the late 1960s. A significant influx of young people into California took place in the early 1960s, and, by 1968, San Francisco and Los Angeles had become hotbeds of radicalism. Greater participation in university education, civil rights issues coming to a head, the war in Vietnam, the influence of counter-cultural figures on the young and the prevalence of psychedelic substances were among the drivers of this.

While some of these factors may have also played a part in protests that took place in other parts of the world, not all of them would have been so relevant and other important factors were therefore at play. There was a general intensity of social unrest and mistrust of and antagonism towards political regimes, especially against militarism and traditional political authorities. Mass movements in 1968 were wide ranging, including women's liberation activism, anti-nuclear protests and the dawning of the environmental movement.

The year was extremely significant in the civil rights movement in the US, where revolutionary movements such as the Black Panther Party emerged. Some elements of the civil rights movement were willing to resort to violence by this stage, as they felt themselves very much in battle with an institutionally racist state which treated black people with violent contempt. It is important to state, however, that most of the civil rights movement in the US in the 1960s was peaceful. In addition, the Black Power movement, with which the Black Panthers were aligned, used a variety of methods of activism to achieve the goal of empowerment for black citizens. The state was more likely to dish out violence against peaceful black protesters in this period than be the recipient of violence from black campaigners.

In February 1968, three African Americans were shot and killed and 27 other activists injured when nine highway patrol officers opened fire on civil rights protesters on the South Carolina State University campus. The protesters had been demonstrating against racial segregation at a bowling alley. The event is known as the Orangeburg massacre. None of the police, who claimed they were being shot at – despite none of the students having guns – were convicted. However, one of the protesters, Cleveland Sellers, was convicted on a charge of rioting and served a seven-month prison sentence. It took 25 years for the governor of South Carolina to pardon him.

Other civil rights protests in the US in early 1968 included sit-ins in food outlets that discriminated against black people by refusing to allow them to sit, and Los Angeles high school pupils staging walk-outs of classes to protest against discrimination of Mexican American pupils. Just as the civil rights movement was gaining ground and interest across the country in spring 1968, the civil rights leader Martin Luther King was assassinated.

Dr King, who received the Nobel Peace Prize in 1965 for combating racial inequality through non-violent resistance, had been campaigning against the Vietnam War and poverty among all ethnicities, as well as for racial equality. The event he had been planning prior to being gunned down in April 1968 was a national occupation of Washington entitled 'the Poor People's Campaign'. White supremacist James Earl Ray pleaded guilty to the murder, but a subsequent case brought by Dr King's family concluded that US government agencies were probably conspirators in the politically motivated assassination.

Following the murder, protests took place in more than a hundred cities across the US. Members of the political establishment and other civil rights activists spoke to calm the situation by encouraging people to follow Dr King's example of non-violent activism.

Other flashpoints of protests in 1968 included Mexico, Czechoslovakia, Poland, West Germany, Spain, Italy and France. In some settings, capitalism-supporting states were the target of protests by left-wingers, while in others poor civil rights under communist regimes were targeted by protesters.

Protests in Mexico were sparked by the apartheid-era South African team being included in the Olympics in Mexico City. Dozens of teams threatened to boycott the games because of the white supremacist country being allowed to participate and, as well as Mexican students, black civil rights activists were involved in the activism. The Olympics Committee ultimately backed down and the South African team was rejected.

Other ideological issues were also at play, including disenchantment of the educated younger generation with the old political and social order, just as in many parts of the world that year. An important part of this was the women's liberation movement within Mexico, with young women playing a critical part in the summer of activism. Numerous protests were held against the Mexican government and clashes took place between the students and the police. The army were also brought in and occupied the National Autonomous University of Mexico. An October demonstration in Tlatelolco Plaza in Mexico City, attended by men, women and children, culminated in the police and army shooting dead more than 100 citizens.

A political shift in Czechoslovakia in 1968 was short-lived but ultimately laid the ideological foundations for fundamental and lasting revolution decades later. The 'Prague Spring', as the 1968 period of liberalisation was known, happened in the context of the country being part of the Soviet bloc, which it had been since 1948. At the time of the Prague Spring the official name of the country was the Czechoslovak Socialist Republic.

The start of the 'spring' was actually in January, after Alexander Dubček was elected First Secretary of the Communist Party in the country. His aim was increased rights for citizens and a process of democratisation. Dubček's progressive reforms included greater freedom of speech and freedom of movement as well as greater freedom for the media. A decision was also made to divide the centralist state of Czechoslovakia into the Czech Socialist Republic and Slovak Socialist Republic.

The partial decentralisation of the economy was fundamental to Dubček's reforms, but this alarmed the Soviet regime which, in August 1968, sent in half a million troops as an occupying force. The Soviet tanks and those from other Warsaw Pact countries rolling into the country led a large number of citizens to flee the country.

Those who did not leave and supported Dubček's reforms attempted to resist what was effectively a military coup in a largely non-violent manner. Curfews imposed by the Soviets were ignored and street signs were turned around or painted over to confuse the invaders. There were also several public suicides where people set themselves on fire as a form of protest against the occupation. The only reform that survived after the Soviet invasion was the creation of the Czech Socialist Republic and Slovak Socialist Republic.

It took more than 20 years from the Prague Spring for the country to gain liberation from Soviet rule. The Velvet Revolution was a non-violent uprising which lasted two months at the end of 1989. Those involved in widespread demonstrations against the Communist Party of Czechoslovakia, which had enjoyed one-party rule, included older dissidents who had been part of the Prague Spring as well as university students.

In March 1968, two months into the Prague Spring in neighbouring Czechoslovakia, there was political unrest in Poland. The '1968 Polish political crisis', as it has been called, was a mass movement involving academics, writers and students. It was driven by a range of events, experiences and frustrations. These included inflation of food prices, especially meat, and reduction of wages. Those who spoke out about poor living standards were persecuted by the state. Anti-Semitic policies and suppression of free speech were other key drivers of the unrest. The Prague Spring, before it was crushed, had given the Polish dissidents hope that democratic reforms could be introduced.

As well as the global context of political unrest at the time, there had been growing concern for some time in Poland among the intelligentsia about political control over universities and censorship of authors. A number of activists, writers and academics had already been persecuted by the Communist Party for their activism and a play called Dziady, written in 1824, was banned on account of it apparently being anti-Soviet.

In a meeting in Warsaw at the end of February, members of the Polish Writers' Union condemned the ban and other attacks on free speech in the country. They also discussed a rise in anti-Semitic incidents in the country, encouraged by politicians. The removal of dissidents from the University of Warsaw a few days later led to violent suppression of a rally by up to 1,000 students by both uniformed and undercover police. This only spread the unrest to other colleges.

An anti-Jewish campaign that started in 1967 related to a power struggle within the Communist Party in Poland. An attempt by the ultra-nationalist Minister of the Interior Mieczysław Moczar failed to overthrow the Władysław Gomułka government, but the anti-Semitic purge led to the expulsion from Poland of thousands of Jews, including many from government or government agencies.

Following the violent crackdown on dissidents in March 1968 and beyond, many more people emigrated from the country or were expelled or arrested. The protests continued throughout March and April 1968 and the state responded by culling entire academic departments. Despite the violent crackdowns, arrests and expulsions from the country, protests occurred in a number of locations. The protests spread to small towns by the middle of March, though dissidence in the country was ultimately crushed.

Nevertheless, 1968 was a turning point in Poland's history. Factors that drove the uprising – such as authoritarian control, censorship and poor living standards – ultimately laid the foundations for the Communist Party's power being swept away in 1989.

Student protests in West Germany in 1968 were a response to authoritarianism, in a context where many former Nazis worked for the state and universities. Kurt Georg Kiesinger, the chancellor of West Germany at the time, was himself a member of the Nazi Party. As well as seeking to get the country to confront its Nazi past and remnants in power, the students protested against inequality in the country, conditions in the developing world, the Vietnam War (the West German government supported South Vietnam economically), and the power of the right-wing press.

Activism by students increased from 1966 through 1967 and climaxed in 1968, when schoolchildren and union members also participated. Protests were crushed violently by the police, which amplified their intensity. However, the existence of different groups with different missions appeared to be a factor in the overall disintegration of the general movement in 1968. Nevertheless, the protests did have a long-term moral and cultural impact on the country, with the ideological positions of the activists filtering into public and political discourse.

The most explosive and arguably successful activism in Western Europe in 1968 took place in France in the spring and summer. The protests and other actions did not just involve students but also school pupils and millions of workers from across France. However, in spring 1968, university campuses were where the fault-lines in French society became clearly apparent.

The main activism was in May and June of the year, but in March police surrounded a building at Paris University at Nanterre occupied by students, left-wing activists, poets and musicians. Those present were discussing class discrimination as well as university governance and funding. The protesters left the premises peacefully, but the university disciplined some of the students after the event.

Tension between students and the university administration grew over the coming weeks, culminating in the institution being shut down by the administration at the start of May. Protests then spread to the Sorbonne, where students protested against the closure of Nanterre. Police invaded the university as a result.

Things escalated when France's national student union and a union for academics marched in protest about the police's actions. As thousands of students and academics marched towards the Sorbonne, police charged, attacking peaceful marchers with batons. To defend themselves, some marchers used any materials they could find to make barricades. Some responded by tearing up paving stones and hurling them at the police, which forced a brief retreat. However, police subsequently used tear gas on the crowd and charged with batons again. Of around 20,000 marchers, hundreds were arrested.

The following day, school pupils and workers joined the students and academics at the Arc de Triomphe to demand that criminal charges against the arrested students be dropped, police leave the Sorbonne and both the Nanterre and Sorbonne campuses be reopened. A false report that the campuses were to open again led protesters to disperse as students returned to their campuses. On doing so, however, they found that police were still occupying the institutions.

Three days later, on May 10, police and police reservists were hit by missiles after a march was blocked. After negotiations were attempted and broke down, the police attacked the protesters, many of whom sustained injuries. Hundreds of arrests were also made. The protest and police response were broadcast on the radio, which appears to have encouraged public sympathies for the protesters and ultimately increased the size of the movement. Police were accused of using agent provocateurs, who threw petrol bombs and burned cars.

By May 13, a one-day general strike and mass demonstration took place against the government and the police's response to activism. More than a million people marched through Paris, which led the prime minister, Georges Pompidou, to announce the reopening of the Sorbonne and release of the detained students. After the university reopened, it was occupied by students, who declared the prestigious institution an 'autonomous people's university'.

The protest movement continued to grow, with hundreds of

popular action committees established in a matter of weeks, taking up grievances against the state. The size of the worker contingent of the protest movement increased markedly, with a wave of occupations and strikes sweeping the country. By the middle of May, workers had occupied around 50 factories and the number of people striking had swelled from around 200,000 in the middle of the month to 10,000,000 within a week – a sizeable proportion of the country's workforce.

The strikes were not simply for more pay and were not prompted by the union movement but were about a fundamental political shift in society and working practices. Calls were made for the resignation of President Charles de Gaulle and his government and claims put forward that workers should take over the running of some factories. Unions were, in some cases, regarded as establishment collaborators – with attempts by union leaders to end the strikes by negotiating significantly higher pay, workers reportedly jeered union officials and continued to strike.

By May 29, things were so tense in France that de Gaulle was anticipating an attack by protesters on the Élysée Palace, the official residence of the president of France, and he fled. He reportedly told his son-in-law, Alain de Boissieu, that he did not want blood to be shed in his defence. An announcement was made that de Gaulle was going to his country home. However, he simply disappeared via helicopter without even telling government colleagues where he was going. This led the prime minister, Georges Pompidou, to exclaim: "He has fled the country!" This was subsequently proved to be true — he had fled to Germany.

The protests by the students and workers paralysed the French government, with the expectation of imminent violent revolution. This had particular resonance, given the bloody ten-year long French revolution at the end of the 18th century. However, rather than people being beheaded by guillotine, the biggest problems for the government were simply related to workers withdrawing their labour. Getting petrol and accessing money in banks became a particular problem.

At the headquarters of the French military in Germany, de Gaulle met General Jacques Massu, who persuaded him to go back to

France rather than exile himself in Germany. On May 30, de Gaulle was persuaded by Pompidou to dissolve the National Assembly and call an election.

Calling an election on June 23, de Gaulle demanded that workers return to work. He threatened to instigate a state of emergency if they continued to strike. As a show of strength, with the military close by, an orchestrated 800,000-strong march of his flag-waving supporters walked down the Champs-Elysées just as de Gaulle finished his speech. At this point the opposition party agreed to the election.

The revolutionary mood quickly deflated and people returned to work, student demonstrations ceased, the police retook the Sorbonne in June and, in the aftermath of the protests, de Gaulle's government banned some left-wing groups. In the June election, de Gaulle was returned to power, with his party winning by a landslide.

In mid-July, on Bastille Day, some new demonstrations, led by left-wingers, bubbled up in Paris but police acted quickly to suppress them, with many protesters hospitalised. The UK and West German governments filed formal protests about alleged crimes committed by the police, including the indecent assault of two British schoolgirls by police officers.

The following year de Gaulle left office after the French public voted in a referendum against his reforms. He had made a promise to resign if his reforms were rejected. The reforms were concerned with decentralisation and altering the way the Senate operated. The Senate would have been weakened and this would have limited its ability to block legislation the government wanted to introduce. Therefore, a reform that seemed democratic, decentralisation, was bundled in with reforms to erode political scrutiny.

Readers will note parallels between the events of 1968 and more recent unrest and battles in various parts of the world. Uprisings against oppression, from whatever side of the ideological spectrum, are routinely crushed and undermined, but, unless the underlying drivers are dealt with intelligently, the energy behind comes back in a new way rather than being completely eradicated.

Malicious and violent responses by authorities to protest will always be remembered, but in this era of digital media they are much easier to broadcast. This does not mean that counter-cultures will always get their way, as the power of the establishment is often too great – and what they have to lose is too great for them to back down. Concerns about contagion of uprising have amplified in the era of social media and this may affect how rapidly and brutally authorities deal with protests.

The following chapter looks at a variety of uprisings referred to as the 'Arab Spring' and examines the impact of these and of state responses to the movements.

Chapter 5 – Attempts at liberation: Part 2

The 'Arab Spring' and beyond

The series of uprisings known as the 'Arab Spring' or 'Democracy Spring' started in late 2010 and spread rapidly in 2011. It is important to note, however, that the protests and unrest which were most prominent from 2010 and 2011 did not appear out of the blue. They represented the boiling point of tensions and activism that had been building for some years in the Middle East and North Africa. They also relate to socio-politico-religious tectonic plates which had begun to shift – and still are shifting.

With conflict still ongoing in Syria at the top of news bulletins for much of the time I have been working on this book, some would contend that the Arab Uprising continues today. However, as I have watched rebel forces and civilians alike be bombed by Assad and Russian forces in Syria, it has been hard to regard it as much of a spring. The term Arab Winter has been used to refer to the aftermath of the uprisings, which have been crushed relentlessly in many places. It is worth remembering, however, that it took more than 20 years for the Prague Spring to germinate into ultimate and lasting revolution, and underlying drivers of the Arab Spring are still very much a reality.

What we have seen unfold in Aleppo during the last year or two could be viewed as one aspect of the Arab Spring turning to autumn and then winter, but the Arab Spring started very differently. Armed conflict in the streets and missiles raining down upon houses and hospitals is what many people will remember of the Syrian conflict, but it is worth revisiting the start of the diverse uprising and recalling the myriad of more peaceful activities that became known as the Arab Spring.

Some of the methods of uprising are comparable to those seen in the 1960s, which from a distance would, for some, have given the movements a nostalgic air. Vocal demonstrations, silent protests, strikes, sit-ins, protest camps and civil disobedience took place. Self-immolation also played a dramatic role, as in a 1963 protest against the persecution of Buddhists by the South Vietnamese government.

Other aspects of the Arab Uprising – and means of dissemination – were only possible because of digital media and internet technology. Social media was key to the spread of movements and confidence. As effectiveness of political messaging of activists requires widespread dissemination, those in distant places sharing news on social media played a part in the uprisings, though without being at risk of persecution and state violence.

While in 1968 protesters had to hope that international media picked up and ran stories, and articles took at least a day to appear in newspapers, during the Arab Uprising news spread around the world in seconds. This not only empowered protesters but made citizens on social media around the world feel involved in a way not seen previously in multi-country mass protests. This immediate global engagement with conflicts is something that has changed forever but, unfortunately, some states have few qualms about attacking their citizens while the world is watching.

Furthermore, the massive bloodshed seen on social media may have desensitised many viewers to the horrors of war and conflict. Curiously and disturbingly, images of violence, blood and dead bodies from overseas are sometimes shown on UK television by broadcasters that would not show the same sort of images from violent British incidents.

As well as desensitising viewers to overseas horrors, there has also therefore been a sense of dehumanising the distant 'other'. It is questionable that this process helps us recognise the part Western governments, and therefore taxpayers, play in overseas conflicts. A related issue is the way the mainstream media now has to compete with social media in terms of immediacy and intensity of coverage.

The brutality of coverage of social media and traditional outlets can both humanise and dehumanise. Some of the most powerful output from Syria in recent years, and from Gaza during quite recent Israeli airstrikes, has been children on social media talking about their worlds being torn apart.

Countries where uprisings associated with the 'Arab Spring' have taken place include Tunisia, Egypt, Syria, Libya, Morocco, Yemen, Bahrain, Kuwait, Lebanon, Oman, Jordan, Saudi Arabia, Sudan and Mauritania. In some places dissent has been violently crushed, while in other places shifts have occurred resulting from uprisings. However, in others all out civil war has taken place in the wake of unrest. In Syria, this 'civil war' has involved forces from a number of different countries, groups and factions.

I will discuss some of the individual circumstances that led to unrest in specific countries, and particular state responses, but key factors included human rights violations by brutal authoritarian regimes, political corruption, shortcomings of democratic processes, economic problems impacting on citizens (such as unemployment and inflation) and religious divisions.

Tunisia, where the Arab Spring is credited as having started, experienced mounting social and political tension in the years leading up to the Tunisian Revolution, which started in 2010. Sit-ins, rallies and strikes were met with dozens of arrests, numerous injuries and some fatalities in 2008, but the spirit of dissent was not crushed as the realities of poor living conditions, high unemployment, inflation and state oppression did not change.

The act in Tunisia, on December 17, 2010, which lit the fuse of the Arab Uprising, was a young street vendor called Mohamed Bouazizi setting himself on fire. His self-immolation was a response to the confiscation of his stock and his experience of being harassed and humiliated by state officials. He took 18 days to die from his injuries. In a six-month period after Mohamed Bouazizi's death, more than 100 Tunisians tried to kill themselves by self-immolation and the event also inspired, for want of a better word, numerous self-immolations in the Middle East, North Africa and Europe.

Mohamed Bouazizi's act of suicide was followed by a series of street demonstrations, which were brave in that climate of oppression where free speech was not tolerated. The police and security forces killed dozens of Tunisian protesters in an attempt to crush the uprising.

The Tunisian Revolution, also referred to as the Sidi Bouzid Revolt (named after the city where it began) or the Jasmine Revolution, proved to be a success. It resulted in President Zine El Abidine Ben Ali being driven from office on January 14, 2011, after 23 years in power. It ultimately also led to legitimate democratic elections in the country. Though elections took place during his rule, they were far from free, fair or transparent. Amid protests against his regime, Ben Ali fled to Saudi Arabia in mid-January 2011 with his wife and some of his children. Other family members were arrested while attempting to leave the country.

In late January 2011, the Tunisian government, via Interpol, issued an international arrest warrant for Ben Ali, his wife Leïla and other family members. He was accused of taking money out of the nation illegally and illegally acquiring property and other assets abroad. Video footage revealed that Ben Ali had stashed money and jewellery at his palace. He also had millions of dollars in Swiss bank accounts, which were subsequently frozen.

In June 2011, a Tunisian court sentenced Ben Ali and Leïla to 35 years in prison for charges of theft and unlawful possession of cash and jewellery. The following June, still in absentia, he was given a sentence of life imprisonment for inciting murder and violence. In April 2013, he received an additional life sentence for the violent repression of political protest. Ben Ali acknowledged through a lawyer in 2016 that his regime made "errors, abuses and violations". He remains, at the time of writing, in Saudi Arabia. The Saudi government has failed to respond to requests to extradite the couple. Ben Ali currently resides in Jeddah, where Idi Amin lived in exile from Uganda until his death.

In January 2011, there was unrest in Oman, Yemen, Syria, Morocco and Egypt. On January 25, less than a fortnight after Ben Ali was ousted, thousands of Egyptian protesters gathered in Cairo's Tahrir Square to demand the resignation of President Hosni Mubarak, who had held power since 1981.

As with Tunisia, the unrest in Egypt had been bubbling away for some time, with many protests happening in the preceding years, often organised by the labour movement. Social media was a significant factor in the rise of demonstrations in the country, which brought together young working people and more privileged middle-class students.

The protests in Egypt started on January 25, 2011, and continued for 18 days. Three days into the uprising, the Mubarak government attempted to stop protesters organising via social media by cutting internet access. Despite this, on that day, tens of thousands of protesters were on the streets of Egyptian cities, and Mubarak was shaken enough to dismiss his government. He subsequently appointed a new cabinet, including the first vice-president Egypt had known in three decades.

All presidential power was passed to the vice-president, Omar Suleiman, on February 10, but Mubarak later sought to remain in his role until the end of his term, in September 2011. This was rejected by protesters, who gathered in front of the presidential palace. On February 11, it was announced by the vice-president that Mubarak had resigned and power was being transferred to the armed forces. The military then dissolved parliament and suspended the country's constitution.

Though the military began to relinquish power with the election in March of Essam Sharaf as prime minister, violent protests continued late into 2011 as a result of citizens' concerns about governance and the slow pace of reforms.

On June 2, 2012, Mubarak was found guilty of failing to stop the killing of protesters by the Egyptian security forces during the first six days of the uprising. He was sentenced to life imprisonment for that crime but found not guilty of ordering the violent crackdown on protesters. Charges of profiteering and fraud were also dismissed by the court. The life sentence was overturned on appeal in 2013, and a new charge of complicity in the murder of protesters was later dismissed on a technicality. The only charge that stuck in the end related to corruption.

Mohamed Morsi became the first democratically elected president of Egypt, in June 2012, but only lasted in his position until July 2013. He was also ousted as a result of protests, as well as military intervention. A few months into his presidency, Morsi, who was the candidate of the Islamist 'Muslim Brotherhood', issued a constitutional declaration granting himself the ability to legislate without legal scrutiny or challenge. Soon after this, on December 5, 2012, tens of thousands of his supporters clashed with those who opposed him.

There were other aspects to his authoritarianism, including prosecutions of journalists and attacks on peaceful protesters. These ultimately backfired and led to more protests. On June 30, 2013, protests took place across Egypt amid calls for Morsi's resignation. As a result, the military gave him a 48-hour ultimatum to meet certain demands or they would intervene by "implementing their own road map" i.e. the threat of a military coup. The military kept to their word and he was ousted by a coup on July 3.

The following day the chief justice of the Supreme Constitutional Court, Adly Mansour, was sworn in as acting president. However, Morsi and vocal members of the Muslim Brotherhood refused to accept his removal. Protests led to several hundred deaths, mostly of Morsi supporters. Many thousands of Muslim Brotherhood members were jailed, with a great many sentenced to death or life imprisonment.

A referendum enabled the interim government, in January 2014, to institute a new constitution. In late March of the same year, head of the armed forces Abdel Fattah el-Sisi, who was effectively in power, announced that he was resigning from the military to stand in a presidential election. The election, which took place in May, gave Sisi a landslide victory – against just one opponent — and he became president in June.

Since then Sisi has introduced some tough economic reforms and encouraged some bold cultural changes, including modernising the teaching of Islam to remove a focus on the glorification of violence. He has shown concern about rape and sexual assaults in Egypt and encouraged the police to place more emphasis on tackling these crimes.

In 2015 he became the first Egyptian president ever to attend Christmas mass, and he spoke at the Coptic Orthodox Christmas service in Cairo about unity. He has also focused on duty to the country, encouraging ministers to set an example by arriving at work by 7am. His policies have led to higher prices for many essentials, including fuel. However, his message of the importance of duty and sacrifice appears to have been effective, strengthened by his leadership from the front – he gives half his salary and assets to the state. This is emulated by other officials and some prominent wealthy people. His messages and leadership style seem to appeal to much of the population. In April 2016, he had an approval rating of 79%.

Although much bloodshed has occurred in Egypt and the election arguably gave voters little choice – and the president is a former head of the military and military intelligence chief, some progress has been made. The country is neither ruled by someone who has clung to power for 30 years nor an Islamist regime with little interest in unity of the different communities in the country.

Significantly, Sisi has taken a stance on the Israel-Palestine conflict that is progressive and effective. He favours a two-state solution of establishing a Palestinian state on lands taken by Israel in 1967, but has also risen above past conflicts to reach out to Israel. He recognises the long and bitter Israeli-Palestinian conflict as a breeding ground for extremism in the Middle East and has therefore attempted to act as a bridge between the two sides.

At the start of Sisi's presidency there was an outbreak of fresh hostilities between Israel and Gaza, with Israel responding to launches against it with devastating attacks on Gaza, including on hospitals and schools. Sisi's government characterised Israel's attacks on civilians of the Gaza Strip as "oppressive policies of mass punishment rejecting the irresponsible Israeli escalation in the occupied Palestinian territory, which comes in the form of excessive and unnecessary use of military force leading to the death of innocent civilians."

Under Sisi's leadership, Cairo hosted a number of meetings with Israeli and Palestinian officials to try to bring about a ceasefire between Hamas in Gaza and the Israeli state. Egypt also gave 500 tons of aid, including food and medical supplies, to beleaguered Palestinians trapped in the Gaza Strip. The subsequent ceasefire was brokered by Egypt. The country has since hosted an international donor event intended to raise the billions needed to reconstruct the Gaza Strip after waves of Israeli airstrikes on homes and municipal buildings.

Like Syria, which will be discussed in more detail in Chapter 8,

Libya broke down into war following uprisings. Also, in common with Syria, foreign powers played a role in how events unfolded.

For decades leading up to the crisis, the country was led by Colonel Muammar Gaddafi. He came to power in 1969 at the age of 27, having founded a revolutionary cell within the military. When he seized power in a bloodless coup, it was from the monarch King Idris, who had ruled since 1951, his position supported by the UK and USA, which saw him as pliable and a buffer to Soviet expansion. The monarchy was abolished after Gaddafi seized power, with Libya becoming a republic.

Other significant features of Gaddafi's rule included resisting foreign influence on the country, bolstering relationships with Arab nationalist governments, taking the country towards a form of socialism embedded with Islamic values and nationalising the oil industry. After four years in office, Gaddafi initiated a new system claimed to be 'direct democracy', forming General People's Committees. However, he continued to make key decisions.

Three years later, in 1977, Gaddafi dissolved the Republic and created what he said was a new socialist state 'of the masses'. Despite a claim at that point of occupying a symbolic role in governance, as commander-in-chief he was very much in control.

A significant event that influenced the decades to come, including the way in which the 2011 uprising and subsequent war unfolded, was the 1988 Lockerbie bombing. A Pan American flight travelling from Frankfurt to Detroit was brought down and sections of the plane landed in the Scottish town of Lockerbie. All 243 passengers, 16 crew and 11 people in Lockerbie were killed.

After a lengthy investigation by the FBI and Dumfries and Galloway Constabulary, arrest warrants were issued in 1991 for two Libyans. They were intelligence officer and head of security for Libyan Arab Airlines Abdelbaset al-Megrahi, and Libyan Arab Airlines station manager Lamin Khalifah Fhimah. Eight years later, amid UN economic sanctions, and after lengthy negotiations, Gaddafi handed over the pair. Megrahi was convicted of murder but Fhimah was acquitted. Ten years into his life sentence, Megrahi was returned to Libya on compassionate grounds, having been diagnosed with prostate cancer.

Though a number of groups, including the Guardians of the Islamic Revolution, the Islamic Jihad Organization and the Ulster Defence League, claimed responsibility for the bombing, Gaddafi eventually admitted Libya's responsibility. However, he only accepted responsibility for the actions of his officials and denied ordering the attack.

Assuming that the Libyan state did plan and carry out the attack, a likely motive was retaliation for incidents involving the US in the 1980s. A number of confrontations took place in the Gulf of Sidra, where the Libyan military came off worse against the US. These included Libyan fighter planes being shot down and vessels being sunk. In 1986, US airstrikes were made against Libya in retaliation for the bombing of a nightclub in Berlin frequented by US servicemen. The US strikes on Tripoli and Benghazi killed up to 30 people. The planes involved took off from bases in the UK.

In 1987 Libya began producing mustard gas and Gaddafi commenced a nuclear programme. As well as contending with US confrontations, in the late 1980s Gaddafi faced opposition from Islamist groups, including the Libyan Islamic Fighting Group and the Muslim Brotherhood. A number of plots to kill him in the latter part of the decade were foiled and mosques viewed as incubators of opposition to his regime were raided.

Nevertheless, in the 1990s, Gaddafi was still facing threats from many directions, including a failed coup. The UN sanctions mentioned also had a significant effect on the country in the 1990s.

As well as handing over those accused of the Lockerbie bombing, at the end of the 1990s Gaddafi's engagement with the West began to change. In 1999, Libya reportedly commenced secret talks with the UK government, then led by Tony Blair, aimed at improving relations. Blair would later be criticised for his engagement with Gaddafi over a number of years.

Attempts to rehabilitate Libya on the world stage proved effective, however. After the September 11 attacks in 2001, which he condemned, Gaddafi expressed sympathy for the victims and pledged support for the 'War on Terror' against militant Islamism. With Islamist militants threatening his own regime, this was an easy commitment for Gaddafi.

In December 2003, months after the US-led invasion of Iraq, Libya renounced weapons of mass destruction and decommissioned its chemical and nuclear weapons programmes. The search for weapons of mass destruction was a key claim used to justify the war on Iraq. As a consequence of changing its stance, Libya's relations with the USA and other Western nations improved.

Gaddafi was rewarded in 2004 by a visit from Tony Blair, who shook his hand in front of the cameras and spoke of a "new relationship". It would appear that Libya was rewarded economically too as, just as Blair met Gaddafi, it was announced that British-Dutch energy company Shell had signed a deal for oil and gas exploration in Libyan waters.

The rehabilitation continued in 2004, with Gaddafi invited to the EU headquarters in Brussels, and sanctions against Libya by the union were soon dropped. As well as building bridges with Western nations, Gaddafi also strengthened Libya's relationships with both China and North Korea. Later in the decade he visited Russia, where then prime minister Vladimir Putin joined him in a Bedouin tent pitched in the grounds of the Kremlin.

In 2006 Libya was removed from the USA's list of state sponsors of terrorism and through the latter part of the decade also managed to strengthen ties with countries like Venezuela, which viewed the US as exploitative imperialists. In 2009, invited to address the UN General Assembly for the first time, Gaddafi condemned Western aggression and the exploitation of the developing world. In a speech much longer than scheduled, he called the UN Security Council 'the terror council' and spoke of the bias of the UN towards certain countries, lambasting it for its selective intervention in conflicts.

Appearing to claim to speak on behalf of the 'third world', Gaddafi stated: "From the beginning, since it was established in 1945, the Security Council has failed to provide security. On the contrary, it has provided terror and sanctions. It is only used against us." His narrative about the International Court of Justice was similar: "The decisions of the International Court of Justice, the international judicial body, take aim only at small countries and third world nations. Powerful countries escape the notice of the Court.

Or, if judicial decisions are taken against these powerful countries, they are not enforced."

He went on to suggest that African nations colonised in the past by European countries should be compensated to the tune of $777 trillion by their former colonisers. He argued that, by compensating African countries, Mauritius, India, the Philippines and Latin America would end immigration to Europe from those places.

Linking the history of colonisation and the reality of contemporary migration, he said: "Why are Africans going to Europe? Why are Asians going to Europe? Why are Latin Americans going to Europe? It is because Europe colonized those peoples and stole the material and human resources of Africa, Asia and Latin America – the oil, minerals, uranium, gold and diamonds, the fruit, vegetables and livestock and the people – and used them. Now, new generations of Asians, Latin Americans and Africans are seeking to reclaim that stolen wealth, as they have the right to do."

Changing his tone somewhat from his stance on the September 11 attacks and commitment to the 'War on Terror', Gaddafi also said: "I want to save the citizens of the United States, the United Kingdom and other countries who are fighting in Iraq and Afghanistan. So I tell them: leave Afghanistan to the Afghans; leave Iraq to the Iraqis ... Let there be a civil war in Iraq. If the Iraqis want to have a civil war and fight each other, that is fine. Who says that if the Taliban form a government they would possess intercontinental missiles or the kind of aeroplanes that hit New York? Did those aeroplanes take off from Afghanistan or Iraq? No; they took off from American airports."

The UN speech was generally reported by Western media as rambling and incoherent, not so subtly pushing the idea that Gaddafi was mentally disturbed – a characterisation that continued until the end of his life. However, despite the socialist and Pan-African narratives of Gaddafi at the UN, his actual direction in the lead up to the civil war was towards large-scale privatisation of Libyan industries and resources. This was not, though, matched with political or social liberalisation. Like many charismatic leaders, behind the colourful veneer he was calculating and shrewd.

After the Tunisian Revolution began, Gaddafi initially spoke out in favour of Ben Ali. However, concerned about the possibility of an uprising in his own country, he also implemented measures aimed at warding off protests. These measures included reducing food prices and releasing several Islamist prisoners. This was not, however, enough to head off an uprising, probably because corruption and 30% unemployment were of greater concern to the Libyan population than sectarian tensions.

The Libyan aspect of the 'Arab Spring' started on February 17, 2011, and within three days the protesters controlled most of Benghazi, the country's second largest city. Troops and militia deployed by Gaddafi to recapture the city were repelled by rebel forces. Gaddafi's son Saif al-Islam Gaddafi, who undertook public relations and diplomacy for the regime, appeared on television on February 20 warning of civil war, after protests spread to the capital Tripoli. He blamed the conflict on Islamists and tribal factions, promised reforms, and warned ominously of civil war and the country being taken over by foreigners.

His father subsequently accused the rebels of being influenced by Al-Qaeda and Osama Bin Laden, claiming that hallucinogenic drugs had been put in drinks and pills and blaming Bin Laden and Al-Qaeda for distributing these substances. Somewhat contradictorily, Gaddafi later said that the uprising was a colonialist plot by foreign states, including the US, France and the UK, to control oil and rule the Libyan people. In reality, the first protesters appear to have been civilians such as students, teachers and lawyers, who were joined by police officers and soldiers who had defected.

After the army shot dead hundreds of protesters, several senior politicians and diplomats resigned and some defected to the rebel side. Calls for the government to step down intensified. Gaddafi insisted that he would die in Libya "as a martyr" rather than relinquish power. He said, "forces affiliated to foreign forces" were seeking to "disfigure, undermine and tarnish the reputation of the country".

In late February, the opposition established its own interim government (National Transitional Council of Libya) in Benghazi in opposition to Gaddafi's. By the end of the month the cities of Misrata, al-Bayda and Tobruk were also controlled by rebel forces.

A month after the uprising began, the UN Security Council authorised a no-fly zone over the country and sanctioned "all necessary measures" to protect the civilian population but it also prohibited foreign occupation. Two days later, on March 19, the US, France and the UK began a bombing campaign aimed at Gaddafi's forces. The military intervention was joined by a coalition of 27 states from Europe and the Middle East.

Aerial bombardment by NATO forces enabled the rebels to drive back Gaddafi loyalists from the fringes of Benghazi and take the area along the coast. However, Gaddafi's forces retook most of the northern coastal towns. After a three-month battle in the west of the country the rebels made progress in Misrata, supported by coalition airstrikes. The decisive breakthrough came towards the end of August, when opposition fighters captured Tripoli.

Relentlessly stubborn Gaddafi, however, tried to cling on by shifting, with some of his officials, to Sirte. Others scattered in different directions. Right up to the end, Gaddafi was indignant and questioning of the legitimacy of the opposition movement. Although he did reportedly offer to establish talks with rebel leaders over the formation of a transitional government, this was rejected. Given his actions up to that point it would appear to have been the last gambit of a cornered man rather than acknowledgement of a need for a peaceful solution.

The Colonel's tactic of moving, along with his bodyguards and inner circle, to avoid the shelling failed him on October 20, 2011. When he bolted in a convoy from where he was in Sirte, the convoy was bombed by NATO planes. Many vehicles were destroyed and others scattered in different directions. Gaddafi and his entourage then hid in a nearby villa but this was shelled by rebel forces. The group then fled to a building site and Gaddafi and others hid in a drainage pipe while his guards attempted to repel the onslaught by opposition fighters. Gaddafi sustained head injuries from a grenade.

He was taken prisoner by the militia, who beat him up while filming it. In the mobile phone footage Gaddafi appears to be stabbed in the rear end with a sharp weapon, perhaps a bayonet or knife. His discarded, unconscious and semi-naked body was then taken by ambulance to Misrata, but he was dead on arrival. The

National Transitional Council claimed that Gaddafi was caught in an exchange of gunfire, but other accounts suggest that rebels shot him at close range.

One of his sons, Mutassim, who was a national security adviser to the regime, had been in the convoy but not on the construction site and was found dead later. He and dozens of Gaddafi loyalists appear to have been killed by extra-judicial execution. Though some pro-Gaddafi loyalists continued to fight, sporadically, against the victorious new regime, both Russia and China, which had supported Gaddafi, acknowledged the National Transitional Council as the legitimate government of the country.

Unfortunately, the Libyan uprising and civil war has not had, at the time of writing, a happy ending. Despite legislating against criticising the revolution or the transitional government, or praising Gaddafi, the National Transitional Council did not have legitimacy across the diverse and tribal country. In early 2012, protesters opposed to the Council entered its headquarters and made a number of demands. These included greater fiscal transparency, that officials from the Gaddafi era be sacked and that Sharia law shape Libya's future constitution.

Elections were held in July 2012 and the Council was dissolved and power transferred to a new General National Congress on August 8. The handover date coincided with Ramadan and a crowd gathered in Tripoli's Martyrs' Square with candles to mark the occasion as a time of peace and reconciliation. Nevertheless, tensions remained in the country, not least from militias which had fought in the civil war. The enduring economic problems of the country were other key factors that plunged Libya into its second civil war in May 2014.

At the time of writing, division in Libya persists, with two political factions claiming legitimacy. These are the UN-backed Government of National Accord in Tripoli and the House of Representatives in Tobruk. Each is backed by a variety of militias, with distinctive ideological and tribal origins. To complicate matters further, the lack of an effective government has enabled the Daesh to gather power within the country, where it has committed numerous murders.

In a 2016 report, the non-profit, non-governmental organisation

Human Rights Watch stated that militias affiliated to both competing Libyan governments were engaging in war crimes, including the illegal imprisonment and torture of civilians. Some civilians were trapped in areas of fighting and warring factions shelled residential areas occupied by civilians. By that point thousands of citizens had been detained without trial.

The Human Rights Watch report claimed that some forces used cluster munitions and anti-personnel landmines, which are internationally banned. The organisation also said that the justice system had broken down in much of the country. Militias and criminal groups abducted and 'disappeared' hundreds of civilians, including activists, politicians and workers from non-governmental organisations. Journalists are among those who have been harassed and murdered by armed groups.

These are among the factors driving Libyans from the country to seek asylum elsewhere. This has put economic and political pressure on other states and helped fuel the rise of anti-refugee sentiment in countries which those fleeing enter or attempt to enter. The Human Rights Watch report states that, in 2015 alone, more than 3,100 asylum seekers heading to Europe from North Africa drowned at sea.

While few people would admire Gaddafi's approach to governance or his take on democracy, it could be argued that his authoritarian approach may have kept some volatile forces in the highly complicated country at bay. Some may be tempted to go further and claim – finding 'evidence' in the mess seen in Libya and given the complex tribal, religious and geographical issues – that such a country *needs* an authoritarian 'strong man' leader to hold things together. This sort of narrative was used, and still is used by some, when commenting on conflicts in post-colonial Africa after the retreat of European empires left power vacuums.

However, there are some extremely unsavoury underlying aspects to such a narrative. It suggests that some human communities are somehow inherently unstable, which has echoes in narratives about savages and evolutionism, as discussed earlier in this book. Following such a narrative to its conclusion, if certain human communities *need* an authoritarian regime for relative stability, then it follows that democracy is not appropriate for such societies. This, however, would be a deeply and dangerously flawed conclusion to draw.

The reality is that economic conditions and exploitation, along with weaponry from abroad, have played key roles in the fate of Libya. As with other countries torn apart by conflict, in which civilians are harmed in tug of wars for power, resolving entrenched economic problems and corruption, as well as stemming the flow of weaponry from outside, are more important than racist narratives about the inherent capacity of citizens and their ability to make decisions.

The Bahrain aspect of the Arab Uprising, and the crackdown, demonstrates that authoritarianism is not the answer to complex political, economic and ideological tensions. Protests, which began on February 14, 2011, were initially focused on achieving greater political freedom and better human rights, including equality for Shia Muslims, who make up approximately two thirds of the population but have been ruled by Sunnis.

After three days of generally peaceful protests, tensions and the focus of protests changed on February 17 after police killed four protesters occupying the Pearl Roundabout in Manama. The roundabout, near the financial district of the capital city, had (it was subsequently destroyed by the government) symbolic significance. Composed of six ascending sails joining at the top to hold a pearl, it represented the connection between the Gulf Cooperation Council's six-member nations.

After the killings by the police, some protesters started to demand an end to the country's monarchy. The following day the army opened fired on protesters when they tried to enter the roundabout. One protester was killed. The day after that the protest was allowed to continue and the government appears to have ordered police to stand down. Over the next days the protest movement grew but there was also counter-protests in support of the government calling for national unity.

By February 22 the number of protesters at the Pearl Roundabout site had grown to more than 150,000 – more than 10% of Bahrain's population. The military opened fire on a large group of protesters that day, killing around 20 citizens, with more than 100 injured. By mid-March the government had brought in troops from Saudi Arabia and the United Arab Emirates. On March 15, the ruler, King Hamad bin Isa Al Khalifa, declared a state of emergency and ordered the military to stamp down on the movement. The following day, as soldiers and armed police cleared the protesters' camp at the roundabout, three protesters and three police officers were reportedly killed.

On March 18, the government had Pearl Roundabout monument demolished. It was bulldozed and set on fire. A migrant worker was crushed to death by a falling cement arch in the demolition process. In justifying destroying the roundabout, the government claimed that the monument had already been "desecrated" by protesters.

The state of emergency continued for almost three months to quell the uprising, but as soon as the intervention was lifted, on June 1, the movement continued with several rallies by opposition political parties. A mass rally on March 9, 2012, brought between 100,000 and 250,000 protesters onto the streets. The protesters called for the release of political prisoners and the removal of the King from power.

The government crackdown on dissent has not just been on protesters but also on bloggers. As well as violence directed by state agents at protesters at rallies, the government has subjected citizens in Shia neighbourhoods to late-night raids and detention without due process of law. Thousands of people have been arrested and several citizens have been killed by torture while in custody. Since 2012 there have sporadic bomb attacks, blamed on the protest movement, with a number of police killed and injured.

Chapter 6 – Globalisation, neoliberalism and predation

The other side of the coin to grass roots uprisings in the name of democracy involves the imposition of different values on a society from outside. Sometimes, as in the case of Ukraine in 2014, it can be difficult to work out how much an uprising is driven from inside a society and how much foreign powers are driving events.

Given the complex ways in which identity, community and ideologies are constructed in the contemporary world, the relationship between personal agency and political movements are complicated and hard to unpick. Information flows around the planet faster than ever and, in addition to other significant driving forces such as local economic and political conditions, resistance can be encouraged by a variety of influences that are hard to measure in individuals let alone larger groups.

Observing dissident movements and some other mass movements take off and develop can be like watching large flocks of starlings swirling acrobatically around the sky. It can be both awesome and terrifying, depending on your own perspective and your understanding of what is happening. As fun as it looks to be a starling in such a mass movement, appearing to become a giant single entity, the reality is there are practical and rational factors driving the behaviour.

One is safety in numbers, to reduce the likelihood of an attack by a bird of prey. Another reason is that the position individual birds have in the roost they share that evening, and how warm they will be, is influenced by how they are in the mass flock beforehand. These ornithological observations also have relevance for human mass movements, such as dissident uprisings.

As we saw in the various uprisings known as the Arab Spring, safety in numbers was an important factor in the timing of events. In all cases, there were years and sometimes decades of more muted unrest prior to events coming to a head. Furthermore, the way that the wave of uprisings spread across North Africa and the Middle East appears to be related to a sense of safety in numbers. It was not that societies suddenly felt aggrieved by their own rulers after a Tunisian street vendor set himself on fire, but empowerment in Tunisia sparked empowerment elsewhere. There was perhaps for many a sense of 'now or never'.

The issue of roosting position, as noted in starlings, also has relevance for human political uprisings. During these events, members of the aspiring new order jostle for position. Just as stronger and more dominant starlings get the best perches in the centre of trees, those activists who make the most impact in uprisings and revolutions hope to be rewarded with prized positions in the new regime. This is a risk, of course, as so many uprisings fail to overthrow the old guard. Those fighting against it most energetically are at greatest risk of death, torture, imprisonment or exile should the uprising fail.

To extend the parallels from nature a little, it is worth remembering that the movements of many prey species are driven by the movements and manipulations of predators. Prey animals may do all they can within their repertoire of behaviour and physiological capacities, but ultimately they are at the mercy of the predator's greater capacities. These may be physical or mental. Human beings, for example, are slower, less agile and less good at climbing than a great many other mammals, but our brains, inventiveness and the technology we have created gives us the edge overall. Humans can kill everything from a parasite to a polar bear if equipped with the right tools and knowledge.

In human hunting parties, whether in hunter-gatherer tribes or groups of British aristocrats, the advantages our species has over prey animals are similar. As a species with a complex language and good memory for narrative, information is passed down by word of mouth – and sometimes in books. Children in such communities will have heard hunting stories from an early age and the amassing of pertinent knowledge is one factor that gives them the edge when they finally come to join the hunt.

On the day of the hunt itself, language also gives our species the edge. Prey can be more easily worn down and cornered by predators who can communicate with one another. Tools, such as guns, bow and arrows, spears or even other species we enlist (such as dogs and horses) are other advantages that make up for our species' relative slowness, ungainliness, poor stamina and weakness.

With all this in mind, and bearing in mind that human beings and groups have extraordinarily variable levels of wealth, technology, information, greed, empathy and callousness, we must recognise that *we* are sometimes unwittingly driven by the actions of predators. Just like a group of rabbits startled by a noise and then picked off by a distant unseen gun, or grouse made to take flight and then shot, human movements can be manipulated for the benefit of the greedy, power-driven or ideologically dangerous.

I focused earlier on in this book on the way in which intelligence services cause unrest and conflict to impose the will of their masters, but the CIA is far from the only group to do this. Since colonial times and before, human groups with the most advantages have preyed, in various ways, on other humans, just as we as a species have preyed upon, exploited and exterminated other species.

Colonialism and the racist pseudo-scientific narratives surrounding it have been discussed above, and to most readers these narratives and power relationships seem reprehensible. As thoroughly modern people we might scoff at people in the eras of slavery, imperialism and segregation who accepted these as 'just the way things are', perhaps with their minds furnished with flawed yet comfortable evolutionist and racist narratives. However, if you are reading this on a screen, or next time you glance at your phone, you (as I have to when typing these words on a laptop) should acknowledge that we have not escaped the shadow of that dynamic.

Overt imperialism has largely been replaced by neocolonialism, and national empires handing the reins to multinational corporate empires and international bodies, but the power discrepancies and narratives justifying exploitation are not so very different. Even the perfectly rational response that many readers will be thinking – 'but it's beyond my control' – is sadly not a million miles from, 'that's just the way things are'.

I am not encouraging readers to hurl their iPads from windows – if you do, please finish reading this book first and be careful where it lands – but am merely making the point that the power relationships over workers in other countries, imposed by the likes of Cecil Rhodes, are still very much present. Just as it is important to see through the veneer of the 'civilisation' of Rhodes' era, it is important to see through the veneer of the consumerism, production and international trade of today. When you look beneath the shiny veneer of products, they are actually composed not only of plastic and metal but also entrenched power relationships – sometimes they are dripping with blood.

Of course, it can be argued – and frequently is – that by using the developing world to do so much of the production of consumer goods, powerful and prosperous countries are helping them to 'develop'. There are certainly good examples of Gross Domestic Product (GDP), educational standards and local levels of technology improving in countries that produce a lot of consumer goods for the Western world. However, it should be noted that GDP is a measure of economic activity (the trading of goods and services) in a country as a whole. It does not show how wealth is distributed within that country. The gap between the wealthiest and poorest can increase and the most marginalised can become even more so even as GDP rises.

Furthermore, as well as increasing economic inequality and the resultant social and educational inequality, the poorest in countries with increasing manufacturing productivity are generally those most affected by the side effects of this productivity. For example, overcrowding and environmental pollution can affect both air and water. There are many effects of climate change that are also more likely to hit the poorest harder than the wealthy, including food security problems, the prevalence of zoonotic diseases (which move between humans and animals) and more unstable living conditions. The poorest are also more likely to be driven to migrate, though the wealthiest will find it easier to do so.

Some will argue that, though there is great inequality in the countries we use as factories, ultimately each society as a whole becomes wealthier. Not only does this ignore the realities discussed above but it also has a troubling resonance with some of the evolutionist narratives discussed earlier in this book.

When you pin down the narrative and examine it in the context of economic, political, social, environmental, medical and historical reality, the suggestion is that generations should toil in unhealthy and exploitative conditions for the fortunate as one day those we trample upon will have a bit more money and be trampled on a bit less. This is not too dissimilar to the narratives of evolutionists, who justified colonial oppression and exploitation because somehow darker skinned people had not yet 'evolved' to be like those lighter skinned people who claimed the role of master.

Such narratives are also reminiscent of ideologies within Hinduism that justify oppression, exploitation and violence by saying that some were born to serve and must reincarnate to transcend their status rather than expect progression in their current life. If we consider master and servant relationships globally, taking into account relative power between wealthy countries and poorer countries, and between corporate empires and local workers, we have to acknowledge that we are all part of a global caste system. The global economic system and consumerist structures can mask this, and we rarely see those who make our gadgets, but fundamentally we are in a master and servant relationship.

Within Hinduism, reincarnation offers hope for spiritual evolution, freedom from suffering and transcendence. Within the modern materialistic world, one day becoming prosperous is the hope, perhaps, of billions. With a rapidly growing global population, ecological threats, a greater and greater need for energy to power the life many take for granted, and widespread debt, that dream fades day by day for a huge number of people.

Paradoxically, however, the more that dream recedes for many people, the more alluring it becomes. We see this in the Western world as much as the developing world. As more people in the USA have become impoverished in the last decade or so, the greater the longing for a bygone era when the 'American dream' seemed within more people's grasp. The USA is a nation that has always been unequal and divided – in fact it is a nation built on the blood of dead natives and slaves. It is debatable, therefore, that the so-called American dream was ever more than a pipe dream for most.

Perhaps one of the most significant cultural events in recent years in the US is that many watched prosperity fade, along with the country's status in the world. They have seen through the veneer of the economic system. While some hope desperately that the fortune of their country will be restored, like cargo cult members waiting for wealth from the sky, others have turned their wrath on neoliberalism, encouraged by Donald Trump.

This is quite a conjuring trick by Trump, as he and his family have gained more from neoliberalism and globalisation than most people. Nevertheless, Trump supporters have taken up the mantra of attacking neoliberalism, as though it is an ogre that can be vanquished by chanting.

I would suggest that those in the West experiencing this in recent years have merely been getting a taste of what much of the world has been subjected to for much longer. The USA has been exploiting and depleting the resources of other nations throughout its history, just as Britain and other major powers have for centuries. Even after losing some of the nation's prosperity, US citizens consume more than citizens in most of the world.

However, the unrealistic expectation of consistently rising living standards, combined with a strong sense of entitlement among Americans, appears to have transformed economic ups and downs into an existential crisis for the US. This is probably not helped by identity in the US being so tied up with what you own, what you buy and how much money you have.

In addition to Trump's insincere attack on the system that made him and keeps him a billionaire, another ironic thing is that the USA and the many corporate empires within it have pushed neoliberalism more than any other nation. The very same thing that was seen as a god has morphed, for many US citizens, into a monster.

Another peculiar irony is that, although neoliberalism is a right-wing model, hard-right tycoon turned politician Trump has managed win votes from the left by exploiting and whipping up anti-neoliberalism sentiment. One reason for this could be that the USA has moved so far to the right politically that supposedly left-wing politicians can be portrayed as agents of neoliberalism. Given that, for Trump supporters and American conservatives more generally, the word 'liberal' is often used as an insult, as though a swear word, we cannot rule out the possibility that some people believe that social liberalism is the same as economic liberalism – and therefore neoliberalism. Consequently, it is worth clarifying what is meant by liberalism, economic liberalism and neoliberalism.

Distinguishing between liberalism and neoliberalism

Liberalism is a philosophy based upon the concepts of freedom and equality. Neoliberalism is often deceitfully linked to political and social liberalism in order to accuse those who criticise it of hindering human freedom. In reality, neoliberalism, which promotes freedom of the owners of capital to do what they want with little political intervention, often robs individuals of liberty and hinders social progress towards equality. There cannot be a fair and free market if some, such as Donald Trump or Rupert Murdoch, are born into fortunes and are able to use their power to strengthen their positions further.

The reason neoliberalism has the name it does is because it is seen as a modern reiteration or resurgence of a model of economic liberalism seen in the 19th century. The 19th century 'laissez faire' economic liberalism was eroded by a recognition of the importance of political intervention to curtail the excesses of capitalism, and for certain key resources to be under state ownership. Key aspects of the neoliberal agenda include privatisation of publicly owned utilities, deregulation, free trade, the shrinking of the state to give 'business' (such as the running of prisons and hospitals) to the private sector and cutting the welfare provisions for families and individuals.

Coming to the fore in the era between the economic liberalism of the 19th century and the later neoliberalism agenda was a model based on the ideas of the economist John Maynard Keynes. Putting forth his ideas during the 'great' depression of the 1930s, Keynes challenged the tarnished liberal economics assumption that free markets would provide full employment if workers were flexible in their wage demands. He recognised that demand for products and services was key to national economic activity and that, therefore, regardless of the flexibility of workers, economies were vulnerable to declines in economic activity for a variety of reasons.

According to his school of thought, which became known as Keynesian economics, there is a need to intervene fiscally (with taxes and expenditure) and through monetary policy (the supply of money) to mitigate the risk and effects of booms and busts associated with economic cycles. Keynes' ideas became the policy of leading Western economies from World War Two until the late 1970s.

At times of economic decline, rather than impose swingeing austerity, as UK chancellor of the exchequer George Osborne and prime minister David Cameron did between 2010 and 2016, Keynesian orientated governments invested in projects that spread money around society. Those working on projects have money to buy goods and services, which creates employment for others, who also spend money, and so it goes on – thus creating a multiplier effect on government spending. This therefore mitigates the risks of economic depression while also supporting individuals, families and communities.

The neoliberal era, which came into its own in the 1980s, was a dramatic shift away from Keynesian economics. From that period, driven in the UK by Margaret Thatcher and in the US by former actor Ronald Reagan, the focus was on privatisation, deregulation, attacks on welfare provision and, some would say, an attack on society itself, except, of course, the societies of brokers and asset strippers, who swooped down like birds of prey, sinking their talons into whatever they could grab.

As is often the case when change is imposed by those with little respect for 'ordinary' people, those with the most power, wealth and freedom gained more of these while the most vulnerable suffered the most. In the UK, a great deal was made of the public benefits of floatation on the stock market of resources that were publicly owned, such as British Telecom (which had been part of the Post Office) and British gas and electric utilities.

A great deal was spent on TV advertisements encouraging citizens to buy shares, and many took up the offer and made some money. However, ultimately what happened over time was that shares of formerly publicly owned key utilities ended up in the hands of the wealthy and a few large companies ultimately took over the business, sometimes accused of fixing prices like a cartel.

A neoliberal might talk of the democracy of such flotations, but many citizens will now reflect that a novel little gamble on shares, even if you made £100 or so, is no compensation for the public losing critical resources to the amoral, and at times immoral, market. The fun of being allowed to play a market previously restricted to elites can be seen as a distraction from a massive plunder of the nation's family silver, as well as an attack on socialism.

The term neoliberalism was used as early at 1898 and appeared to some extent in the early 20th century, but it found a new lease of life thanks to Margaret Thatcher's murderous tyrant friend General Pinochet.

Illustrating the distinction between political liberalism and economic liberalism, the term neoliberal was used to describe the economic reforms Pinochet imposed on Chile from the 1970s. Readers will recall that, with the help of the CIA, Pinochet replaced the left-leaning Salvador Allende in 1973 before destroying the stable system in place and killing, torturing and imprisoning thousands of people. Therefore, the use of any term with 'liberal' in to describe the dictator's approach is rather nauseating, in my opinion.

Pinochet's reforms were shaped by a group known as the Chicago Boys, a group of right-wing Chilean economists trained at the University of Chicago by Milton Friedman, a major critic of Keynes and a key figure in the spread of neoliberalism. If thinking abstractly and comparing economic reforms as a medicine, it looks very much like Chile was a testing ground for a potentially dangerous experimental drug. This was a more extreme form of economic liberalism than that seen in the 19th century and, as we have seen, the impact of violently taking over the country's military to test the dangerous new 'medicine' was catastrophic.

The reforms imposed by Pinochet's regime included the banning of trade unions, removal of tariff protections for local industry and the privatisation of the welfare system and state-owned resources. Despite claims from the right that Pinochet's regime created an economic miracle, the reality appears to be that economic inequality significantly increased. Even *if* the 'miracle' had been as claimed, most thinking people would question the idea that something imposed violently and resulting in a massacre, mass imprisonment and torture can ever be described as miraculous.

Born in 1912, Friedman was a student, research assistant and young economist during the Great Depression. Failing to gain an academic post, he took advantage of Franklin D. Roosevelt's 'New Deal', a national government programme of a Keynesian nature. The programme provided work for numerous economists. He was, however, critical of many aspects of the New Deal, including price-fixing and wage-fixing.

He moved into academia in the 1940s and, over the subsequent decades, became involved with right-wing politicians, including acting as adviser to Republican presidential candidate Barry Goldwater in 1964 and President Ronald Reagan in the 1980s. He was also an adviser to UK prime minister Thatcher. Friedman's agenda was the maximisation of the freedom of the free market.

Unsurprisingly, he was antagonistic towards welfare and social security systems and argued that such safety nets created a culture of dependency. He had a remarkably different view from Reagan on some things, however, notably drug use. He took a libertarian stance in relation to both sex and drugs, advocating the legalisation of drugs. Reagan was known for his anti-drug campaigns, having continued the 'war on drugs' started by Richard Nixon in 1971.

Friedman's involvement in Chile's fate does most to tarnish his reputation and raise questions about the ethics, integrity and ultimate value of his free market dogmatism. In the years following the coup, the economy of Pinochet's Chile was failing. Friedman was invited to the country in 1975 to give a series of lectures on economic liberalism and meet members of the regime. That visit was in March, and the following month Friedman wrote to Pinochet, setting out what he believed were the key economic problems facing Chile. Cutting inflation and government spending were core elements of the prescription that Friedman gave Pinochet.

In the letter, he said: "Cutting government spending is by far and away the most desirable way to reduce the fiscal deficit". He said it would strengthen the private sector and lay the foundations for "healthy economic growth". Viewing inflation, rather than a murderous tyrant being in power, as the problem facing Chile,

Friedman said in the letter that rising unemployment was a price to pay to cut inflation. Fond of medical metaphors, he talked about the value of "shock treatment".

Given what the population had already been through by that stage, it seems extraordinarily callous that Friedman also suggested that the dictator supported trade by suspending the law against sacking employees. Soon after this, Jorge Cauas, a Chicago School graduate taught by Friedman, became Minister of Finance. This was followed by other Chicago School graduates taking roles as Minister of Economy, Minister of Labour and Pensions, Minister of Mining and President of the Central Bank, and also filling the role of Minister of Finance on other occasions.

Over the subsequent years, foreign investment was attracted to the dictatorship, where employment rights, including the right to industrial action, were cut further. GDP *did* rise but working conditions declined. Comparing Chile's economic condition in the mid-1970s to a "plague" Friedman was more concerned with pushing (or trying out) his economic model than the atrocities that Pinochet and his regime carried out. Having supported Pinochet's regime, it is fascinatingly narcissistic that, years later, Friedman suggested that he and his bitter economic prescription ultimately led to the end of Pinochet's rule and the movement towards a democratic government.

In 1991, a year after Pinochet left office, Friedman stated: "I have nothing good to say about the political regime that Pinochet imposed. It was a terrible political regime. The real miracle of Chile is not how well it has done economically; the real miracle of Chile is that a military junta was willing to go against its principles and support a free market regime designed by principled believers in a free market ... Now, at long last, Chile has all three things: political freedom, human freedom and economic freedom. Chile will continue to be an interesting experiment to watch to see whether it can keep all three or whether, now that it has political freedom, that political freedom will tend to be used to destroy or reduce economic freedom."

For me, the detachedness that enabled Friedman to view Chile as an experiment – his own personal and egotistic experiment – is chilling. It reminds me of US-backed experiments on populations, whether the social science scrutiny of Project Camelot or the CIA's mind control programme, Project MKUltra. In the latter, a bewildering array of experiments were conducted on people, often illegally. Drugs and various techniques, including torture, were used in an attempt to improve the CIA's ability to interrogate and force confessions. Sometimes hallucinogens were given without subjects' knowledge and sensory deprivation, isolation and even sexual abuse were used to torture individuals.

Experimenting in this way on the public perhaps did give some observers some insights. However, it was a sadistic and unethical programme with consequently tarnished results. Similarly, Friedman's experiment on the captive and brutalised Chilean population to dogmatically impose and test his anti-Keynesian model was unethical. Furthermore, the conditions of the Chilean people were such that it is questionable that any insights gained would be widely applicable.

Friedman claimed to be delivering a free market system, but in a true free market the citizens – whether employees, vendors or purchasers – must have freedom. The Chilean people lacked that freedom and pay was artificially suppressed as the tyrant in power could simply crush employee rights and impose extreme austerity, while citizens were too terrified to protest. All Friedman's and his followers' covert social experiment showed was that if you find a society living under the regime of a murderous tyrant, you can force feed them unpalatable economic 'medicine'.

Almost as chilling as Friedman's callous disregard of the rights and safety of the people of Chile as the country was used as a testing ground for his rather toxic drug is the fact that the 'success' in Chile enabled the Friedman dogma to be rolled out to other countries – including the UK and the United States. The medicine was already of questionable efficaciousness by the time the UK and US were made to swallow it, and yet take the medicine those societies did.

Friedman's 'marvellous' medicine, or toxic drug – depending on your point of view – is still very much in our system, and Trump's election and appointment of rich allies into positions of power was not the antidote to neoliberalism many might have hoped for. Trump shouldered his way into power on the back of promised infrastructure projects that might sound Keynesian. However, he and his cronies are some distance to the right of Keynes, who was actually far from being a socialist himself.

In reality, Keynes' concern was that if capitalism is not made to work effectively then systems are more vulnerable to the incursion of socialism. He has, however, often been described by those on the right as a socialist. This is a straw man fallacy. Linking Keynesian economics to socialism is a lazy way to attack perspectives and policies that might be described as Keynesian, and therefore block initiatives that help people and strengthen communities.

Globalisation and neocolonialism

Just as contemporary economic realities, such as relationships between Western consumers and assemblers in the developing world, are complex, interconnected and dynamic, the above terms are too. It is worth pinning down each term to help us to understand forces that both hold what we call civilisation together and pull systems and societies apart. They are key aspects of the veneer of civilisation, while also being moving parts within the machinery of civilisation that shake systems around and cause alarm.

Globalisation is a term that is used a great deal, and the reality of it affects almost everybody, yet it has widely different meanings for different people. The Oxford English Dictionary defines it as: "the process by which businesses or other organizations develop international influence or start operating on an international scale." Wikipedia has a much broader definition, more aligned with that which I learned as an anthropology student. This definition goes beyond the commercial towards the complexity of contemporary human life: "the process of international integration arising from the interchange of world views, products, ideas, and other aspects of culture."

Given that a key part of globalisation is the movement of ideas around the world, it is interesting in itself that the world of commerce managed to hijack the term, in terms of the Oxford English Dictionary's primary definition. The Merriam-Webster dictionary also gives primacy to the business aspects of globalisation in its own definition: "the state of being globalized; especially the development of an increasingly integrated global economy marked especially by free trade, free flow of capital, and the tapping of cheaper foreign labor markets."

Despite the help of these dictionaries in locating globalisation firmly within the world of trade and money, this is not how the term emerged. The specific term can be traced to at least the early part of the 20th century. In a 1930 book called *Towards New Education* by W. Mackenzie and M.M. Boyd, the term is used to refer to a global or holistic view of human experience within education. Over the succeeding decades the term was used sporadically by social scientists and other commentators in quite different contexts and therefore with slightly different meanings.

Given many of the factors that drive the broader anthropological definition of globalisation favoured by Wikipedia were changing just as rapidly as commerce, it is interesting that, by the 1980s – when the term became more widely used – it was locked for many to narrow business connotations. The evolution of transport technologies and telecommunications, as well as the more rapid and frequent movement of people around the world coupled with easier, cheaper and faster ways of publishing and sharing information and ideas, transformed human culture as much as business.

Trade and human experience are of course linked, but the cultural aspects of globalisation should not be understated, as the following example illustrates. Vinyl discs produced in the US, stuffed into crates and sailed to Liverpool docks in the late 1950s, had a profound impact on local kids who got hold of them. Some of those kids went on to create their own records, which were then sent and broadcast around the world, with a huge and permanent impact on all sorts of aspects of human culture.

The musical education, emergence and impact of The Beatles is just one example of how the movement of ideas, arts and technologies – and the easier creation, reproduction and sharing of ideas – can have an extremely positive impact on lives. Teenage girls screaming hysterically at a Beatles concert in 1964 almost certainly would not have been reflecting on the wonders of globalisation, yet that is what they were experiencing.

The mushrooming of the use of the term globalisation, in a business context, in the neoliberal wave of the 1980s, appears to have been influenced by a 1983 Harvard Business Review article entitled 'Globalization of markets', written by the academic economist Theodore Levitt. Putting the term to one side, however, it can be argued that the reality of globalisation pre-dates the 'greed is good' decade by thousands of years.

The economic historian and sociologist Andre Gunder Frank, in his 1998 book *ReOrient: Global Economy in the Asian Age*, suggested the rise of trade links between Sumer (a civilisation located in what we now call Iraq) and the Indus Valley Civilisation (which occupied an area currently under the boundaries of Afghanistan, Pakistan and India). The ancient Greeks can also reasonably be described as pioneers of globalisation – not just the trade of goods but also the dissemination of ideas.

Maritime trade was important to Greece, which needed to import wheat, but ideas and tales also travel with people and products. The Hellenistic period, in which the culture of Greece dominated the Mediterranean and beyond, is generally defined as from the death of Alexander the Great in 323 BCE to the domination of the Roman Empire three centuries later. Greek cultural creativity and influence in the Hellenistic era spanned mathematics, mythology, philosophy, science, theatre, architecture, visual art and music.

These contributions to human culture are still studied on 'classics' degrees in universities around the world, even as contemporary Greece struggles with economic decline often associated with economic globalisation and neoliberalism. This reality is an illustration that globalisation is much more than the movement of relatively transient goods and money, but of ideas and arts which have enduring, profound and often unpredictable impacts.

For example, Sigmund Freud, discussed earlier in this book, was greatly influenced by Greek myths created many centuries before he was born. In turn, Freud's ideas have influenced many aspects of human culture, including advertising, literature, film and the emergence of political focus groups. They would have also fed into the Facebook and Cambridge Analytica data harvesting scandal, which enabled hard-right political movements to manipulate the psychological vulnerabilities of susceptible voters by microtargeting them with questionable information, which they then disseminated to their social media contacts. More will be said about this later.

Another important step on the road to the globalisation we experience today was what has been dubbed the 'Silk Road' or 'Silk Route', an ancient transportation channel starting in China and passing through Central Asia, West Asia and Africa to Europe. This network of trade routes was not only key to exchange of goods through Asia and beyond but also to the exchange of ideas and therefore the development of culture within the countries involved.

It is certainly the case that the Silk Route had considerable impact on the development and transformation of culture in China, Persia, Arabia, the Indian subcontinent and Europe. By culture in this context I do not just mean arts, but also politics and the dissemination of philosophies, technologies and religious ideologies.

The movement of information and ideas and the impact this had actually makes the Silk Route more like what used to be called the 'information super highway' than simply a fabric distribution network. Thousands of years before computers or phones, it arguably represented a living internet, albeit a slow one.

The spreading of religious and other ideologies, as noted above, in relation to the Silk Route, often lacks some of the more materialist definitions of globalisation which emerged in the 1980s and 1990s. Many of the definitions from that era were not only narrow but extremely optimistic and, ironically given the neglect of ideologies, idealistic. As definitions have attempted to become more all-encompassing, they have also communicated darker aspects of globalisation.

Some might argue that the world has just become more complicated and darker, but I would assert that the world was always complicated and the veneer of civilisation has always been thin. However, the speeding up of movement and cultural exchange can amplify tensions, spread dangerous ideas (as well as diseases) and also increase inequality and ecological threats. Nevertheless, we are living in a fascinating time *because* of rapid cultural exchange. Even if we are alarmed by ways in which globalisation impacts negatively upon communities economically, as a species we enjoy the fruits of ideas and technologies flowing around the world.

In 1990, the sociologist Anthony Giddens defined globalisation as: "the intensification of worldwide social relations which link distant localities in such a way that local happenings are shaped by events occurring many miles away and vice versa." The same year, Martin Albrow, another prominent British sociologist, stated: "Globalisation refers to all those processes by which the peoples of the world are incorporated into a single world society, global society."

Professor Albrow's definition has the potential to alarm those who believe in and are fearful of a 'New World Order' driven by a shadowy 'Illuminati'. Ironically, fears and fantasies about this mythical group have largely been spread through the 'World Wide Web'. Readers who have read my book *Psychopathic Cultures and Toxic Empires* will be aware of my scepticism towards a New World Order driven by a secret cabal. The online myth-peddling around this can fuel prejudice as narratives are often steeped in anti-Semitism. One of the problems of the largely unchecked spread of 'information' around the world is, as we saw with the fake news churned out to smear Hillary Clinton in the run up to the 2016 US election, attractiveness to primed recipients and sheer volume, giving credence to blatant lies.

Given the complexity of culture and identity and the unpredictable ways in which ideas move around the world and transform as they do, the idea of a single world society seems flawed to me at this stage. While it is true that, as a species, what one human community does has an impact on others, this is not the same as saying that we are a singular body. Narratives about unity are positive, such as those expressed earlier in this book where notions of hierarchical groupings of different 'races' were challenged, but there can be commonality in our humanity without a single world society. One might hope that the empathy we feel for people from different backgrounds can increase over time, but global communications and easier travel can support distinctiveness rather than invariably lead to some horribly dystopian uniformity.

In 1992, yet another sociologist, Roland Robertson, referred to "the compression of the world and the intensification of the consciousness of the world as a whole." This is extremely interesting in that it creates the idea of global consciousness as like a living entity transformed by a process. I like that definition, but by creating a sense of unity, even if there is also a sense of being compressed and perhaps even heated up like something in a test tube, we do not yet come to terms with the conflict that can be created when different ideologies clash. For me, at this stage, any definition of globalisation should include something about a clash of ideas, which can be positive as well as negative.

Robertson's definition does not disclude other species. If we recognise that the global consciousness includes that of other species, it would be comforting to think of unity and intensification. However, the stark reality is that one particular species is responsible for a vast number of others being eradicated and endangered. It is difficult to speak of unity when a significant number of species are being destroyed by the actions of one or when many human groups are endangered while others are living in luxury and relative safety.

Two interesting commentators on globalisation, with very different perspectives, are Joseph Stiglitz and Thomas Friedman. Stiglitz is an economist, currently teaching at Columbia University. He was chief economist of the World Bank from 1997 and 2000. He is also a former member of the Council of Economic Advisers, an agency which advises US presidents. Friedman is an American journalist and author, and three-time winner of the Pulitzer Prize. It is worth summarising some of their contributions as this allows us to look at globalisation from some quite different angles.

Stiglitz is a strong critic of advocates of laissez faire economics, who he dubs 'free market fundamentalists'. He is also critical of the International Monetary Fund (IMF), which is meant to promote financial stability, high employment and sustainable economic growth, as well as reduce poverty around the world. During his stint as World Bank chief economist, he developed the view that the IMF acts against the interests of developing countries rather than truly supporting them. He won a Nobel Prize in Economic Sciences in 2001 and used his acceptance essay to make some damning statements about the IMF and the neoliberal agenda.

Referring to his motivation at the World Bank in relation to impoverished developing economies and concerns he developed, Stiglitz stated: "I had no strong agenda, other than doing what I could to promote the development of these countries, in ways which did as much as possible to eliminate poverty. But as I quickly became engrossed in the problems of development, a variety of issues surfaced, the most important of which was the intellectual framework with which development was to be pursued."

Alluding to a trip to Ethiopia aimed at supporting development, Stiglitz also said: "I saw the IMF advocate policies of financial market liberalization which made no sense, in which it argued that the country's budget was out of balance – when in my estimate that was clearly not the case – and in which it had suspended its program, in spite of that country's first rate macro-economic performance. More broadly, the IMF was advocating a set of policies which is generally referred to alternatively as the Washington consensus, the neoliberal doctrines, or market fundamentalism, based on an incorrect understanding of economic theory and (what I viewed) as an inadequate interpretation of the historical data."

In the essay, Stiglitz also stated: "The IMF was using models that failed to incorporate the advances in economic theory of the past twenty-five years, including the work on imperfect information and incomplete markets to which I had contributed. Most importantly, they had departed from the mission for which they had been founded, under the intellectual guidance of Keynes – they actually promoted contractionary fiscal policies for countries facing an economic downturn – and they advocated polices like capital market liberalization, for which there was little evidence that growth was promoted, while there was ample evidence that such policies generated instability."

In 2002 Stiglitz published a rather incendiary book that caught the attention of not only economists but a broad range of readers. The name of the book, *Globalization and its Discontents*, echoes the title of Freud's *Civilization and its Discontents*, discussed earlier. In the book, Stiglitz discusses his time as chief economist at the World Bank and his stint as chairman of the Council of Economic Advisers, when he advised Bill Clinton.

Picking up the themes addressed in his Nobel Prize acceptance essay, Stiglitz argues in *Globalization and its Discontents* that the IMF's policies are empirically flawed because the theories underpinning them are also flawed. He contends that what has become known as neoliberal economics is no different from the 19th century laissez faire economics that created so much political instability and which the Keynesian approach has sought to remedy.

In both 19th century laissez faire economics and the neoliberal era spanning the late 20th century and early 21st century, the role of government is diminished, pay is suppressed and there is a reliance on wealth created for the economic elite to trickle down to alleviate poverty. In each case, the latter is a fallacy. In reality, the result is increasingly pliable and desperate workers, as we are seeing in this era where many people are on zero hours contracts, pay a high proportion of income on rent and have an ever-diminishing chance of buying property.

These realities have the greatest impact on the children of the poorest who, as well as having a myriad of disadvantages in early life, will have the greatest apprehension of taking out the vast loans often required to attend university. The inequality enabled by neoliberalism therefore becomes more and more entrenched. For those in countries with great poverty, few legal rights, no welfare state safety net, strong organised crime syndicates, high levels of corruption and routine violence towards striking workers, the neoliberal dream is even more of a nightmare.

Stiglitz recognises globalisation as a reality but argues that how well it works for specific societies depends on how well it is managed. Just as Keynes believed that economies do require state intervention if they are to be sustainable rather than destabilising to societies, Stiglitz argues that, rather than have the process of globalisation managed by international bodies such as the IMF, the governments of each country, focusing on the unique needs and characteristics of their environment, should manage the pace of change.

This is at odds with the IMF approach of imposing economic liberalisation, as though it is a panacea, at a pace which destabilises economies and negatively impacts primarily on the poorest. Stiglitz points out that international institutions like the IMF and World

Bank lack the accountability of national governments, and these bodies impose conditions on societies without members of those societies being able to challenge them.

The IMF was not designed to be a promoter of laissez faire economics but was a Keynesian initiative, envisaged as a means to enable societies to grow towards full employment. The World Bank, which was formed at the same time, in 1944, was designed to alleviate poverty by providing loans for capital programmes in the developing world. Founding father Keynes did not envisage it as an agent to help impose market liberalisation on societies, opening them to exploitation by powerful companies and individuals.

Despite the problems of the IMF and World Bank Stiglitz raises, he does not believe that they should be abolished – rather reformed to give nations greater control over the pace of change and ensure greater protection for workers and greater investment in health and education. Rather than a 'one size fits all' model, Stiglitz suggests that different countries should be able to follow different paths and democratic systems should be strengthened to enable citizens to have maximum control over the economic trajectory of their societies.

Furthermore, rather than countries in most debt to the IMF and World Bank being further destabilised by having to raise taxes and cut public spending to pay debt down, Stiglitz advocates debt relief. He suggests that, because such loans primarily gave wealth to foreign investors and local elites, such as government officials, it is unfair that local workers should suffer through higher taxes. Loans and resultant debts have been used to manipulate countries to accept reforms that are ultimately detrimental to workers and society. Structural adjustment programmes (loans from the IMF and World Bank) have ultimately led to reduced health, nutritional and educational levels in countries on which they have been imposed.

Stiglitz makes the point extremely clearly that his book is designed to open debate. He is not antagonistic towards globalisation and recognises that it has helped many millions of people, but he also recognises that situations can and should be managed much better. He is by no means an anti-globalisation campaigner but someone from inside the establishment who, like Keynes before him, realised and articulated the dangers to societies of blindly pursuing free market dogmatism.

The neoliberalism pushed by Milton Friedman, and then by proselytisers like Margaret Thatcher, has led to greater inequality, poverty and political instability as well as slow growth. Stiglitz wrote his book several years before George Osborne became chancellor of the exchequer in the UK and imposed some of the most swingeing austerity seen in decades on an environment reeling from the credit crunch. Unfortunately, the alarm bell that Stiglitz rang, though it chimed around the world, did not stop Osborne and many others from imposing policies that hurt the poorest.

In 2002 Stiglitz wrote: "The results of the policies enforced by the Washington consensus have not been encouraging: for most countries embracing its tenets, development has been slow, and where growth has occurred, the benefits have not been shared ... Those who have followed the prescriptions, endured the austerity, are asking: 'When do we see the fruits?'" Certainly, in the David Cameron and George Osborne era, those who suffered the most from globalisation, through losing jobs to overseas companies, loss of work stability and austerity policies that cut public provisions, were not seeing the fruits.

The benefits of neoliberalism and globalisation not being shared throughout society supported the resurgence of the hard-right in many countries, who jumped at the opportunity to spread poison about immigrants. In the UK, David Cameron was so concerned about the United Kingdom Independence Party (UKIP), a hard-right anti-EU party taking Tory votes, that he pledged a referendum about the UK's membership of the EU.

Rather than, as Cameron would have hoped, vanquishing the then fringe party made up, in his words, of "fruitcakes, loonies and closet racists", the pledge of the referendum just gave more prominence to UKIP, who were featured incredibly often on BBC news and debate shows for a party that had no Westminster MPs. It could be that, to begin with, the BBC, which suffered from falling ratings on tired old shows such as *Newsnight* and *Question Time*, thought bringing antagonistic UKIP figures into the limelight would be a spectacle and therefore boost viewing figures and social media impact.

In reality, they gave a continuous and priceless platform to what, for some, became the acceptable face of the hard-right. UKIP did not have the thuggish look of groups like the EDL and the British National Party, but mainly seemed to attract old posh men in yellow or red trousers and tweed. With the greater media prominence of UKIP, anti-immigration and anti-EU narratives became normalised, and by 2016 we had the shock marginal Brexit vote in the UK, closely followed by the shock election of Donald Trump in the US.

A clearly complex cluster of variables led to the UK lunging to the right and ultimately opting for Brexit and the US, despite his not winning the popular vote, ending up with Donald Trump in the White House. The impact of economic globalisation and neoliberalism were certainly important factors, but perhaps even more significant were the ways in which politicians exploited anger, hardship, fear and frustration to put the blame on immigrants rather than those, very much like themselves, who had gained considerably from both globalisation and neoliberalism.

Former commodities trader Nigel Farage and international businessman Trump were hardly victims of or long-standing opponents of neoliberalism. However, by focusing on very visible aspects of globalisation – immigrants – both were able to whip up enough alarm to gain support for their personal agendas. The irony is that being made to be fearful of some aspects of neoliberalism – a relentlessly right-wing ideology – the public in the UK, US and elsewhere allowed their political and economic systems to shift much further to the right.

By opening the doors on the private worlds of the IMF and World Bank, Stiglitz sought to bring those detrimentally affected by their policies into the debates. Rather than people being passive victims of heavy-handed intervention, which often leads to greater exploitation, Stiglitz wanted those whose lives are most intensely affected to be informed and, ideally, become part of the debate.

Given that *Globalization and its Discontents* became a best-selling book and the wider public now talk about globalisation perhaps as much now as they spoke about the ego and unconscious in the wake of Freud, I would suggest that Stiglitz has been successful in that ambition. However, as politicians have been successful in getting a significant proportion of the electorate to focus on immigration more than broader aspects of globalisation and the neoliberal agenda, there is much further to go with this. If we return to Freud, while it is true that many people have used words like 'ego' over the past century, it is also the case that people have frequently done do so without having read his work – and often without really understanding what he meant. There could be a parallel with terms like liberalism, globalisation and neoliberalism.

I do not believe that the majority of citizens who, encouraged by politicians and wannabe politicians, become alarmed by immigration, are fundamentally mean-spirited or racist. It is the nature of the economic system and politics that all of us have a partial view of events, and this can be exploited by the powerful. Rather than look into bank accounts and see the tax returns of the politicians and media magnates who manipulate our perceptions, we just have the world immediately around us to go on. For many, the most noticeable things about the world around us are changes in who lives near us and works with us, accents around us changing and shops and other businesses changing.

My concern is that there has been a massive sleight of hand going on by certain elites who claim to be anti-establishment. While attention has been put on immigrants, those who already had the most wealth and power have managed to consolidate their positions. Predatory capitalists and hard-right politicians alike – and they are often the very same people – thrive on chaos, conflict and division. They have had a lot to feed on in recent years. While the spotlight has been put on immigrants and the movement of refugees, the neoliberal system has continued its plundering march.

Neocolonialism is the use of economic, political and cultural pressures to exert influence on other countries. While citizens in centres of power such as the UK and US have been encouraged to look upon immigrants as the source of problems, elite groups in our countries have been a major source of problems in the developing world. While some people in prosperous countries have been troubled by victims of globalisation coming into their countries to find work or seek refuge from war, the most powerful in prosperous societies have been plundering resources from less powerful nations.

Thomas Friedman's books, articles and documentaries have covered an extremely broad range of subjects, including Israel, terrorism, globalisation, the Kosovo war, China, Iran, oil and the environment. His 1999 book, *The Lexus and the Olive Tree*, discusses the tension between the drive for prosperity, which necessitates development and change, and the desire to maintain identity and maintain traditions. The Lexus, a fairly luxurious car made in Japan, is juxtaposed in the title with the olive tree because Friedman associates the Lexus with progress and prosperity and the tree with the maintenance of tradition and identity.

The desire to preserve traditions, or to recreate traditions, seems to be stronger when one's society or community is facing rapid change, such as those brought about by globalisation. This certainly could help explain why anti-immigration movements and nativist movements often use 'golden age' narratives to whip up strong feelings and mobilise people.

An interesting parallel to local attempts to preserve traditions has been observed by anthropologists in people who move abroad for work. They may be forward-thinking people who embrace change, but once in a strange land the desire to recapture traditions from their homeland can be strong. This desire can also increase the tendency for immigrants to seek fellowship with those from their former country.

Both of these dynamics, though perfectly rational and understandable drives, can collide with the other and exaggerate perceptions of the strangeness of the 'other'. Anti-immigration narratives often talk of those from other cultures 'not integrating', but the desire of newcomers to hold on to their traditions and identity should surely be understandable to those who, alarmed by change, are doing the same.

It is ironic that those who try so hard to recreate their traditions have so much in common, despite the distinctiveness of the traditions they cherish. There is a core desire that can lead to greater empathy if the cultural differences can be appreciated and bridged – and the manipulations of anti-immigration politicians and agitators is ignored.

Friedman argues that globalisation itself can bring peace between countries. He puts forward a thesis in *The Lexus and the Olive Tree* called the 'Golden arches theory of conflict prevention'. The golden arches in question are the symbol of the fast-food chain McDonald's, which is often seen as an embodiment of all that is wrong with globalisation. In his golden arches theory, Friedman makes the incredibly bold claim that no two countries with McDonald's restaurants have fought a war against one other – the underlying suggestion being that countries most embedded in globalisation would no longer go to war – at least not with one another.

Friedman's suggestion is that the existence of McDonald's in a country is indicative of the existence of a middle class, which suggests that the particular country has reached a certain level of economic development. This acquired position as an 'economically developed' country would somehow prevent it from going to war. The reason for this, Friedman ventures, is that as globalisation binds countries together into a complex web of shared commercial interests, such countries have too much to lose to fight one another.

There are quite a few problems with this particular idea of Friedman's, not least that it is simply not true. Countries that have McDonald's *have* fought with one another. Even if that were not the case, when Friedman wrote the global mushrooming of McDonald's restaurants was part of very recent history. Warfare, on the other hand, has been going on for much longer than cheap burgers being sold in the vicinity of images of a maniacal looking clown.

Furthermore, countries going to war (and communities breaking into civil war) routinely had complex ties and co-dependencies that were incredibly expensive to break. Friedman's hope and logic are endearing, but his assumption that the world revolves around the interests of multinational burger vendors is flawed. The fact is that conflict often lacks rationality, and war is rarely halted because it is expensive. If nobody else gains, the military-industrial complex does. Moreover, above and beyond any loss to the burger and fries business, there is the small matter of millions of lives that can be lost in war.

It is interesting to note that in the very year that *The Lexus and the Olive Tree* was published, NATO bombed the country then known as Yugoslavia. Yugoslavia did have McDonald's restaurants at that point, though they were demolished by protesters on the first day of the NATO raids. Other examples of conflicts involving countries with McDonald's include India and Pakistan (who fought a war over Kashmir), Russia and Georgia, Russia and Ukraine, and Israel and Lebanon. Panama also had a McDonald's in 1989 when it was invaded by McDonald's epicentre, the USA

Friedman has since suggested that his golden arches theory of conflict prevention was not meant to be taken as seriously as critics who diligently proved him wrong believed. His tongue was in his cheek in a more obvious way in the title of his subsequent book on globalisation, *The World is Flat: A Brief History of the Twenty-First Century*. That book was published just five years into the 21st century, making it an exceptionally short history.

The title *The World is Flat* is a reference to Friedman's idealised vision of the global market as a level ground, in which commercial competitors have equal opportunities. Friedman takes the reference from Indian entrepreneur and politician Nandan Nilekani, who reportedly said to him that the commercial 'playing field' was being levelled. A key thing that has levelled the field, according to Friedman, is that the internet has removed the geographical barriers to the market, enabling businesses in far-flung places to compete more effectively, and those such as India and China were quite suddenly able to compete like never before.

The reality of global trade enabled by modern communications technologies was very old news by the time *The World is Flat* came out. Many businesses had been using the internet for two decades. Although Friedman is clearly pro-globalisation and firmly believes in the free market, the timing and the focus on his book is interesting and suggests a strong patriotism. Given his focus on the rising commercial potency of countries such as China and India, there is a sense that he is trying to rouse the US to wake up and compete. On the one hand, he seems genuinely excited about the changing global market, which would appear to vindicate his early cheerleading for globalisation, but at the same time he is clearly a cheerleader for the USA.

In the book, Friedman goes through events and developments

which he argues have been key to an apparent flat market. I will outline some of these. The fall of the Berlin Wall in 1989 marked the end of the Cold War and opened up the Eastern Bloc for business. Stating, "when the walls came down, and the windows came up", Friedman referred to the ability of people in former 'communist bloc' countries to use personal computers with Microsoft Windows operating systems. This ultimately enabled people to connect more effectively to one another and across vast distances.

The availability of Netscape's web browser (Netscape Navigator) was another key event for Friedman. Though to many readers now it will mean either nothing or seem as far away in time as the Soviet Bloc in eastern Europe, it was the dominant web browser in the 1990s and helped deliver hundreds of millions of people to the internet.

Our ability to upload content onto the internet, such as blogs and open-source software like Wikipedia, is another significant development that Friedman notes. The open-source movement in software is significant in itself, but the model also applies to other collaborative projects enabled by the web, such as those relating to open-source pharmaceutical discovery and other areas of science. Other open-source applications include electronics, engineering and fashion.

Another key driver of a level playing field is outsourcing, which has also been supported by the internet. This is the process whereby companies split different aspects of their work into component parts so that some can be subcontracted to make things more efficient and cost-effective. Using the example of drug discovery, not only is it now common for pharmaceutical giants to have research and development in one part of the world and manufacture done elsewhere (see offshoring later), but innovation in relation to novel mechanisms of drug delivery and formulation, for example, can be outsourced to smaller companies that specialise in those areas of research. It can be cheaper and quicker to use small innovative firms for this than retain vast research and development operations.

Offshoring, which means the relocation overseas of an organisation's manufacturing or other processes, for example a call centre, has become much more common since Friedman's book came out. The extent to which a company can claim a product has been made in a particular country becomes a contentious issue when materials are processed in one country and components made in various other countries by subcontractors.

These phenomena and related ones built on these over the decades obviously have benefits to human beings generally, in that they enable easier communications and help technologies to evolve. However, even the rose-spectacled Friedman recognises that there are threats associated with these, though he seems primarily concerned with threats to US companies. Commenting from an anthropological perspective rather than a patriotic one, I am more broadly concerned with threats to societies, habitats, ecosystems and the erosion of workers' rights.

For the USA to retain a dominant position, Friedman advocates a number of things that echo the laissez faire liberalism that Keynes challenged in the early 20th century. He argues for a more adaptable workforce, which would enable people to be more flexible in what they can do. Workers would also need to be open to switching jobs and employers frequently over the space of a career. It is interesting that companies can be viewed as the primary beneficiaries of economic globalisation, with barriers to market diminished, costs cut and risks reduced – yet it is ordinary people, often drowning in debt, who have to make themselves more and more flexible and shoulder a huge amount of uncertainty.

In *The World is Flat*, Friedman updates his widely disputed 'golden arches theory of conflict prevention' by introducing his 'Dell theory of conflict prevention'. He states: "The Dell Theory stipulates [that] no two countries that are both part of a major global supply chain, like Dell's, will ever fight a war against each other as long as they are both part of the same global supply chain." The idea is that economic interdependence between nations stems from large companies (such as the computer giant Dell) having supply chains in multiple global locations, and these countries will not want to go to war as this would cause them to lose wealth.

The weaknesses of this theory are not dissimilar to the McDonald's-centric one already discussed. War does not simply happen because it is economically affordable, and war is not prevented because it is expensive. If only the world was as simple as this. There is a myriad of complex historical, cultural, economic and political reasons for wars. Wars and invasions happened before globalisation and during the age of globalisation.

My sense is that Friedman is so enchanted by globalisation and sensitive to criticisms of it that he puts forward these rather flaky ideas that somehow globalisation means the end of war. In fact, globalisation is key to how conflicts have emerged in recent decades and in the modern manifestation of terrorism. For example, recruitment of young people into Daesh or so-called Islamic State has been facilitated to a very large extent by the capacity to upload information to the web, discussed earlier.

Though the developments in interconnectivity that Friedman outlines are realities – indeed they were some time before *The World is Flat* was released – the general thesis is flawed. As has been mentioned, Friedman's approach is US-centric, and it is also blind to much of the world. Disciplines such as anthropology, human geography, environmental science and economics have shown for some time that globalisation has an extremely uneven impact on societies and within societies.

There are only so many resources to go around and globalisation actually helps those who are good at finding ways to plunder to do so more easily. The masses, especially in the poorest areas, come off badly from globalisation and neoliberalism. Even in prosperous settings such as the US and UK, the poorest get scant benefits and great levels of uncertainty from economic globalisation.

It is all very well Friedman saying that workers should be flexible in what they will do – as if the poorest haven't always been so – but, in many settings, all flexibility can do is sustain you from day to day. You are far less likely to get a share of the fruits of economic globalisation if you were not lucky enough to start out with distinct advantages.

Sitting in an office in New York, with news from all over the place streaming into one's eyes, it might seem as though globalisation is a smooth and equal process helping the world to 'evolve'. For a child in no shoes, with no access to school, who expresses his or her 'flexibility' by rummaging through toxic rubbish on landfill sites, things are extremely different. For them, the fruits of globalisation they see are the bits of metal they hope to scavenge from old computers and other electrical appliances discarded in the US or Europe but ending up on a polluting rubbish dump 'outsourced' to Africa, India, Pakistan or Vietnam.

Chapter 7 – When the veneer is torn away

The last chapter focused on tensions between the fruits and negative impacts of globalisation and the conflict-laden ideology of neoliberalism. These concepts, and debates around them, help us to look through the veneer of contemporary civilisation to the economic, political and ideological battles being waged. In this chapter, the focus is on dramatic examples in which the veneer of civilisation was brutally torn away, leading to human communities being torn apart.

Readers will notice, in the following examples, many of the elements already discussed coming into play, such as racism and dehumanisation, economic battles, political volatility, religious conflict and the impact of external pressures.

When I was growing up, World War Two seemed like distant history. I can remember feeling that it was too long ago to warrant the level of attention it received. I grew to resent comedy about it, documentaries about Hitler and people who appeared obsessed with the war. I lived in a world of video games, rapid innovation in music, satirical comedy and general excitement. From my brightly coloured and ever-changing world of fun, people in black and white Pathé newsreels – from a time when people fell for ludicrous frothing dictators – were in a different world that could never come again. Even films about the war made decades after it ended seemed incredibly dull and irrelevant to me.

It is strange actually that I saw *the* war, as it was referred to when I was as child, as so far off. I was close to my grandparents, one of whom had been a prisoner of war before finally returning and marrying my grandmother, who also served in the army during the war. My other grandmother had the veneer of her seaside existence torn away on her 16th birthday, the day Britain joined the war.

I didn't resent *their* stories, but somehow their particular stories were in colour in my mind. The films, documentaries and news footage, though, were from a bygone black and white age. Another reason it is strange that I saw it as so far off is that war was played out on the news every evening in a myriad of different places – in horrific colour. However, those places and events seemed as remote to me at that point as the rabid-looking Hitler seemed absurdly unique, and therefore not likely to be emulated or echoed again.

If I am honest with myself, I must acknowledge that I had in my mind a simplistic evolutionist model of life. Yes, terrible things happened in the past, but we are not so daft now that we would ever let something like that happen again, might have been my view if I was forced to spell it out.

Wars and conflicts I saw on the television news as a child did allow glimpses through the veneer of civilisation and periodically challenged my assumptions about progress, but they were remote and could never be like World War One or World War Two. These various conflicts in distant places were confusing to me but did not scare me much. Although we had some Irish Republican terrorism on UK soil, the impact of British attacks on other societies had not really come home to roost at this point.

My grandmother whose 16th birthday was ruined by Hitler was less optimistic and more suspicious than me. At some point before I was born she had become suspicious about some Irish men sharing a house next door to her in east London. Her suspicions were mocked until the police dug the garden up and found a cache of weapons. This did not worry her too much, having lived in a pub in London through the blitz. As my other grandmother, barely five feet tall and perhaps six stone, said after the 2005 terror attacks on London, where I was living: "Londoners survived the blitz, we aren't going to let these bastards win."

Perhaps the huge wars of the early 20th century made other wars and conflicts seem less consequential. The existence of nuclear bombs worried me as a child but that was a futuristic threat and not like the cruel sadistic brutality of the two world wars. Us all being wiped out together was less monstrous to me than certain people separated off because of their ethnic origin and taken to death camps. It was not the guns and bombs of the two world wars that repulsed me, but the way in which groups were singled out, dehumanised, starved, tortured and killed with such sadistic planning and industrial-scale execution.

I'm sure many readers will recognise reading these paragraphs that my childish denial of the possibility that anything like the two world wars could happen again reflected the horror of these sickening human tragedies. Even though all I had to go on was stories, films, documentaries, photographs and recordings of broadcasts, it was terrifying enough. It was much easier at that age to immerse myself in fun things and imagine that the future could only be even better than the present than to reflect on much more horrific realities.

The realities were, and are: World War Two wasn't actually that long ago; there are many people alive who were hugely affected by it; if we are not careful the same sort of dynamics can play out again; and *all* wars reveal a capacity for human beings to do the most sadistic things to one another. Furthermore, human beings can do the most sadistic things to those they have been living peacefully alongside for their whole lives.

I am not judging my childhood self, or anybody else, for attempting to create psychological and emotional buffers to ward off the horrors of wars that happened before we were born, or those occurring in our lifetimes. If the opposite was true, and children and adults lived in terror that the wars and tyrants of the past could return at any point, then societies could be very unstable.

If it were not for the resilience of children and the speed with which culture can transform, we might be perpetually dragged back into the shadows of the past. One of the benefits of humans having the life spans we do is that it is possible to turn over to fresh pages that are not splattered by the horrific events of the past.

However, lessons from the tragedies of wars were always passed on to younger generations though word of mouth, whether in stories, songs or poems. This also happens through material culture in the form of, for example, paintings, tapestries and pots depicting battles. These can seem heroic, tragic or morbid, depending on the perspective of the observer. However, the 20th century was the first time in history that footage and audio of war and the victims of war could be recorded for posterity. It is extremely difficult, if not impossible, to evaluate the impact this would have, both positive and negative.

The quality of film and audio recording happened to improve rapidly in an era of two world wars, and continued to do so in the subsequent decades. Overseas reporting also expanded as a discipline, with the war correspondent becoming a familiar sight on news bulletins by the time I was a child.

It is possible that, as with CCTV cameras, there was a hope that ubiquitous observation could prevent atrocities or their escalation. In Chicago in 1968, as police brutally clubbed anti-war protesters to the ground, campaigners chanted: "THE WHOLE WORLD IS WATCHING. THE WHOLE WORLD IS WATCHING." This was an exaggeration, as a much smaller proportion of people outside the prosperous US had access to television, but certainly a vast number of people did see it.

It is questionable, however, that the visibility of war and other brutal events does make them stop any quicker or be less brutal. It is also debatable that seeing wars unfold so often on news bulletins made people, overall, more concerned about war. It could be that it desensitised us or led us to assume that war is just a normal part of human life.

The Rwandan genocide

The first war that really broke through my mental barriers and shattered the impression I had developed that human societies would evolve as fast as music and video games, was one in Rwanda, which resulted in a sickening genocide. I think it shocked me more than other wars I had seen on the news because of the ethnic cleansing aspect, and also because people who had lived and worked alongside each other for their entire lives were bludgeoning and hacking one another to death in the street.

The veneer of civilisation was torn away for me in the most repugnant and terrifying way. If a previously functioning society could rapidly tear itself apart, perhaps any society has the ability to abandon civilisation in favour of barbarity. Perhaps the torture implements that had both fascinated and terrified my sister and I when we visited dark museums as young children could return. Perhaps this glittering world of flashing lights and music we live in could be shattered. Between 1990 and 1994, when all hell was breaking out in Rwanda, rave was still quite big in the UK and Britpop was in the ascendancy. Images of the Rwandan war created a discordant tone, to say the least.

In the 24 years since the Rwandan genocide, in which approximately 800,000 people were slaughtered in a 100-day period, this event has stayed in my mind and affected my perception of not only other conflicts but also any circumstances in which people are treated differently because of their ethnicity. It became a marker in my mind of how far people are capable of falling, just as for older generations World War Two was a constant reminder of humanity's capacity for industrial-scale cruelty and violence.

When there are discussions about conflicts in Africa, people often do one (or both) of two things, grounded in ignorant and often racist assumptions. One is to bring up the concept of tribes, usually before making the dull assertion that, 'Africans will inevitably fight with each other' as a result of ancient 'tribal' histories. The other blinkered assertion often made, rarely grounded in research, relates to the fallacy that Africans live more peacefully when there are 'civilised' white colonialists to keep the 'tribes' from fighting. Ironically, this sort of racist narrative has much in common with the narratives of those who commit genocide.

I have heard these sorts of assertions made by 18-year-old university students and by 60-year-old professionals. Examples like Rwanda have the potential to teach such people that they have got it terribly wrong. However, in order to gain that awareness, they need to look into it carefully and with open minds. Culture and conflict in Africa is much more complicated that just tribal histories. Economics, inequality, colonialism and political manipulations have generally played highly significant roles, not least in the build-up to the Rwandan genocide.

To understand the Rwandan civil war of the early 1990s and the genocide it is necessary to understand the historical context. The earliest known inhabitants of what is currently known as

Rwanda were the Great Lakes Twa, a semi-nomadic community of pygmy hunter-gatherers. The Twa settled in the region several thousand years ago. However, between 700 BCE and 1500 CE, a number of Bantu-speaking groups moved into the area and cleared forest for agriculture, and the Twa lost a great deal of their forest habitat, shifting their settlements to the slopes of mountains.

The 'Bantu' is a term that describes more than 500 ethnic groups in Africa who speak one or some of the hundreds of Bantu languages. Bantu groups exist from central to southern Africa. Both Hutu and Tutsi are Bantu and the distinctions between these groups grew over time. In the Rwanda context, they can be better understood as constructed class or caste divisions rather than racial or 'tribal' distinctions.

It is possible that differentiation of Hutu and Tutsi happened prior to the movement of Bantu into Twa territory but this process could have happened after the migration. This has not been proven either way but what is known is that differentiation and resultant conflict were amplified in recent centuries.

It appears that, before the 17th century, the Bantu population in the area was split into clans composed of both Hutu and Tutsi, but by around 1700 the population had divided into eight kingdoms, some amassing more power than others. One such group, the Kingdom of Rwanda, became the dominant power from the middle of the 18th century.

As the kingdom expanded north and west in the late 19th century, divisions grew between the Hutu and Tutsi. Though the Hutu was by far in the majority within the kingdom, they were primarily peasant agricultural workers, while the royalty was primarily Tutsi. However, at this stage there appears to have been some fluidity between groups and some Hutu had the status of nobility. Divisions increased, however, with the influence of European colonialists.

The influence of European colonial powers in the territory became significant towards the end of the 19th century. The Berlin Conference of 1884 (also known as the Congo Conference) was a meeting of imperial powers about dividing up Africa. The conference assigned the area to Germany. As was common in the colonial era, the invading empire used existing systems of power, in this case the Rwandan monarchy, to rule the territory.

After the defeat of Germany in World War One, a different European power, namely Belgium, became the colonial master of both Rwanda and neighbouring Burundi. The Tutsi supremacy over the Hutu was only strengthened under the new colonial regime. The distant Belgian society, which was highly stratified, formalised a rigid ethnic distinction of the citizens of the colony in 1935 by introducing identity cards that defined people as either Tutsi, Hutu or Twa.

In the years leading up to this, the Belgians also reinforced divisions by enabling Tutsi chiefs to take control of grazing land historically used by Hutu. Although the colonisers initiated developments in areas such as education and health, the Hutu were not the major beneficiaries of 'development' in the country and many were driven in the 1930s into forced labour

A class distinction that had grown over the centuries had been, under colonial rule, cemented into something that appeared like a racial or tribal distinction. This construction over time of a rigid distinction between people is an excellent example (or warning) from history about how 'racial' categories can be constructed, leading to division, conflict and – in this case and in Rwanda – ultimately genocide.

For the marginalised Hutu in the 1930s and 1940s, Catholicism became a strong draw. Faith and the support of the Catholic Church was significant in the emancipation movement which gathered potency. Though many people today view Christianity as a force of repression, it has been extremely significant in movements designed to shake off oppression, not least in Caribbean emancipation and independence movements.

Liberation theology, which has been a significant force for good in Latin America, is concerned with strengthening the oppressed and bringing about positive social and political change. Though it reflects the teachings of Jesus found in the Bible, it has been opposed by the conservative Roman Catholic establishment and the political right-wing, which views it as a Marxist initiative. However, the current Pope has recently expressed a more positive view of liberation theology.

In Rwanda, Catholic missionaries were sympathetic to the plight of the Hutu and sought to strengthen their position in relation to the economically and politically dominant Tutsi. One way in which this shift in power happened was through the creation of a new Hutu intellectual elite. As well as improving the educational opportunities of Hutu generally, the Church produced many Hutu clergymen, who helped progress the emancipation movement.

The historically constructed distinctions between Hutu and Tutsi were dramatically reinforced, ironically, by the Hutu in a 1957 document called the *Bahutu Manifesto*. Written by nine Hutu intellectuals, the manifesto defined the Tutsi and Hutu as different 'races'. The full title of the 10-page political manifesto was *Note on the Social Aspect of the Indigenous Racial Problem in Rwanda*. Addressed to the Belgian vice-governor general of Rwanda, the document called for the liberation of the Hutu people from both the colonialists and the Tutsi. The document referred to the "monopoly which is held by one race, the Tutsi" and stated that "statistical law" requires that power should shift to the majority Hutu population.

A Tutsi attack in 1959 on Hutu sub-chief Dominique Mbonyumutwa was the spark that led to a bloody revolution lasting two years and that changed the face of the country. Mbonyumutwa was not killed in the attack, but rumours that he had been were enough for Hutu revolutionaries to begin killing Tutsi. The revolution started with riots and arson attacks on premises occupied by Tutsi.

There was retaliation from Tutsi but the Belgian powers had decided, no doubt to protect their own interests and lives, to back the Hutu. Less than a year into the revolution, the Belgian administration replaced most Tutsi chiefs and sub-chiefs with Hutu, and the Tutsi King, Kigeli V, was stripped of his power and reduced to figurehead status.

The Belgians also organised elections, which took place in the middle of 1960 and resulted in a landslide Hutu victory. This led to King Kigeli fleeing the country and the establishment of a Hutu-led republic, independent from Belgium.

During the revolution, many Tutsi fled Rwanda, with most moving to neighbouring Burundi, Zaire, Uganda and Tanzania. However, rather than be content with settling in those countries, where they were deemed refugees, displaced Tutsi formed militia designed to violently overthrow the Hutu regime. Incursions by these groups ultimately failed and led to the Hutu killing more Tutsi in reprisal. The largest such incursion by the Tutsi took place towards the end of 1963. After it was repelled, Hutu forces killed thousands of Tutsis still living in Rwanda.

By 1964, within five years of the revolution starting, around 330,000 Tutsi had left Rwanda, which was a large proportion of Rwanda's Tutsi population. To put this in context, the population of the country at this point was just over three million. Those Tutsis that remained in the country had the status of second class citizens and were frequently subjected to violence because of their ethnic classification. There were no more attacks by Tutsi refugee militias in the decades that led up to the civil war of the 1990s, though the strengthening of Tutsi capacities started in the 1980s, during military activity in Uganda.

In that decade, around 500 Rwandan refugees in Uganda, led by Fred Rwigyema, who had been exiled from Rwanda at the age of three and grew up to lead the Rwandan Patriotic Front (RPF), fought with Uganda's National Resistance Army in the Ugandan Bush War. The success of this led to the overthrow of Ugandan president Milton Obote, who had been deposed by Idi Amin 14 years before.

The Rwandan exile soldiers remained in the Ugandan army after Yoweri Museveni, who they helped seize power, became president of the country. However, they were, and had been all along, plotting and gaining the experience for an invasion of Rwanda aimed at deposing the Hutu regime. Within the Ugandan army, the Tutsi exiles created a covert RPF network which enabled Rwigyema, in October 1990, to lead a group of 4,000 men into the country of his birth. He was killed three days into the incursion.

The Rwandan army, supported by French forces and soldiers from Zaire, repelled the RPF invasion. After a tactical retreat, led by Rwigyema's former deputy Paul Kagame, the group embarked on a mission to recruit Tutsi refugees. Once the RPF had gathered strength and morale, it commenced a guerrilla war against Rwandan forces. The conflict prompted new attacks by Hutu against Tutsi still living in Rwanda.

There was also a rising tide of protests in the country, which by the middle of 1992 helped push President Juvénal Habyarimana towards peace negotiations, though these were opposed and undermined by Hutu hardliners. These hardliners were behind massacres of Tutsi citizens in 1993 and these led to an RPF offensive which took the guerrillas close to taking Kigali, the country's capital.

The RPF subsequently returned to negotiations with the government and signed a peace agreement known as the Arusha Accords, named after the city in Tanzania where negotiations took place. These five protocols to end the civil war were signed, in August 1993, by the Rwandan government and the RPF.

The Arusha Accords established transitional government composed of the RPF and five Rwandan political parties that had made up an interim administration in place since the previous year. The Accords included agreement on the repatriation of refugees, the rule of law, a power sharing agreement and the ultimate merging of government forces and rebel militia, in addition to an agreement that RPF solders would make up 40% of the Rwandan army and account for at last half of the officers.

The agreement stipulated that the transitional government and national assembly would be established within 37 days of the Arusha Accords being signed and general elections would be held within 22 months. President Habyarimana was not committed to the deal, which would reduce his power considerably. It seems more than possible that he never intended to honour the agreements. Hardline Hutu nationalists were also antagonistic towards any power sharing agreement.

Two months after the Arusha Accords were signed, the UN Security Council commissioned Resolution 872 to establish the United Nations Assistance Mission for Rwanda, with a view to supervising the implementation of the agreement. This meant around 2,500 UN military personnel in the country as a peacekeeping force. Tragically, the peace agreement did not hold and the death toll exceeded anything that had happened in the country previously.

In the background, a growing group of Hutu hardliners had been plotting a 'final solution' to wipe out all Tutsi. A significant event that catalysed the genocide to come was the assassination of Juvénal

Habyarimana and fellow Hutu Cyprien Ntaryamira, the Burundian president. The pair were travelling in a plane shot down by two missiles in April 1994, on route to Kigali. It is still not clear who was responsible for the attack but Hutu extremists and RPF troops were the key suspects.

The 100-day genocide that was to follow commenced on the orders of the interim government, led by Théoneste Bagosora. A Hutu military officer, Bagosora had never accepted the power sharing agreement or the influx of Tutsis into the military. He was present at the Arusha negotiations but reportedly said he would return to Rwanda and "prepare for the apocalypse" after the Accords had been signed. His covert goal, and that of other Hutu hardliners, appears to have been, for some years, genocide.

Bagosora had been establishing sleeper paramilitary (genocidal massacre) units called 'Interahamwe' in communities across the country. These have often been described as 'self-defence' units, but the term actually translates to "those who work together". This sounds all very cooperative and warm, but it contained a sinister euphemism. By the time of the genocide, it was apparent from radio broadcasts encouraging attacks that the word 'work' was being used as code and really meant 'to murder people with machetes'.

Using the Interahamwe network, Bagosora had been arming the Hutu population with guns and a vast number of machetes. It has been established that between early 1993 and the following March more than half a million machetes were imported into Rwanda. These weapons played a major role in the genocide. Bagosora and other plotters also prepared by drawing up lists of early victims of the impending bloodbath, including not only Tutsis but also moderate Hutus.

The genocide began the day after the plane was brought down. Rwandan soldiers, police and local militia set about killing Tutsis and moderate Hutus. The moderate figures were seen as agents of an unacceptable power sharing agreement and potential threat to the new order of hardliners. Checkpoints were erected so that ID cards, showing ethnic classification, could be checked and Tutsi quickly identified and killed. As well as the machetes imported for the purpose of the genocide, Hutu civilians were encouraged to use clubs or other blunt objects to kill their Tutsi neighbours.

People who refused to take part in massacres were routinely killed. I describe human groups in which people are pushed into becoming part of a cruel and destructive system, as part of psychopathic cultures, in other writing. Psychopaths only account for a small percentage of the population in any nation, and it is important to stress that most psychopaths do not kill. Psychopathy is an inherent brain abnormality and therefore it cannot be the case that a large number of citizens suddenly become psychopathic killers. In Rwanda, people were whipped into a violent frenzy by malicious leaders, a history of oppression, fear and a disturbing inclination of human beings towards conformity.

The process was also aided by ideologies that encouraged citizens to view part of the population as dangerous, evil, the source of all problems and, critically, essentially different. Racist narratives and ideologies connected with relative worth appear to be one of the easiest ways of encouraging people to dehumanise and harm other citizens. Just as we have seen elsewhere in recent years, elements of the media help push racist narratives, and this can help lay the foundations for the brutality which follows.

Some readers might be thinking: "If, as you claim, race is just a construct, and the Hutu and Tutsi have the same ancestry how can *this* be described as racist?" This, however, is precisely the point. To discriminate against certain people as a result of some imagined essential difference, but based on superficial characteristics or historical cultural factors, is the definition of racism. And to attempt to wipe those people off the face of the planet because of construction of them (and their construction of themselves) as essentially different is exactly what genocide is.

The development of greater and greater distinctions between the Hutu and Tutsi over the centuries, leading to social stratification, a caste system, resentment, conflicts and ultimately genocide, can be seen as an horrific illustrative fractal of a larger reality. It just happened to be that the amplification of otherness and conflict occurred in an era where events could be documented, but it would appear reflective of the fundamental human problem of what happens when unity disintegrates into division, dehumanisation of the other and conflict. This is one reason why I think Rwanda is as important a lesson from history as the rise of Nazism.

It is perhaps easy for some in 'the West' to imagine that what happened in Rwanda has no bearing on the life they live or where they live. However, if they consider the way in which political leaders, elements of the media, far-right antagonists and terrorist groups construct and amplify a sense of otherness and foster division, it is clear that this grotesque example from not so long ago has relevance for all sorts of societies.

It is critical that we can recognise narratives of division before open hostility breaks out. The rise and nature of hate crime we saw in the UK around the 2016 referendum about membership of the EU was inextricably linked to the narratives of political antagonists, such as UKIP and Britain First, and from the hard-right media.

In Rwanda, rape was used as a weapon of war and genocide. Propaganda from the leaders of the genocide portrayed Tutsi women as sexually seductive and in league with the Hutus' enemies. Hutu women, as well as men, were involved in the attacks on Tutsi women and also on moderate Hutu women. Just as with other pathological human cultures, anyone conforming and implicated can become psychologically and emotionally corrupted.

The use of sexual violence as a weapon of war had an additional danger and cruelty in that era as HIV was a significant problem in that part of Africa and there was not the antiretroviral therapy that is available now. The large number of rapes during the genocide led to an increase in HIV infections of both mothers of young children and babies, who were born with the virus.

The RPF ended their ceasefire once the genocide of Tutsi citizens in Rwanda started. They managed to steadily capture territory in the north of the country by surrounding cities and cutting off supply routes. UN interventions aimed at bringing peace were rejected, with RPF leader Paul Kagame refusing to negotiate while Tutsi citizens were being slaughtered.

In July 1994, the RPF captured the city of Kigali and, with the continued advancement of the RPF, the interim government fled into Zaire and both the civil war and genocide were stopped. During the period of genocide, up to 70% of the Tutsi population in Rwanda were murdered, which was approximately one fifth of the country.

After the RPF took control, Kagame became *de facto* leader of the country before becoming vice-president later in 1994. Steps were taken to bring those involved with the genocide to trial but there was also work to promote reconciliation between Hutu and Tutsi. Nevertheless, around two million Hutu who had fled Rwanda after the RPF victory remained outside the country, with many living as refugees in Zaire, as it was called at that point.

In late 1994, the International Criminal Tribunal for Rwanda (ICTR) was established by the UN. The tribunal was given jurisdiction over genocide, war crimes and crimes against humanity. Genocidal rape, as a weapon of war, was included in the cases heard. Dozens of people have been convicted in a large number of trials within the tribunal process.

The focus of the tribunal has been on those most heavily involved with the genocide, such as political figures behind it, but media figures also received lengthy jail sentences for their part in the atrocities. In 2003, Ferdinand Nahimana and Jean-Bosco Barayagwiza of Radio Télévision Libre des Mille Collines (RTLM), were both found guilty of genocide, incitement to genocide and crimes against humanity. Prior to co-founding the radio station, Dr Nahimana was a prominent Rwandan historian. Barayagwiza was a trained lawyer and civil servant.

The radio station, which aired from July 1993 until the following July, had been supported by the government's Radio Rwanda. As well as inciting attacks on Tutsis and moderate Hutus, the station incited hatred about Belgians and the UN. In a largely illiterate population, the radio station was an especially powerful platform of propaganda.

Hassan Ngeze, editor of magazine *Kangura*, was found guilty of the same offences as the broadcasters. The word kangura means to wake other people up. The publication was established in 1990, after the RPF invasion. It was funded by state intelligence and military officers, as well as members of the MRND political party. It began life attacking the RPF and ultimately became the mouthpiece and encouragement of genocide.

In a similar way to how fake news attacking Hillary Clinton was amplified by both poorly informed and consciously malicious people on social media in 2016, the poisonous messages of *Kangura* were disseminated by word of mouth. Articles were read in public meetings and during Interahamwe rallies.

Hassan Ngeze was also a correspondent for and shareholder of RTLM. In addition to calling for murder in editorials and on the radio, publishing lists of people to be killed and organising militia, Ngeze was alleged to have led and participated in murder, torture and mass rape.

Initially both Nahimana and Ngeze were sentenced to life imprisonment and Barayagwiza to imprisonment for 35 years. Four years later, on appeal, their sentences were reduced to 30 years imprisonment for Nahimana, 32 years for Barayagwiza and 35 years for Ngeze.

Théoneste Bagosora, who had fled to Zaire once the RPF had taken control of the country, was indicted in 1996. After the genocide, he lived in refugee camps and worked to rebuild the Hutu military, with the intention of completing the genocide. After he moved to Cameroon, along with other prominent Hutus, Bagosora was arrested. He faced 13 thirteen charges, including genocide, crimes against humanity and war crimes.

Along with other figures, Bagosora was also accused of making lists of intended victims and supporting the media outlets that incited hatred. In 2007, Bagosora and two other senior Rwandan army officers were convicted of crimes against humanity and war crimes.

Bagosora was held responsible for several political assassinations as well as orchestrating the mass murder of Tutsi citizens. He was also found guilty of rape and a string of other crimes. He was sentenced to life imprisonment, but this was reduced to 35 years on appeal.

Of 95 individuals indicted by the ICTR, there have been 61 convictions. There are a number of pending cases of individuals captured more recently and also some fugitives yet to be caught.

One of the longest sentences handed down after the atrocities was to politician Pauline Nyiramasuhuko, a trained social worker who had become Minister for Family Welfare and the Advancement of Women. She incited troops and militia to carry out rape during the genocide and she also incited murder, including the burning alive of a group of women.

Nyiramasuhuko appears to be the first woman ever brought to trial by an international tribunal. She was charged with conspiracy to commit genocide, complicity in genocide, direct and public incitement to commit genocide and crimes against humanity. Sentenced to life imprisonment, Nyiramasuhuko will not be eligible to apply for parole for 25 years from when she was sentenced, in 2011.

Nyiramasuhuko's son, Arsène Shalom Ntahobali, was an Israel-born Interahamwe leader. Between 1990 and 1994 he helped develop a detailed plan aimed at exterminating the Tutsi. This plan involved the training of militias, distribution of weapons and drafting of the lists of those to be murdered. He also played an active part in the genocide once the plans were carried out between April and July 1994 near his family home which, under the instructions of Ntahobali and his mother, was used to identify, separate off and kill Tutsi.

During this time, he was involved in the murder of numerous Tutsi citizens. Before they were taken for execution, the victims were often forced by Ntahobali and his mother to strip naked. He was also alleged to have been part of a group that went to the University Hospital of Butare where they abducted and killed Tutsis who had gone there to seek refuge and medical assistance. He is also reported to have raped a Tutsi woman at the hospital. Ntahobali was sentenced to life imprisonment with no possibility of parole.

Kagame went on to serve as president from 2000 and also won presidential elections in 2003 and 2010. A new constitution was drafted in 2003 and subsequently approved by a referendum. The constitution enables presidents to serve for seven-year terms and provides for a two-house parliament. It is also supposed to promote multi-party politics.

The constitution is also supposed to prevent Hutu or Tutsi political dominance, stating that "political organisations are prohibited from basing themselves on race, ethnic group, tribe, clan, region, sex, religion or any other division which may give rise to discrimination". However, Human Rights Watch has said that this clause, along with other pieces of legislation introduced by the Kagame government, effectively make Rwanda a one-party state, "under the guise of preventing another genocide".

Chapter 8 – When the veneer erodes in a key strategic centre

Syria is much more than a key strategic centre, where powerful empires of the world, local factions, rebel groups and government forces have one of the most complex and bloody tug of war battles the planet has known. It was a key centre for the development of human civilisation.

More than 10,000 years ago it was a centre of Neolithic culture and the place where agriculture was pioneered. The emergence of agriculture does not just mean that a human group understood the habitat well enough to exploit the capacities of the land, but that they cooperated – and therefore communicated – well.

Syria's success culturally and agriculturally stems from being part of an area known as the fertile crescent, a region of relatively moist and fertile land. Other modern countries with territory within this area include Iraq, Egypt, Lebanon, Palestine, Cyprus, Jordan, Israel, Turkey and Iran. The advantages of the fertile crescent, sometimes called the cradle of civilisation, in nurturing human societies, led to some important technological and social developments. These included writing, the wheel, irrigation systems and glass.

Dating back to the fifth millennium BCE, the settlement of Hamoukar in north eastern Syria was an important centre for obsidian production, a material used in a variety of tools, including weapons. The settlement became one of the largest cities of Mesopotamia. Specialisation of labour appears to have been instrumental to its success.

There is archaeological evidence that Hamoukar was destroyed in approximately 3500 BCE. Thousands of clay bullets have been found alongside slings during excavations conducted in the last decade. There is an eerie echo from this early evidence of urban warfare and that we have seen in Syria in recent years.

Another Syrian city to flourish in the late Neolithic and bronze age was Emar. This success was enabled by its strategic position making a shipping point. In the third millennium BCE, the city was under the influence of the rulers of Ebla, which was one of the earliest known kingdoms of Syria. Ebla itself is not far from what we now call Aleppo, which has been in the news so much in recent years.

Ebla was a major centre from around 5,000 years ago until around 1600 BCE, though the city was destroyed more than once. There were, consequently, three distinct kingdoms over time. The Elba Empire was a major power, comparable to ancient Egypt, developing from a small settlement to a significant trading empire and then becoming an expansionist power. The reach of Ebla's control appears to have spanned Anatolia, Mesopotamia and Damascus.

Excavations of the former city state have unearthed what appear to be gifts from Pharaohs, proving Ebla's contact with Egypt. Artefacts have also demonstrated links to Sumer, Cyprus and Afghanistan. The oldest library known to have existed in the world was found in the ruins of Ebla. The third Elba kingdom was by destroyed by the Hittites.

As we look at the complexity of the conflict in Syria and the many different forces, dynamics and ideologies involved, it can sometimes seem that things are too complex to ever be solved. However, it is worth reflecting on the fact that Syria has been fought over by the Babylonians, Sumerians, Egyptians, Eblaites, Akkadians, Hittites, Hurrians, Mitanni and Amorites.

Though it is clear from this history that Syria has consistently been seen as a place worth fighting over, it would be wrong to suggest that conflict for Syria is inevitable or somehow war is in the blood of Syrians. To imagine that either of those things are true ignores the history of Syria and the impact of outside forces on the country.

It is possible to go through many examples from Syria's history to keep reinforcing the point that the geographical position of Syria and its resources and cultural and ideological complexity have long been vulnerabilities. However, a more positive way of looking at this is that Syria over the millennia has had a myriad of great things going for it, not least a rich and diverse cultural heritage.

The vulnerability Syria experienced through the millennia has some similar root causes to vulnerabilities it has experienced in recent years. As a key part of the cradle of civilisation, the tragedy of destruction in Syria, whether in 1600 BCE or 2016, is a loss for human civilisation generally. Although the fracturing of such an important civilisation with such a rich history is an appalling regional tragedy, it is also a tragedy for humankind.

The destruction of the three Elba kingdoms may have been brutal and quite sudden, twice involving fire, and contemporary Syrians have some of the most 'advanced' weapons ever developed to worry about. They also have a medieval death cult with access to modern firepower to contend with, not to mention what might rain down from the sky at the whim of politicians thousands of miles away.

Amid this horrific marriage of brutality and advanced weapons technology, citizens in a country once at the pinnacle of civilisation were forced to cower in rubble or flee for their lives. Many of those killed or turned into refugees were young children. Those Syrians lucky enough to escape are portrayed as savages by newspapers that exhibit less linguistic sophistication than toilet wall graffiti and less care than cave art. Much to the shame of many Brits, then prime minister David Cameron described refugees who had made it to France as a "bunch of migrants" in 2016. He also used the term "swarm" to refer to people who had their homes, lives and countries destroyed.

It seems highly likely that such dehumanising language in fearful reports about refugees, often filmed on their plight crossing countries or attempting to cross seas, encouraged some who voted for Brexit in the 2016 UK referendum. Rather than help refugees as fully as they should, politicians weaponised refugees to fuel fear and bigotry. Those on the right, including the far-right, who pushed smearing narratives about Syrian refugees, avoided putting the existence of these people in context. If they had, it would have been much harder to weaponise their plight.

The context and complexity of the Syrian conflict

The proximity of Syria to such different countries has helped make it one of the most ethnically diverse countries in the region. It neighbours Turkey, Iraq, Jordan, Lebanon and Israel. Distinctive groups include Syrian Arabs, Armenians, Assyrians, Kurds, Greeks and Turks.

The extent of religious plurality might surprise those in the West who mistakenly assume that all problems in the country are to do with Islam. Religious groups that have lived side by side in the country include Sunnis, Christians, Jews, Alawites, Mandeans, Druze, Shiites, Salafis and Yazidis. That is not to suggest that conflict in the country has simply been the result of religious differences. In any conflict, including those where ideologies play a part, power, control of land, money and the character of key figures routinely play significant roles.

The full current name of Syria is the Syrian Arab Republic, but prior to the early 20th century it was ruled by the Ottoman Empire. After breaking from Ottoman control during World War One, the country briefly – for a few months – became the Kingdom of Syria, led by King Faisal. The short reign was ended by the Battle of Maysalun in summer 1920, after which French general Henri Gouraud established an administration.

French control was referred to as a 'mandate' as opposed to colonial rule, at least by the French. The idea was that France would act as a benevolent trustee until local people, who had been so long under the Ottoman Empire, would be in a position to maintain an independent state.

Under French control, six distinct Syrian states were created. These were Aleppo, Damascus, Alawites, Jabal Druze, the Sanjak of Alexandretta and Greater Lebanon. The latter became Lebanon in 1926.

The way in which Syria was divided up by the French was informed by realities of sectarian complexities. However, there was widespread hostility to the French action, which was seen to cause division. As a result of this hostility and antagonism to the French administration generally, there was unrest across the imposed and fabricated Syrian states. Contagion from a 1925 revolt starting in Jabal Druze led to what has been called the Great Syrian Revolt.

In 1930, with the French administration still in place, the state of Syria was declared the Republic of Syria. Six years later, a Franco-Syrian Treaty of Independence was signed, although this was not ratified by the French. Nevertheless, territories that Syria had been divided into, apart from Greater Lebanon, did become part of the Republic by 1938. In autumn 1938, the French caused a new problem, however, which is yet to be resolved. They turned Alexandretta into the Republic of Hatay, which joined Turkey the following year. This was not acceptable to Syria and the matter is still disputed.

Syria proclaimed independence again in 1941 but it would see a few more years and the establishment of the United Nations before this would be achieved. In 1945, as France bombed Damascus and attempted to detain democratically elected Syrian leaders, the country's prime minister Faris al-Khoury was at the founding conference of the UN in San Francisco, where he presented his country's claim for independence from France. It took one more year and a combination of pressure from Syrian nationalists and the UK for France to withdraw its troops.

Despite the imposition of power on the country by the Ottoman Empire and the occupation by France, it is important to say that Syria is not a passive country. Syrian forces, with those of other Arab countries, invaded Palestine in 1948. This enabled them to attack Jewish settlements on Palestinian land. Syrian troops were ordered by president Shukri al-Quwwatli to the front, "to destroy the Zionists". The hope driving the attack was to stop the state of Israel from being established.

This intervention ultimately failed and Syria, in a state of unrest and vulnerability, was subject to a military coup by Colonel Husni al-Za'im in 1949. The volatilities continued, however, and two further coups took place, by Colonel Sami al-Hinnawi and then Colonel Adib Shishakli. In 1954 Shishakli was also overthrown by coup and Syria was returned to a parliamentary system.

Despite the movement back towards parliamentary democracy, power in the country was still in the hands of the military and security services. Power centred in that way did not strengthen the country but added to the unrest in Syria and vulnerability of governance as well as the economy.

Like other settings where economic and social volatility became a breeding ground for nationalism, such movements grew in the country. This can be problematic in any country but for one with such different ethnic identities this can be especially volatile and divisive.

As is often the case when an unstable economy impacts most on the poorest, socialist movements also came to the fore at that point. Those who fared worst economically were often those from the most marginalised of religions, and these groups were among those most loudly calling for reform of the country.

The shift towards the left took a dramatic turn in 1956 when the country's leaders signed a pact with the Soviet Union. The regime required military equipment, which the Soviet Union would supply in exchange for political leverage. As has often been the case in Syria's history, an apparent strength then became a vulnerability because Turkey became increasingly concerned about its neighbour's rising military capability. There was a particular concern within Turkey that Syria might attempt to reclaim İskenderun, in the Hatay Province, but UN attention averted war.

Turbulence within and around the country did not disappear, however, and in 1958 the

president, Shukri al-Quwatli, and Egypt's Gamal Abdel Nasser announced that the countries would be merged. Nasser was a leader of the 1952 Egyptian Revolution and subsequently became president of the country. The union between the two countries formed the United Arab Republic (UAR).

The UAR was hoped to be the first step towards a pan-Arab state. The Arab Socialist Ba'ath Party backed the union and there was strong support for it from Arabs in Syria. However, it is important to understand that, rather than representing a dramatic shift to the left, the UAR was designed to prevent just that.

Prior to the union being created there was a great deal of concern in the West about Syria becoming a communist state. Nasser told Syrian leaders that they needed to remove communists from their government but the Syrians argued that a union with Egypt would be the best way to eradicate the 'communist threat'. Though he did not favour complete union with Syria, such was Nasser's fear of communism encroaching that he agreed to the UAR plan. Similarly, the Syrian Ba'ath Party was alarmed by the burgeoning strength of the Syrian Communist Party in the context of its own relatively unstable position.

The union between the two countries was short-lived. Syria left the union in 1961 after yet another coup. However, Egypt continued to retain the UAR name until a decade after Syria seceded.

Nasserism, as an Arab nationalist ideology, continues to have an impact almost 50 years after his death. Ba'athism has also been a potent force over the decades. As well as Syria, Iraq under Saddam Hussein is a notable example of Ba'athism being aggressively imposed.

Though there are drives behind Ba'athism that can be thought of as left-wing, it rejects key aspects of Marxism, such as class conflict and the primacy of the proletariat. It shares more with early 20th century European fascism than with movements aimed at increasing equality. The emphasis is placed on the battle for Arab independence rather than class struggle.

Ba'athism means 'renaissance' or 'resurrection', the revival being Arab culture and power. With the use of one-party states to foster this 'progression', the focus is certainly not on the rights of the individual. Where Marxism is relevant, it is in relation to societal transformation. However, it seems unlikely that Marx would have endorsed such a brutal system in which citizens are sacrificed to either Arab identity or the authoritarian state. It is far from liberatory.

Syrian Army officers were behind the 1961 coup, after which the country reverted to being the Syrian Republic, later becoming the Syrian Arab Republic. Despite the army's attempt to enable governance by existing parties, divisions within the army had impacts within politics and made for instability. A fresh coup took place just two years later.

The 1963 coup was launched by the military committee of the Syrian Regional Branch of the Arab Socialist Ba'ath Party. Those behind the coup were emboldened by a 'successful' coup by the Iraqi Regional Branch early in 1963. I put successful in inverted commas as the Iraqi coup, in which Saddam Hussein played a role in progressing, was followed by violent purges against the left-wing and some of the most vicious and systematic torture ever documented.

Allegations have been made that the CIA supported the February 1963 Iraqi coup, though evidence of direct involvement has not been proven. The political violence after that coup was a key part of the social volatility that led to another Iraqi coup towards the end of the same year.

In Syria, there were broad areas of social unrest which fuelled the 1963 coup in that country. The growing middle class became increasingly frustrated by the dominance of the traditional elite and peasants were frustrated by the way elite landowners managed the land.

A crossover of values and frustrations within the new middle class and military, both seeking to take power from elites regarded as inept, and the growing anger of the underprivileged minorities, gave strong foundations to the Ba'athist Revolution. There were tensions between the Ba'ath Party and the military, but the party knew that it needed military support and protection in order to take power.

One of the key figures in the military committee that planned the coup was Hafez al-Assad. He later became prime minister of Syria and then president of the country for almost three decades.

In the months after the coup, military institutions were taken under Ba'athist control, despite the inexperience of most of those granted that power. Many Nasserist officers were removed from powerful positions and pro-Nasser newspapers were closed down. In July 1963, there was an attempted coup by the Nasserists, with the help of Egyptian intelligence. The coup failed, hundreds were killed at the time and several participants were arrested and executed afterwards. This marked the decline of Nasserist influence in Syria.

Though in the era after the Ba'athist coup, Hafez al-Assad was involved with transforming the military to make it a Ba'ath institution, through re-education and purging, he ultimately played a key role in stripping away the power of the Ba'ath Party establishment. A coup in early 1966 ousted the national command of the Arab Socialist Ba'ath Party. Neo-Ba'athists deposed the traditional party in favour of a neo-Ba'ath regime.

The neo-Ba'ath movement, which had been strengthening for several years, represented a shift from a pan-Arab movement concerned with identity and the protection of national interests towards autocratic regimes held in place by military might and political violence.

In the new regime Hafez al-Assad became defence minister under General Salah Jadid. Under Jadid there was an attempt at rapid reform in Syria. Jadid's regime took a harder, tougher line towards Israel and aligned itself with the Soviets. However, the era was one of further instability and economic problems. The Ba'ath Party's reaction to unrest was to ban other political parties and therefore crush political debate and dissent.

The popularity of the regime among citizens was further reduced after the Six-Day War in 1967, which involved Israel and Egypt (still called the UAR), Syria and Jordan. Tensions between Israel and its neighbours had been bubbling away for almost two decades since the 1948 Arab–Israeli War but the 1967 conflict was triggered by a specific issue.

In May of that year, the Egyptian president Nasser received reports from the Soviets that Israel was massing troops on the Syrian border. The reports were false, but Nasser responded by massing his own troops in the Sinai Peninsula on Israel's border. The Israeli prime minister subsequently repeated declarations made a decade previously that closure of the Straits of Tiran to vessels heading to Israel would be an act of war and justification for war. The Straits of Tiran, narrow sea passages between the Sinai and Arabian peninsulas, were important routes for Israel to receive oil from Iran.

Despite the threat, Nasser declared the Straits closed to Israeli shipping and blockaded the route. Oil tankers attempting to pass through the Straits asked to submit documents stating that the cargo was not heading to Israel.

Days after this, Israel launched what it said were pre-emptive airstrikes against Egyptian air bases, destroying most of the Egyptian air force. Israel also launched a ground attack into the Gaza Strip and the Sinai, leading to Nasser evacuating the Sinai. Israeli forces inflicted killed many Egyptians and seized control of the Sinai Peninsula.

Syria and Jordan were at this point asked by Nasser to attack Israel. However, intervening took its toll on Syria and Jordan as well. Israel retaliated against Syria and occupied the Golan Heights and counter-attacks against Jordan led to the seizure of the West

Bank and East Jerusalem. During the six-day conflict more than 20,000 Egyptians, Syrians and Jordanian were killed but less than a thousand Israelis. There have also been long-term consequences for the many Palestinians who fled the West Bank and Syrians who fled the Golan Heights and became refugees.

Having called previously for a hard line against Israel, Jadid was significantly weakened by the short war and was ousted three years later by Hafez al-Assad, the father of Bashar al-Assad. The bloodless coup that removed Jadid was known as the Corrective Revolution.

From Assadism to sadism

After seizing power, Hafez al-Assad became prime minister (1970 to 1971) and president. In the early days there appeared to be genuine desire to bring together different parts of the fragmented society, including those who were opposed to the previous administration. He demonstrated a willingness to listen, visiting villages and engaging with citizens. Cutting food prices by 15% proved, as you would expect, a popular move.

There was also a sense that the repression of the past was softening and the state's tone towards critics of the Ba'athists was changing somewhat. A state of emergency that had been in place since 1963 allowed the state to exert extreme control over the press, to the extent that few existing newspapers were Ba'athist. Political dissidents were subjected to 'court' proceedings outside of the normal, more transparent, judicial system. Many dissidents had been sent into exile or jailed in previous years. In Assad's early days in power he suggested a change in the treatment of political dissidents, but Human Rights Watch has estimated that, in Hafez al-Assad's rule, at least 17,000 people were 'disappeared' without trial.

The large and oppressive security services that grew under Jadid's rule were scaled down, though arguably to maximise Assad's own control. Even if the oppressive state of previous years was made to appear, to some, less menacing, the Assad regime was far from a democracy. His regime allowed a vote on his rule every seven years. However, Assad was always the sole presidential candidate. Each of the four times he was 're-elected', Assad apparently gained between 99% and 100% of the votes.

All the evidence suggests that Assad's rule has the characteristics of a cult of personality. Like Trump more recently, the family of the ruler also became key – though not democratically elected – figures in the regime. This level of fortress-like insularity in rulers and nepotism is sometimes driven by conditions like narcissism and paranoia.

Also, like Trump, Assad's inclination was to weaken the powers of the party and institutions of governance to maximise his personal control. However, unlike Trump, who was quickly confronted with complex checks and balances aimed at preventing dangerous demagogues from destroying US democracy, Assad had no such barriers. Despite early suggestions of listening to the public and to dissent, Assad was actually intolerant of debate and dismissed those who questioned him.

There are also interesting parallels with Putin in his enthusiasm for projecting a strong-man image across the country and beyond. Pictures of the president in heroic scenes could be seen in public places across the country. In the West, we tend to find photos of Putin half naked on a horse, holding a fishing rod or clutching a big fish funny. A world leader trying so hard to seem physically tough can appear ridiculous. However, Putin is no idiot and he must know that these sorts of images impress certain segments of his society.

In the case of Assad senior's Syria, the country had just been through so many years of uncertainty that such images could not offer the sense of strength and stability that had for so long been lacking. The pictures may not therefore have been entirely narcissistic. However, Assad's naming of numerous places and institutions after himself and his relatives, and children being forced to sing songs praising the president, do underline the cult of personality associated with the regime. As we have seen with Kim Jong-un in North Korea, the great leader was sometimes depicted as having supernatural qualities.

Again, this attempt at manipulation of citizens might seem transparent and ludicrous to many readers, but when we consider what was to follow it makes more sense that Assad would play on religious iconography to bolster his power. Syria was and still is, after all, a deeply religious country founded on a bedrock of both ethnic and religious complexity.

Over the years the Assad regime was seen to be allowing a favoured elite to become more numerous and wealthier, while many were not only economically disadvantaged but also felt that their cultural group was neglected. Sunni Muslims, the majority group of the population but progressively divested of power over many years, were particularly aggrieved. Although a state had been created where there was no official political opposition to challenge decisions, Sunni groups were effectively the opposition to the Ba'athists.

Sometimes it can appear to people, in part from media representation, that violence and unrest in countries in which there are many Muslims stems from nothing more than different religious views. However, the experience of Syria can help us understand and show that issues such as inequality, poverty and corruption of the elite are at least as important factors in volatile cultural situations. Religion can play a powerful role but so too do more mundane issues that affect all divided and unequal societies. Scarce resources are also another key factor in some settings.

The Islamist uprising in Syria, which began in 1976 and went on until 1982, though with resurgences afterwards, was an attack on the authority of the Ba'ath Party and Hafez al-Assad's regime. It was characterised by violent Sunni insurgency. Most of those involved in the uprising appear to have been members of the Islamist Muslim Brotherhood. Off-duty soldiers were targeted, as were civilians.

The tension and potential for conflict had been rising for more than a decade. There was conflict between the Muslim Brotherhood and the Ba'ath Party after the Ba'athist coup of 1963. The regime responded by outlawing the Muslim Brotherhood the following year. This did not make the problem go away and in 1964 and 1965 industrial action and rallies took place across the country in Syria's major cities. Though these were suppressed by the military, the movement survived and adherents became more radicalised. The town of Hama became a particular hotbed of opposition to the Ba'athist state.

A significant decision by Hafez al-Assad in 1973 inflamed the tensions and lit the fuse which led to the Islamist uprising. A new constitution that year made it possible for a non-Muslim to be president of the country. The Muslim Brotherhood responded by organising demonstrations in Hama, Aleppo and Homs. Assad, who had previously appeared in imagery with Muhammed, was dubbed "the enemy of Allah". Some Sunni officers accused of plotting against Assad were arrested but he was forced to backtrack on the constitution change.

In October 1973 Assad and the Egyptian regime were humiliated once again by Israel. The two countries launched an attack on Israel that became known as the Yom Kippur War, the Ramadan War (because of its timing) and the October War. Early gains were quickly lost and the war was lost in just three weeks, after which Israel retained control of the Golan Heights and the Sinai Peninsula. If Assad hoped the surprise attack would support the 'strong man' image he sought to project, he was mistaken. His rule, though oppressive, was far from stable.

In 1976, Assad's regime began the Syrian occupation of Lebanon. This ultimately lasted until 2005. The occupation was designed to undermine the Palestinian guerrillas in Lebanon. The Syrian action was welcomed by some in Lebanon but rejected by Druze-led allies of the Palestinian guerrillas. In the autumn of 1976 the Arab League decided to expand an Arab peacekeeping force in the country, and it became a much larger Arab Deterrent Force, most of whom were Syrian soldiers. The Assad regime was, from then on, subsidised for its occupation and its invasion was legitimised.

Within Syria itself, the Islamist insurgency continued. After Assad's occupation of Lebanon there were assassinations of a stream of prominent Syrian officials and military officers, as well as highly educated professionals. As most victims were Alawis, a Shia sect long oppressed by Sunnis and regarded as non-Muslims by the Muslim Brotherhood, the Brotherhood are prime suspects for the killings.

In 1979 up to 83 cadets at Aleppo Artillery School were killed by gunmen from the Tali'a muqatila (fighting vanguard), a Sunni Islamist group that grew out of the Muslim Brotherhood. Following this attack there was an upsurge in Islamist terror attacks on Alawis, Ba'athists, military vehicles and barracks, police and places of business. Muslim clerics who spoke out about the killings were also targeted.

Strikes and protests also took their toll on the Assad regime. In March 1980, around the 17th anniversary of the Ba'athist coup, mass action took place across Syrian cities. The Muslim Brotherhood played a key role in the unrest but a variety of both religious and secular organisations participated in the protests. Demonstrations were met with a violent military crackdown in Aleppo, where tens of thousands of soldiers were dispatched and hundreds of protesters killed. Several thousand more were arrested.

A few months later, at the end of June 1980, Assad came under attack at a diplomatic function in Damascus. Two men threw grenades and aimed machine gun fire at him. The would-be assassins managed to get away. The Assad regime reacted with extreme violence, with Assad's brother, Rifaat al-Assad, orchestrating the slaughter of Islamist inmates at Tadmor Prison in Palmyra the next day. Estimates of those killed vary but the number is believed to be more than a thousand. They were killed by gunfire and grenades – the weapons of the assassination attempt.

Assad also responded through legal sanctions, making membership of the Muslim Brotherhood a crime punishable by death within a few weeks of the attempt on his life. Members were given a month's grace period, in which they could turn themselves in. Those who did turn themselves were primarily university students, academics, teachers and other professionals.

With the regime's frustration with its inability to maintain order, people with no connection to crimes were often punished for terror attacks. For example, a 1980 attack on soldiers in Aleppo led to the army killing scores of residents at a nearby block of flats. In the following year, around 400 residents of Hama, aged 14 upwards, were killed by government troops after an attack on an Alawite village nearby.

The Alawite community was a significant support base of Assad, occupying key roles in the armed forces and intelligence services. The attack on the village was therefore an attack on a source of Assad's military might.

The insurgency continued, and in the autumn of 1981 there were three car bomb attacks in Damascus against state targets. Hundreds were reported killed in the attacks, where were assumed to have been carried out by the Muslim Brotherhood.

Things escalated and came to a head in 1982. A massacre in Hama led to thousands of civilians being killed, along with insurgents and soldiers. After the Brotherhood managed to take control of the city the state bombed it for almost a month. Estimates of the numbers killed vary enormously but the figure was certainly in the tens of thousands, within a city with a population of 250,000.

Though some saw the bombing of Hama as the defeat of Islamist insurgency in Syria, Assad continued his purge for years, with thousands of accused Brotherhood supporters tortured, killed or going missing. This brutal crackdown on what was the only real opposition did not turn back the tide for Assad as, as well as Brotherhood-supporting Sunnis, large swathes of the population rejected the legitimacy of his rule. This included some former Ba'ath Party members.

Nevertheless, some still supported Assad right to the end of his reign. These included public employees, obviously dependent on the regime, but also peasants and elements of the middle class. Essentially supporters were those who most benefited from Assad's policies or successfully indoctrinated by the ideological position imposed by the regime.

In 1983 Assad had a heart attack, and, during a period in which he withdrew from public life, there was a power battle between Rifaat and the military leadership, with the younger brother attempting to position himself for power. This tussle for power ceased upon Assad's return to health and public life. A possibility existed that Rifaat would be prosecuted for attempting to depose his brother but he was ultimately exiled by sending him on an open-ended working visit to the Soviet Union.

Syria's economic health in the 1980s was also problematic. By 1984 there was a serious food crisis, with the country lacking basics such as flour, bread and sugar. The lack of availability of food and other necessities in shops led to rapid inflation and a growing black market, with goods smuggled with apparent ease from Lebanon.

Efforts to tackle the smuggling and black market were not helped by the involvement of Rifaat al-Assad in the trade. He used the Defence Detachment, which he commanded, to smuggle in millions of dollars of goods a week. An anti-smuggling squad established in the summer of 1984 seized almost four million US dollars of smuggled goods in its first week.

By the early 1990s, there were some improvements in the economy, with improvements in GDP and balance of trade, but inflation was more than 15%. Efforts to liberalise the economy led to investment from overseas, especially from Persian Gulf states, in infrastructure projects.

By the mid-1990s the economy was faltering again, however, with a recession, and in 1998 a global fall in the price of oil took its toll. Although a rise of the price of oil the next year was beneficial to Syria, the country experienced one of the worst droughts in a century with crops dramatically hit. Assad, who gained momentum early on from those working on the land, took emergency measures to support farmers, but the wider economy still struggled.

Hafez al-Assad's first choice to succeed him was not his youngest son Bashar. Rifaat had been the most likely successor but his attempt to grab power when his brother was recovering from a heart attack ended that possibility. His oldest son Bassel was Hafez's next choice but he was killed in a car crash in 1994. Soon after Bassel died, Hafez began to prepare Bashar al-Assad for succession. The president-in-waiting was just 29 years old, however, and this led to disquiet among Syrian officials, some of whom were consequently demoted. Bashar became president six years later when his father died of a heart attack.

Bashar al-Assad's rule

It wasn't just his age that made Bashar an unlikely candidate for the presidency of Syria. In a dictatorship so dependent on military might, gaining experience in and then leading armed forces and intelligence services was a well-trodden path. His father had served in the Syrian Air Force as an aviator before moving into roles that combined military prowess and politics. Bashar had instead trained as a doctor, which is something his father had also wanted to do but had been prevented from by financial circumstances.

Bashar al-Assad's only early military experience was as a doctor in the Syrian Army, but he soon moved into specialist postgraduate medical training in the field of ophthalmology. For this, he moved to London, where he appears to have been regarded as a diligent and courteous young doctor. He was in London undergoing postgraduate training for two years before his older brother was killed and his grooming for presidency began. This tragic accident rapidly took Dr Assad from the pristine and precise world of the Western Eye Hospital and liberalism of London into the chaos and butchery of Syrian politics.

In addition to not experiencing combat, Assad had also not studied politics, economics or law, which tend to be helpful to political careers. He was instead learning his 'trade' from a brutal dictator who had many years' experience of failing the people of Syria.

Having moved back from London, Bashar was hot-housed for the presidency and the military leadership elements of the role. There was also a PR campaign to get the public and military elites to accept him. Entering the military academy at Homs soon after returning would have been designed to build a sense of his legitimacy as well as develop his awareness. The former medic, described as sensitive by an ophthalmology specialist who trained him, was rapidly pushed up the ranks and by 1999 was a colonel of the Syrian Republican Guard. This is an elite force responsible for protecting the president.

There is nothing in his background that suggested Dr Assad had been harbouring ambitions to lead the country of his birth. To be plunged into that world, at such a chaotic time in Syria's history and the history of the Middle East, must have been beyond daunting.

A couple of things needed to be fixed to allow the nepotism to be successful. Some of the older military commanders were retired off and more sympathetic ones promoted, and the Syrian constitution was altered to bring the age at which someone could be president down from 40 to Bashar's age of 34.

Just as his father had decades before, Bashar al-Assad communicated a desire for a fresh and more transparent political climate in Syria. Within months of Assad junior coming to power, the Muslim Brotherhood indicated a hope for positive change, issuing a statement that rejected violence as a means of political change and calling for the country to become a democracy. There was also an increasingly higher level of debate around the country about the future of Syria, in what has been called the Damascus Spring.

The Damascus Spring started in June 2000 following the death of Hafiz al-Assad but had been snuffed out by autumn 2001. Assad had responded to the statement of the Muslim Brotherhood and a rising tide of debate across the country by shutting down one prison and releasing hundreds of political prisoners. However, it wasn't long before the Damascus Spring turned back into winter as Assad grew into the role of tyrant that his father clung to for so long. Freedoms dangled in front of people like a carrot were rapidly snatched away.

The Damascus Spring wasn't a time of violent revolution but of healthy political debate and hope for a new beginning for the country. This was enabled by the emergence and growth of talking groups that met in houses in Damascus and beyond. These muntadayāt (salons or forums) discussed politics and broader social issues. Though long-standing opponents to the Assad regime and Ba'athist reformers played key roles in the salon movement, and there was also significant input from intellectuals. The status of women, education and wider Middle Eastern politics were among the issues discussed in salons.

The salon movement led to the crystallisation of political demands for the new Assad regime. In the Statement of 99, which was signed by 99 Syrian intellectuals, a call was made to end the state of emergency which had been in place since 1963. The intellectuals also called for the abolition of martial law and dissolution of the special courts for those deemed dissidents, the release and pardoning of political prisoners and for exiles to be free to return to Syria without being arrested.

The signatories also demanded the right for citizens to form political parties and for Article 8 of the Syrian constitution be repealed. These demands were extremely significant as Article 8 stipulates that the Ba'ath Party leads the state and society. The signatories were therefore effectively calling for Syria to become a democracy.

The Statement of 99 was issued towards the end of September 2000 and in November hundreds of political prisoners were released and Mezze prison was closed. However, in the following year the regime returned to its habit of jailing accused dissidents and also targeted salons, shut them down and imprisoned those involved with forums.

It could be that genuinely reformist instincts of the young president were suppressed by conservatives in the regime. Or it could be that Assad's status as a moderniser was as questionable as his meteoric rise through the military ranks. Assad had not learned to enable a democracy but to lead a violent dictatorship, and this is exactly what he did. In doing so he led the country into being then setting off one of the most brutal and complex bloodbaths ever seen in the turbulent country.

This return to overt tyranny did not destroy the drive for change, however, and intellectuals released statements that echoed the sentiments of the Statement of 99. In fact, over time the intellectuals became increasingly outspoken about the regime. Some forums continued to operate, despite those behind salons receiving lengthy jail sentences.

By 2005 things were coming to a head. In February of that year Rafic Hariri, the former prime minister of Lebanon, was killed, along with 21 other people, in an explosion in Beirut. A number of Hariri's bodyguards and the former minister Bassel Fleihan were among the dead. The Syrian state was widely blamed for Hariri's assassination as in the months before the attack relations between Hariri and Assad had severely deteriorated to the level of threats from Assad.

The UN implicated Syrian officials but the Assad regime denied involvement in the bombing. In a December 2005 television interview, former Syrian vice-president Abdul Halim Khaddam implicated Assad in the assassination of Hariri and stated that Assad had threatened Hariri months before the murders.

Following the murders and links made to the Assad regime by the UN and others, Syrian intellectuals became more outspoken and calls for democratic change intensified.

Towards the end of 2005 a declaration from most of the opposition in Syria was issued, calling for democratic reform. The Damascus Declaration was signed by members of the Muslim Brotherhood as well as several prominent intellectuals. The Assad regime responded in January, saying that it would release five people imprisoned for involvement in the Damascus Spring.

Assad, however, proved unwilling to make significant changes in the country, despite pressure from within Syria and from the international community. As a result of his rigidity in the face of widespread criticism and condemnation, the country hurtled towards breakdown. Over the following years a rising number of people fled the country as refugees. A great many went to Turkey, despite the assumption by the far-right in Western Europe that all Syrians were desperate to move to 'our' countries.

In 2011, as Arab and North African states contended with the Arab Uprising and the drive for democratic change, Assad's Syria descended into what became known as the Syrian Civil War. Large-scale protests in Syria at the end of January 2011 reiterated calls for reforms, including the end of the state of emergency and civil rights. A subsequent protest, in early February, passed without violent state intervention.

However, a two-day event in mid-March, the most extensive in the country in decades, resulted in a violent crackdown against the protesters. Nevertheless, protests continued. As elsewhere in the Arab Uprising there was a sense that citizens opposed to the tyrannical regime were getting somewhere and this was *the time* things could finally shift for good.

Members of the international community condemned Assad's response to rallies and the Obama-led US government imposed sanctions against Assad's regime in April 2011. This was followed up by an Executive Order from Obama in May 2011 concerned with the property of senior officials of the government of Syria. The Order was designed to block members of Assad's regime from transferring wealth within the US or removing wealth secreted in the US.

By the following month, there was an apparent softening of Assad's position, no doubt influenced from mounting pressure within the country and the response of members of the international community. He indicated an openness to reform and dialogue within the country – the very thing his regime has stamped down. Sudden nice guy Assad also at that point called on Syrian refugees to return from Turkey, promising them amnesty if they did so. Rather than acknowledging fundamental problems in his regime driving unrest, Assad claimed at that point that a small number of people were sabotaging the society.

It would appear though that one did not have to resort to aggression to be a 'saboteur' of Assad's regime as in the summer of 2011 the cartoonist Ali Farzat was attacked for satirical cartoons mocking the regime. The cartoonist had both of his hands broken and was smashed in the head.

Amid a strengthening tone of condemnation from outside the country, including from then US Secretary of State Hillary Clinton, who said Assad had lost legitimacy, and Obama, who urged him to step down, Russia remained supportive. The Putin-led government vetoed UN Security Council resolutions that could have led to UN sanctions or military intervention.

With the UN's hands tied by Russia, Assad was able to continue his tyranny, despite his claims that he was open to reform and dialogue. By January 2012, Assad was blaming foreign countries for unrest in his country, rather than just a small number of Syrian 'saboteurs'. In a speech on January 10 he claimed victory was imminent. From the start of the uprising in January 2011 until the end of the following January more than 5,000 protesters and civilians were killed.

Once again paying lip service to democratic reform, in February 2012 the regime claimed it had 90% public backing for a draft constitution that included a 14-year limit for a president to be able to rule (in total). This was met with scorn by members of the international community. While making claim to working towards reform, the death toll in the country continued to rise. The EU introduced new sanctions in early 2012.

Russia maintained its support for the Assad regime and in July 2012 Putin's foreign minister, Sergey Lavrov, suggested that Western powers were provoking civil war by their response to the regime. His assertion was that Western powers were blackmailing Assad.

Very soon after this, the Red Cross said that fighting in Syria was so widespread that the conflict could be declared a civil war. This status meant that those involved in fighting would become subject to the Geneva Convention. The possibility of war crimes prosecutions for Assad's regime and other combatants was therefore heightened. Up to 20,000 people had been killed by this point. The start of the civil war is now generally regarded as March 15, 2011, when there was a violent government response to protests.

Multiple factions have been involved in the war in Syria, and the conflict has been complicated by the fact that a faction fighting against another at one front was allied with them when fighting a common enemy elsewhere.

Those involved in the war over time have included the Syrian government, an alliance of Sunni Arab rebel groups, the primarily Kurdish Syrian Democratic Forces, Salafi Jihadist groups and the Islamic State of Iraq and the Levant (known as ISIL but I prefer to refer to all so-called Islamic State groups as Daesh because they do not represent Islam and are not a state).

Key opposition forces include the Al-Qaeda-affiliated al-Nusra Front and the Free Syrian Army (which contains Islamist groups linked to al-Nusra). Despite these links and components, the Free Syrian Army has been deemed a moderate faction by Western politicians and therefore has been able to receive weapons and support through CIA-run programmes. Fighters from Turkey have been on the side of Islamist rebel forces and the country has provided weapons to opposition militants. Saudi Arabia appears to be the key funder of the opposition fighters, with some estimates of billions of dollars going towards the war.

A distinct part of the conflict that has found itself against not just Assad loyalists but also the al-Nusra Front and Daesh is the Syrian Democratic Forces. While most of the fighters are Kurdish, it has brought together Arab, Assyrians and Armenians. Unlike the Islamists backed by Wahhabi Saudis, these forces have been fighting for a democratic Syria.

Daesh, though Islamists and antagonistic towards Assad's regime, have been in conflict with other Islamists. Those groups who do not conform to its own ultra-conservative puritanical agenda are an enemy to be destroyed. Daesh, and what was its emerging 'caliphate', was at one point extremely powerful in the country, by 2014 controlling most of its oil and gas fields. Since then it has been weakened in both Syria and Iraq to the extent that it would be grandiose for leaders to speak of a caliphate now, even if it seemed like a reality not so long ago.

It should be recognised, however, that Daesh is above all a set of dangerous ideologies – and ideologies cannot be destroyed by bombs and bullets. The deluded ideologies of Daesh have not gone away and can rear their ugly heads in terror attacks at any point. While the Daesh media message a few years ago was to call young adherents to fight in Syria, the current approach now seems to radicalise people willing to attack targets in countries that would-be killers already live in.

A US-led coalition, known formally as the Combined Joint Task Force of 'Operation Inherent Resolve', began to bomb within the country in 2014, aiming for Daesh fighters. In addition to the US, countries within the task force that have conducted airstrikes in Syria include Australia, Bahrain, Canada, France, the Netherlands, Jordan, Saudi Arabia, Turkey, the United Arab Emirates and the UK. The task force, which has also focused with great success on Daesh fighters in Iraq, is made up of military personnel from more than 30 countries.

Allies of Syria have included the Lebanon-based Shi'a Islamist group Hezbollah and Iran. Although Iran has denied the presence of its combat troops in Syria, insisting that its role has been limited to providing military advice to Assad's forces to help them tackle terror groups, there have been claims of several thousand Iranian troops in the country. Iran has also provided the Assad regime with financial support of at least 15 billion dollars and technical support. Shia fighters from Afghanistan and Pakistan appear to have had a strong presence in the country during the war.

Russia has played a significant role in the Syrian conflict, targeting both Daesh fighters and rebel forces opposed to Assad's regime with airstrikes. Civilian targets have also been hit repeatedly by Assad's forces, Russian airstrikes and other forces.

Syria, the US and Russia are not part of the Convention on Cluster Munitions and do not recognise the ban on these weapons. Cluster bombs are a particular threat to civilians as they often leave unexploded 'bomblets' which can kill and cause life-changing injuries long after they are dropped.

Chemical weapons, including sarin, mustard agent and chlorine bombs have been used within the Syrian war. The Ghouta attacks in 2013 was one widely reported incident that led to a UN fact-finding mission to investigate chemical weapons attacks. The inspectors found that sarin had been used in four sites. Following the Ghouta attacks, amid widespread condemnation, work commenced destroying Syria's chemical weapons cache.

A UN report in 2016 said Assad's forces dropped chlorine bombs in April 2014 and March 2015. It also said that Daesh had used sulphur mustard on the town of Marea in 2015. The April 2017 Khan Shaykhun chemical attack, after which our TV screens were filled with small children affected by the chemicals, led to the Trump administration launching its first attack against Assad's forces. The Khan Shaykhun attack, involving toxic gas involving sarin or a related agent, killed at least 74 people and hundreds more were injured.

The Assad regime denied the chemical attack and the Kremlin attempted to explain the existence of the dangerous chemicals after a Syrian airstrike by claiming that Syrian missiles hit a warehouse belonging to rebels which "may have contained a rebel chemical arms stockpile". The Syrian strikes were made on April 4, 2017, and three days later the US launched 59 cruise missiles at Shayrat Air Base, which intelligence suggested was the source of the attack.

It would be impossible to do justice to the complexity of Syria and the war in a book let alone a chapter. It is not a place I have conducted fieldwork and, even if I had, I'm sure I would still have a partial picture and my representation would not please everyone. My perspective is anthropological and humanitarian. Like most people, my concern is with the people of Syria, including the refugees who escaped the carnage or attempted to and were killed. No military force involved comes out of it looking good.

Inevitably as a person living in the UK, much of the news I have absorbed about Syria in my life has come through the filter of British media organisations. I cannot change where I was born but my disciplines of anthropology and journalism have at least helped me realise the shortcomings of different outlets and understand how national intelligence services can shape media output during conflicts.

Even if we cannot read Syrian newspapers, many of us have been able to see the narrative and spin from Syria coming through the Kremlin-backed Russia Today. We can also see the activity on Twitter of the many accounts supporting Putin, just as we can see the repetition of the narrative of those set up to support Trump.

Rather than be blinded by the narratives of these bots and propagandists, it useful to monitor them to see what line they are taking and which they are attacking. The opposite of what they are vehemently claiming is often the likely reality. In their effort to spin the news and muddy the waters, these mechanical parrots can unwittingly give the 'game' away.

By early 2013 Assad was claiming to be open to a political solution while at the same time maintaining that the war was caused by "enemies" of both Syria and God, from outside of country. He said these people would "go to hell" and be taught a lesson. As he said this his own country was looking like hell on earth and it is questionable that Dr Assad was learning much from history.

Anger towards Assad was not just coming from the oppressed within the country or the international community but from the core Alawite support, which was shedding blood to keep Assad in power but felt betrayed by him. A significant event was the defeat of four military bases in September 2014. His own cousin, Douraid al-Assad, demanded the resignation of the Syrian Defence Minister after the massacre by Daesh of hundreds of government troops captured after taking the Tabqa Air Base.

Alawite protesters demanded the resignation of key military figures. Another cousin of the president, Hafez Makhlouf, was removed from a powerful security service role. He was subsequently exiled to Belarus. Those within Assad's inner circle believed that the regime would collapse. Relatives of Assad were themselves victims of the war, with several killed in early 2015. Assad had no qualms about detaining members of his family, and some family deaths could have just as easily been at the hands of Assad's regime rather than enemy forces.

Perhaps like rats fleeing a sinking ship, amid numerous government defeats and the plummeting popularity of Assad, several Assad relatives, Alawites and powerful figures were leaving the country. In spring 2015, Ali Mamlouk, the intelligence chief, was placed under house arrest for alleged involvement in a plot, with Rifaat al-Assad, to depose the president.

While paranoia and attacks, legal or otherwise, on imagined plotters are common in unstable regimes, in Assad's case there certainly were people seeking to remove him from office. The former medic's efforts to exert his authority on a divided country and hold together an unstable regime were proving ineffectual. It took a more experienced politician well-grounded in strategy and military intelligence and with a cold ruthlessness to keep him in place. That person, Vladimir Putin, had long supported Assad but in September 2015 the level of support was markedly increased.

Prior to September 2015, Russia has been training Syrian troops and providing the regime with weapons. In the build-up to direct Russian involvement in the war, Putin played down the expectation of his military intervention. However, when Russia did enter the war, at Assad's request, Putin admitted that military intervention by Russia had been planned for some time.

Putin's justification for Russia entering the war was to stabilise the "legitimate power in Syria" and create "the conditions for political compromise". Given that Assad was the one who was uncompromising in his attempt to cling to power at all costs, and given the opponents to the regime were diverse rather than a monolithic block, Putin's statement seems strange. It would perhaps be correct to describe it as completely dishonest. He was backing up a 'leader' widely regarded as dangerously inept and as callous and anti-democratic as his father before him.

Equally disingenuous, Assad claimed to favour a diplomatic solution but said that this would not be possible while Syria was occupied by "terrorists". This put his genuine political opponents and those inspired to push for democracy since the Arab Uprising began in the same category as Daesh. It also reinforced Assad's long-standing claim that those seeking to topple him were either from outside or a few bad apples inside who could be disregarded by calling them terrorists.

Whether or not Assad believed his own rhetoric, by the autumn of 2015 it was clear for all to see that the country was fractured, in chaos and the leadership was not fit for the job of leading a functioning country.

Daesh fighters had become a significant force in the country but Assad forces and Russia appeared more concerned with attacking Syrian rebel forces. Despite this, towards the end of November 2015,

Assad claimed that the Russian air campaign did more damage to Daesh in the country than the US-led coalition had achieved in a year.

Having been party to attacks on Syria rebel forces, by January 2016 Putin said that the Russian military would support anti-Assad rebels that fight Daesh. The Russian defence ministry subsequently said that their air force was striking in support of 11 groups of democratic opposition, totalling seven thousand people.

Suggestions had been made that, as of early 2016, Putin was one of many world leaders urging Assad to step down. If a report in the Financial Times on January 22 of that year was true, it could help explain Russian air support of anti-Assad militants in the battle against Daesh. The article, citing anonymous "senior western intelligence officials" said that General Igor Sergun, a leading figure in Russian military intelligence, had delivered a message to Damascus from Putin requesting that Assad resigned. The story was denied by Putin's press secretary Dmitriy Peskov.

To add to the intrigue, General Sergun died in mysterious circumstances soon after the time he was alleged to have delivered the message. On the Kremlin website on January 4, 2016, a message from Russian defence minister Sergey Shoygu stated that the 58-year-old had "died unexpectedly" on January 3. The online message and news release did not specify the cause of death. The Lebanese media outlet *Ya Libnan* subsequently reported that the general was killed in the country in a "complicated secret mission" involving a number of Arab and Middle Eastern intelligence agencies.

Without question, Putin's support is one of the key factors – if not the key factor – enabling the Assad regime to remain in place throughout the war. As the conflict in the country was to a large degree caused by the actions of Assad and his father before him, keeping him in place has locked in the toxicity and disease rather than dealt with it.

From the end of February 2016, following talks in Munich, a ceasefire was agreed. It was established by the International Syria Support Group (ISSG), composed of foreign ministers and representatives from numerous countries and international organisations. Countries in the ISSG included China, Egypt, France, Germany, Iran, Iraq, Italy, Jordan, Lebanon, Oman, Qatar, Russia, Saudi

Arabia, Turkey, the UAE, the UK and the US. The Arab League, the EU and the UN also participated.

The co-chairs of the ISSG, Russia and the US announced the Terms for a Cessation of Hostilities in Syria on February 22, 2016, pledging that "the cessation of hostilities will be monitored in an impartial and transparent manner and with broad media coverage."

A few days later, on February 26, 2016, the UN Security Council adopted a resolution demanding that all parties comply with the terms set out by Russia and the US. Daesh and al-Nusra were not included in the ceasefire and therefore positions believed to be occupied by those group could still be targeted.

A cynic might, quite reasonably, suggest that this exclusion from the ceasefire would enable Assad and his Russian allies to attack rebel-held areas, while claiming that they believed targets were Daesh fighters. However, nobody at that stage suggested getting Daesh around a table to agree a ceasefire that included them. The puritanical apocalyptic death cult has never been known for its ability or willingness to negotiate.

In the following month, the Assad forces, with Russian and Iranian support, captured Palmyra from Daesh. The Free Syria Army and their allies captured al-Ra'i from Daesh in early April 2016, although the town was recaptured within days. Fighting in the country escalated again, and by July 2016 the ceasefire was widely accepted be over.

A second ceasefire was attempted in September 2016 but this only lasted just over a week. Again, this was established by the US and Russia and again Daesh and al-Nusra were excluded from the terms.

Reasons for that ceasefire failing included Assad's forces continuing to bomb non-Daesh areas, resultant danger to humanitarians trying to deliver aid, and a botched British-US airstrike aimed at Daesh but killing 60 Assad troops. The Syrian and Russian forces were also negligent, including when they killed 14 civilians and destroyed 18 food trucks by bombing the humanitarian group the Syrian Arab Red Crescent.

By December 2016 there were reports that Assad's forces had reclaimed much of Aleppo from rebel forces. As explosions shook what was left of the crumbling buildings, with citizens cowering in the ruins, the Assad regime presented it as the liberation of the city.

A ceasefire from December 2016 lasted officially until mid-February 2017, although in reality rebel forces and Assad's troops were fighting almost immediately after the agreement was reached. Three days into the ceasefire, Syrian forces fired upon Israeli jets over Golan Heights and claimed to have brought one down.

A US airstrike on a school housing displaced citizens killed 150 civilians on March 20. A claim that the building was occupied by 30 Daesh militants has been rejected by the UN. A March 2018 UN Independent International Commission of Inquiry on the Syrian Arab Republic report states: "The international coalition should have known the nature of the target and failed to take all feasible precautions to avoid or minimize incidental loss of civilian life, injury to civilians and damage to civilian objects, in violation of international humanitarian law."

The April 2017 US attack on Shayrat Air Base, following the chemical attack on Khan Shaykhun, mentioned above, was launched without authorisation from the UN Security Council or US Congress. A Kremlin spokesman subsequently said: "President Putin regards the American attacks on Syria as aggression against a sovereign state in violation of the norms of international law." In the absence of a comma after 'state' in reported quotes, this statement can be read a different way to that which was probably intended. Both readings are probably correct.

In early May 2017 a ceasefire was implemented within the country. An agreement, which was rejected by some groups but signed by Russia, Iran and Turkey, involved the establishment of four 'de-escalation zones' in areas dominated by different factions. A criticism is that the implementation of the zones divided the country on a sectarian basis.

Through the summer and autumn of 2017, a focus by Syrian and Russia forces on Daesh was ultimately effective. In early September, a three-year siege of Deir ez-Zor was broken by Assad forces, with Russian naval and air support. Within two months, Syrian forces had full control over the city and captured Abu Kamal, which is in the east of Syria close to Iraq.

On December 6, 2017, the Kremlin declared that Syria had been "completely liberated" from Daesh and just a few days later Putin visited Syria. During his visit, Putin stated that he had ordered the partial withdrawal of Russian forces from the country and Russian foreign minister Sergey Lavrov suggested later that month than US forces should leave Syrian as soon as the terrorists had been entirely eliminated.

Interestingly, as Assad forces, backed by Russia, have continued to target beleaguered rebel forces in 2018, the justification expressed through propaganda channels has been that these are simply terrorists. Due to the previous battles with Daesh in the country, it has been a relatively simple act of distortion to suggest those left fighting against Assad are either Daesh terrorists or comparable to them.

One reason I wanted to devote an entire chapter to Syria is to put what has happened over the years in context. Once we understand the context, it is clear that one does not have to be a Daesh terrorist to oppose Assad, given that opposition to his regime predates the Daesh incursions into Syria by quite some time.

While towns and cities have been reduced to rubble and broken buildings, the cultural complexity and historical tensions that led to the war are no more simple than they ever were. It is possible, however, that broadcast news viewers find themselves with something akin to compassion fatigue, and after a while are vulnerable to propaganda depictions of all anti-Assad combatants being basically the same.

Towards the end of February 2018, Assad began an operation to capture rebel-held Ghouta, staring with an air campaign. Ghouta is an area surrounding the east and south of Damascus. On April 7, 2018, a chemical attack was reported in Douma, a city within the region.

The Douma attack killed at least 70 people and hundreds more were injured. Due to the rapid onset of symptoms and the nature of the symptoms, doctors on the ground and chemical weapons experts suggested that a combination of chlorine and another gas or a nerve agent, perhaps sarin, was used. Medical and monitoring groups reported seeing Syrian Army helicopters dropping barrel bombs, which were suspected to be the source of chemicals.

As with other attacks, the Syrian government denied the use of chemical weapons and claimed they no longer have such materials in the country. The Kremlin claimed that the attack did not happen and video evidence for it was staged and directed by the UK intelligence service. The notion that a troop of exceptional child actors could be magicked up by MI6 in a country reduced to rubble is clearly something Putin thought his Western apologists would fall for and parrot on social media. He was correct. Rebel forces who were actually there clearly believed it to be real, however, as within a day of the attack they agreed a deal with the Assad government to surrender the area.

In the absence of a clear path of action from the UN Security Council, tension between the US and Russia rapidly escalated, with Donald Trump engaging in childlike Twitter threats, which suggested a US attack was imminent. On April 11, he tweeted about "nice and new and 'smart' missiles." Russia should "get ready" for. The following day, after Russia's ambassador to the UN said the USA would "bear responsibility" for any "illegal military adventure" Trump back-pedalled by tweeting that he "never said when an attack on Syria would take place. Could be very soon or not so soon at all!"

As it turned out, Assad and Russia had a week to prepare for the reprisals. On April 14, after much debate in the countries concerned, the USA, UK and France launched missile strikes on four Syrian government targets. These included Barzah scientific research centre, a military installation storage site and a military bunker. Both Russian and Syrian air defence systems were used and at least one missile was successfully intercepted.

There was much talk in the media about World War Three prior to and immediately after the missile attacks but, as of the time of writing, tensions appear to have subsided and Trump has been more concerned with his battles with the FBI, domestic critics and antagonising Iran.

Although the Organisation for the Prohibition of Chemical Weapons (OPCW) was invited to send a team to investigate the Douma attacks, they were repeatedly blocked from accessing the relevant sites. On April 14, inspectors were prevented from entering the site by Syrian and Russian forces. Another attempt three days later was blocked by a large crowd at one site, while at another the OPCW reconnaissance team was driven away by gunfire. Yet another attempt to inspect a site, on April 19, was blocked. Finally, on April 21, two weeks after the incident, the OPCW was allowed to access the site and collect samples. At the start of May, as this book was about to go to print, the OPCW managed to get more samples and is in the process of writing their report.

Impact of the Syrian civil war

It is too early to assess the true impact of the war on society and politics in the country or international relations. What can be said with great certainty is that the impact of the conflict is huge – it will have a long-term impact on the stability of the region and could help shift the tectonic plates of super-powers in the world.

Like other conflicts in which many international factions become involved, and which much of the world can see unfolding on television and social media, this war is likely to leave a scar on human consciousness. However, this visual memory of a wound affecting many might not prevent similar conflicts happening elsewhere. If those who committed atrocities before the war and breached international law during the war get away with what they have done, then they and others have little disincentive from committing such atrocities again.

The death toll is one way of looking at the impact of a war, though this can be extremely difficult to calculate and numbers are routinely disputed. If we consider the fire at Grenfell Tower in North Kensington in London in June 2017, and the lack of a reliable and trusted death toll in the months afterwards, we can see some of the issues in microcosm. Despite the written history of which organisations were involved in different aspects of the refurbishment of the tower and management of the block, difficulties remain in apportioning blame to specific organisations, let alone individuals.

Grenfell is one tower in the centre of a modern metropolis, with CCTV around the building, yet knowing who was in the building when the fire raged through the flats has proved problematic. Syria is a large and diverse country, with an unstable and inept government, porous borders, people coming to the country from all directions, and a lack of CCTV in many places. It is therefore possible to appreciate that obtaining an accurate death toll and discovering who or what is responsible for each person killed is a mind-boggling endeavour.

Even when a body is found, knowing who is a combatant and which faction, if any, they were associated with, as well as which 'side' is responsible for their death, is extremely difficult. Understanding the myriad impacts of the war on society is more difficult still. Some impacts, such as on health, could potentially be reliable measures of impact, but to measure this well we would need enough health professionals on the ground and conducting research in places to which refugees have fled.

Estimates for the number of deaths in Syria as a result of the war vary but most go above 400,000. The Syrian Observatory for Human Rights estimates that between March 2011 and March 2018 between 353,593 and 498,593 were killed. As of February 2016, the Syrian Centre for Policy Research estimated the death toll to be 470,000, with five times that number wounded.

From what is known at this point, it is estimated that more than 100,000 of those killed were civilians. The number of medical professionals killed stands at more than 800. Most of those deaths have been attributed to Assad's forces.

'Wounded' estimates do not take into account those harmed by disease and health neglect as a direct result of the war, nor do they consider the mental health impact of living through the war or fleeing the country and becoming refugees. As we know from the aftermath of other wars, including the Vietnam War and the conflict in Somalia, it can take time for the mental health impacts of war to reveal themselves. In the immediacy of conflict and while fleeing violence, the mind can be amazing at holding itself together, but severe problems can become apparent later on.

During the war, infectious diseases that are unusual in the modern world were found to have spread in areas held by rebels. These areas appear to have suffered neglect before the war and some of the diseases we associate with previous centuries were therefore already at a high level in those areas. Infectious disease outbreaks were encouraged by poor sanitation, lack of access to decent water and the deterioration of living conditions. Children, often unvaccinated, were hit hardest by the outbreaks, which have included dysentery, tuberculosis, polio, diphtheria, typhoid, measles, whooping cough and hepatitis.

Since the civil war started in 2011, it has been estimated (by the UN) that in excess of six million people have fled the country. In addition to those who have managed to get out, around the same number of people have been displaced and remain within the country. In 2016 the UN said that, of 13.5 million Syrians requiring humanitarian assistance, more than six million had been internally displaced within the country.

To put the death toll, numbers of people wounded and refugee and displacement rates into context, the population of Syria was around 20 million before the war started. Although some of those killed were combatants and aid workers from outside the country, these numbers paint a picture of sheer devastation within the cradle of civilisation.

The civil war has been devastating to heritage sites in the country, with many completely destroyed and many more severely damaged. Archaeological collections held in museums have also been looted. Of six UNESCO World Heritage Sites in the country, all but one has been damaged. Damage to heritage sites has been by means of shelling, looting, deliberate destruction and cultural annihilation. In its apocalyptic and puritan attempt to wipe away any religious perspective that does not conform to their rigid notions, Daesh has destroyed several sites and artefacts. They destroyed temples, statues and tombs in Palmyra, as well as statues in Raqqa and numerous churches within the country.

In terms of taking in Syrian refugees, I'm ashamed to say that the UK has taken a tiny amount – roughly the same as Brazil has received. Turkey has received more than three million, Lebanon more than two million and Jordan more than a million. Germany is the largest host in the EU, taking in around 600,000 Syrian refugees, which is more than Saudi Arabia's 500,000. Several other countries have received well over 100,000 Syrians since the war started, including the UAE, Iraq, Kuwait and Egypt. Sweden has received more than 100,000 and Hungary, Canada, Croatia and Greece have each received over 50,000 Syrian refugees.

Despite the propaganda peddled by the far-right, and by opportunist politicians attempting to look 'strong' by pandering to xenophobia, as of spring 2018 the UK has received fewer than 11,000 Syrian refugees.

Chapter 9 – From far-right to 'alt-right'

In this chapter I focus on a broad range of movements that can be characterised as far-right and on the newer term, alt-right. The inclusion of certain organisations in such proximity to Nazism and other movements linked to mass murder will be troubling to some readers. For people connected to or supportive of such groups, my words have the potential to trigger anger. However, I would urge them to exercise patience, persevere and consider the reasons why I (and others) use the term far-right in relation to specific groups or movements, and hard-right in other circumstances.

Terms indicating position on the political spectrum inevitably mean different things to different people, in part because *individuals* are in different positions on the spectrum. However, given that many far-right movements have frequently been dishonest and tried to re-write history, it is important to pin down the reality of the movements and locate them accurately based on reality rather than on their claims.

Common features of far-right movements include nativism, nationalism (often combined with Islamophobia), dogmatism, fear of the extinction of one's ethnic group, anti-rationalism, anti-liberalism and authoritarianism.

As the politics of different countries are, at any point, at different positions on the political spectrum, far-right groups in particular settings range from being mainstream to illegal. Even the most violent of groups are sometimes tolerated – and supported by governments – in certain political environments. Sometimes far-right mobs can do things that a government cannot get away with themselves but are useful to them.

To give readers a sense of what I mean when I talk of far-right movements and organisations, I will list some emerging in various parts of the world that can be (and have been) designated as far-right. Emerging in the USA have come the America First Party, American

155

Freedom Party, American Independent Party, American Nazi Party, Christian Nationalist Crusade, National Socialist Movement, Silver Legion of America and the Ku Klux Klan.

In the UK have emerged the EDL, British National Party (BNP), British People's Party, British Union of Fascists, National Action, National Front, British Democratic Party, Britain First, Liberty GB and the Protestant Coalition.

Those emerging in Russia have included Black Hundreds, LDPR, the People's National Party and Russian National Unity. Others in post-Soviet states include Svoboda, the Congress of Ukrainian Nationalists, the Ukrainian National Assembly and the Right Sector in Ukraine; the Estonian Independence Party and Vaps Movement in Estonia; For Fatherland and Freedom, the National Alliance and Pērkonkrusts in Latvia; and in Lithuania the Lithuanian National Union, Lithuanian Nationalist Union and Young Lithuania.

Belgium has contended with the National Front, Rexist Party, Verdinaso, Vlaams Blok and Vlaams Nationaal Verbond, while the Netherlands had the Centre Party and still has the Dutch Peoples Union. As well as the Nazi Party, Germany has contended with the German People's Union, National Democratic Party of Germany, PEGIDA and the Pro-Germany Citizens' Movement. Italy, another former fascist state, has contended with the National Fascist Party, Republican Fascist Party, Italian Social Movement, Tricolour Flame and New Force.

Israel has seen the emergence of the Jewish National Front, Kach and Kahane Chai, Otzma Yehudit and Yachad. Movements emerging in India include Shiv Sena, Shiromani Akali Dal and Maharashtra Navnirman Sena. South Africa has spawned Afrikaner Weerstandsbeweging, Front National, Greyshirts, the Herstigte Nasionale Party and the National Party.

It can be a bit harder to pin down exactly where elements of the alt-right are on the political spectrum, other than overtly far-right. This is a reason why some who see themselves as part of this new wave of conservatism find the wishy-washy term useful. The term alt-right is often used as a linguistic smokescreen to disguise or rebrand activities, positions and people that would historically have been regarded squarely as far-right.

Tamer elements of conservatism that have, perhaps in an attempt to appear less stuffy, got into bed under the alt-right blanket, run the risk of being soiled and infected by the far-right elements cuddled up with them. This has been extremely apparent in Trump's era, where he has gained the endorsement of Ku Klux Klan supremacists and privileged 'alt-right' 'commentators' alike, while also receiving support from desperate impoverished people with no previous links to the far-right.

Nazism, despite its name, was and *is* clearly a far-right authoritarian movement, which has and seeks to victimise people on racial and cultural grounds. It is a form of fascism, and its ideologies are tied up with the deluded scientific racism discussed in Chapter 2. It has also been in constant conflict with the left and social liberalism since it emerged. Nevertheless, something as simple as a misappropriated name, and deliberate distortion to manipulate, continues to cause conflict and confusion.

Nazi appropriation of the term socialism

The full name of the party from which the abbreviation 'Nazi' is derived was a distortion to not only distract people from the reality of the movement but also to attack and smear socialism. The name of Hitler's party was Nationalsozialistische Deutsche Arbeiterpartei, which translates to National Socialist German Workers' Party. While it *is* correct to describe members of that party and those who followed them as nationalists, the socialism aspect is wrong, and yet contemporary Nazi groups often hold onto the socialist aspect of the name. However, they are no more left-wing or concerned with social justice than their Hitler-era predecessors were.

No credible social scientist, historian or political commentator would regard National Socialism as anything but a far-right movement. Hitler and his accomplices outlawed socialism, and the Nazis rounded up and killed left-wingers before targeting other groups. Dachau, the first concentration camp in Nazi Germany, initially held almost entirely left-wingers as political prisoners. Only later were Jews also incarcerated there.

In understanding what Marxism, socialism and communism mean, it becomes extremely clear that Nazism is none of those things. One does not have to desire communism or share Marx's beliefs to understand it well enough and see how the far-right and other elements of the right have distorted it for their own political gain and as a way of attacking the left.

In the name of transparency, I should point out that I do not consider myself particularly left-wing or right-wing, though free market dogmatists would regard me as very left-wing for having the view that some essential resources, such as schools, hospitals, social services, prisons and environmental protection agencies should be publicly owned and overseen by accountable politicians and civil servants. I also regard water as a resource that should be publicly owned.

Nevertheless, I regard innovation as extremely important for our comfort, enjoyment and survival as a species, and believe individuals should be rewarded for their work, innovation and creativity. The centrally planned systems that have existed, such as in the Soviet Union, have not done that. I also recognise that commercial companies are often an excellent way of supporting, encouraging and distilling excellent work, innovation and creativity – which can offer a great deal to help people around the world in a myriad of ways.

On the other hand, I recognise that companies can become so powerful that they lack ethics and have a detrimental impact on people outside and within the organisation. Especially in the neo-liberal era, unethical companies have found it easy to construct their organisational structure in such a way as to avoid all but the most paltry tax contributions. Political donations by companies and links with politicians, sometimes on boards, can make it look as though poor ethics is actively unchallenged. At the same time, lobbying by large companies, in a way that is not transparent, can make it seem as though political systems are corrupt.

To make criticisms of some large corporations in this way is certainly not 'anti-capitalist'. In fact, it recognises that the so-called free market can become rigged against smaller companies. The notion of competition is used to justify a commercial habitat that is anything but a free market. This is not only unjust but robs society of the innovation and value that those smaller companies might otherwise find it easier to provide.

The material and human resources of the planet are finite, and, therefore, when a company uses these in a way that another organisation could be using more effectively and ethically, there are arguments that things could be done differently. When Marx was writing, there were far fewer people on the planet, though the population was younger, but the ecological harm that is now starkly apparent was further away. A stronger argument than ever therefore exists to ensure that resources are used wisely and in ways that benefit the maximum number of individuals – now and in the future. For our species, as well as other animals, plants and ecosystems, it is important that the profit of companies and wealth of individuals is balanced against the costs to our world.

Marx was concerned with inequality and exploitation. Those things concern me too, but turning industries from capitalist companies to state-run organisation does not necessarily make life better for workers or consumers. Furthermore, it has the potential to erode employee innovation and make structures too clunky to be productively creative. However, given the finite nature of resources and the damage that can be done, ecologically and culturally, to some industries, I think there will be stronger arguments in the future to curtail the excesses of some industries and ensure that societies get the best from resources that are our heritage and for which we are custodians.

My view is therefore that now (and for the foreseeable future) mixed economies, where some key resources are managed by the state but where there is also a healthy private sector in which innovation and genuine competition flourishes, work best for societies.

Many people, often unwittingly and through ignorance, repeat the lie peddled by the far-right that anything designed to help the population is 'communist'. For example, in the USA, there are people who associate health systems designed to keep the population strong and alive (and therefore supporting of productivity) with the encroachment of communism. Such a system *is* designed to reduce health inequality, but that is *not* the same thing as promoting global communism with no ownership or class divisions, which is what Marx envisaged.

Karl Marx asserted that the way in which human needs are met, including relationships between people to ensure they can eat, are clothed and have shelter, defines human societies. As the ways in which needs are met change and economic relationships change, human societies become different and this changes the experiences of individuals and their families. Such changes in relationships with the world change both behaviour and identity.

Marx, along with his associate Friedrich Engels, took a broad anthropological and historical view, and concluded that humanity passes through distinct economic and political stages. Class struggle not only defines each epoch but also brings about the next. The Marxist model, which views distinct societal characteristics as a product of how needs are met, is known as historical materialism. It can seem a linear social evolutionist model, but within it there is a recognition that different human societies are likely to be at different stages, though there is, Marx believed, a propulsion towards the end point of global communism.

The stages that Marx suggested humanity goes through on our way to global stateless communism are primitive communism, slave society, feudalism, capitalism and socialism. As will be explained, socialism is distinguishable from communism in Marx's model, despite what people often think. However, the socialism stage is a necessary precursor to the final epoch.

Drawing on the work of and engaging with the perspectives of American anthropologist Lewis Morgan, Marx and Engels asserted that hunter-gatherer societies employed an egalitarian system of common ownership that the authors defined as 'primitive communism'. Their 1884 book, *The Origin of the Family, Private Property and the State in the Light of the Researches of Lewis H. Morgan*, was published a year after Marx died and was completed by Engels, who was Marx's literary executor.

Marx left behind a synopsis of Morgan's 1877 book, *Ancient Society; or, Researches in the Lines of Human Progress from Savagery, Through Barbarism to Civilization*, and these notes shaped the book. Morgan, like Marx, was from a wealthy family and studied law but became so fascinated by the Iroquois, a formerly powerful native American confederacy, that he became an anthropological fieldworker.

Marx and Engels speculated that hunter-gatherer groups that fostered this 'primitive communism' did not support hierarchical social class structures or the accumulation of wealth by individuals. The primitive communism system described by Marx and Engels was observed by later anthropologists, some of whom noted the use of various levelling mechanisms to ensure social and economic equality is maintained.

Behind the creation of levelling mechanisms appeared to be the insight that conflict arises if one person hoards resources, or positions themselves above others. Arrogance is an especially unattractive and dangerous characteristic in hunter-gatherer societies, which require a community approach to work and the sharing of resources for individuals and the community to thrive and survive.

According to Marx and Engels, the 'primitive communism' stage comes to an end as a result of property becoming private, as opposed to owned by the community, and this creates discrepancies between the power and status of individuals. This ultimately, according to the model, makes some people the slaves of others. The shift away from hunting and gathering to large-scale agriculture has been seen as pivotal to the shift to that epoch, as this heightens differences between what individuals possess.

In the slave society phase, not only do discrepancies in status and what people have appear, but a form of state emerges which assists slave owners to maintain and increase their elevated status. Marx and Engels suggested that within that epoch the opposing forces of democracy and authoritarianism start to become apparent.

According to the Marxist model, the slave society era collapsed with the birth of the next phase, namely feudalism. In terms of power discrepancies, there are similarities with the slave society era but rather than expand power by conquering more and more slaves, feudal 'elites' created systems to reinforce and legitimise power and status discrepancies. In this stage, the aristocracy was established, and they fixed their position of dominance by handing status down to offspring. This ceremonial veneer added the semblance of legitimacy to authority and exploitation.

Another aspect of this new stratification of societies was the establishment of theocracy – the rule of people through religion. To enable this to work most effectively, there had to be a shift from pantheistic spirituality to the domination in societies of one religion, ideally with one god. Christianity obviously achieved this, through dogma and persecution, but even Hinduism, which has millions of minor gods as well as one supreme being, was able to use religion to justify a system in which the straitjacket of assigned caste is handed down by birth.

Whether by an invented handed down status or the imposition of power by dogma, the result is that the masses are dominated and impoverished while the powerful increase their power. However, another key aspect of the feudalism epoch was the development of nation states, and this ultimately led to the demise of feudalism and the rise of capitalism.

To support trade between nation states, a new 'class' emerged to act as intermediaries. This merchant and money-lender class gained power and wealth while the old powers weakened. In the capitalist phase, though there are still some aristocrats, power shifted to the capitalist bourgeoisie, who own the means of production. The working class 'proletariat' (wage earners who do not own the means of production) are exploited, just as serfs and peasants were under feudalism.

Key elements of the capitalist epoch identified by Marx were (and *are*) a market economy, the means of production owned by the bourgeoisie, the emergence of democracy (although access to this would at times be dependent on one's wealth or status, including gender status), an imperialist drive to conquer and exploit other countries for resources and impose new regimes, and the drive for both profit maximisation and monopolistic power.

Though innovation and trade are often great things, it is hard to ignore the bloodthirstiness of the system. There is quite a paradox in how our 'highly evolved' capitalist civilisation has such ravenous predation at the heart of it. This reality can remind us of the boys in *Lord of the Flies*, who came from a place of supposed sophistication and refinery but some lunged towards brutality and domination at the first opportunity.

Capitalism was the dominant epoch in Marx's life, as he was born into the age of the industrial revolution, though this reached Germany quite some time after Britain. Marx believed that resentment towards increasing inequality and poverty for a great many would lead the proletariat to rise up and seize the means of production. This would, he believed, lead to the second-to-last phase, namely the development of the socialist state.

The confusion many have about this phase, and its associated terminology, explains some things that are very relevant to much of what has happened in the last century and to right-wing movements and their distortions. It also helps to explain why supposedly communist societies, such as North Korea and China, are so far removed from Marx's vision of equality, yet are often used as ammunition to attack left-wing views or people.

The phase of the socialist state involves the emergence of a centralised state working on behalf of the society. However, this phase has in practice opened the path to authoritarian regimes and a different form of inequality, often with terrible abuses of power. In reality, China and North Korea have powerful state machines, and, for a considerable time, those countries have been stuck in the socialist state phase.

China, like Russia before it, does not appear to be transcending the large-state phase, as the Marxist model would suggest, instead retaining the power of the few through the vast machine of governance, while cherry picking aspects of capitalism. Despite the use of the term communism within and about North Korea and China, those countries are not and have never been at the stage Marx called 'communism'.

Marx believed that the structures of the state required for the shift from capitalism would wither away and societies would move to the epoch of global communism. Class distinctions would vanish, along with political power structures. Marx believed that people would administer their own lives and that there would be no private property and no laws or nations.

Clearly, this has *never* happened, and many would argue that it is not in our nature – as a rather creative but demanding, competitive and aggressive ape. However, rather than being entirely naïve,

Marx's model is arguably grounded in a healthy measure of cynicism about human beings. The model can be seen as an acknowledgement of, and perhaps a safeguard against, a tendency towards selfishness and exploitation, just as hunter-gatherer levelling mechanisms are an acknowledgement of the dangers of division, arrogance and hierarchy.

Regardless of how optimistic Marx may seem to us now, one thing that is certain is that Nazism is a long way from what Marx was getting at. He was concerned with equality and envisaged a global system where no people dominated others. Despite all the drivel and misinformation posted online, Nazism is the opposite of this. It is a supremacist model, which ranks people based on superficial traits, and it has murdered those arbitrarily deemed lesser human beings. Nazism is an authoritarian and nationalistic system, whereas Marx envisaged a time where nobody would have power over anyone else and there would be no nation states.

Marx can be criticised for many things, not least an extraordinary amount of confidence in human beings' ability or desire to create a fair and well-functioning utopia. However, it is completely wrong to link his and Engels' visionary political philosophy to the sadistic agenda of Nazism. The Nazis did not want to build a utopia, but a cruel and rigid dystopia in which people are victimised on an industrial scale.

Nazism rejected Marx's idea of class struggle driving us forward, and instead used propaganda to turn the population against minorities. Had the Nazis in the 1930s been genuinely concerned with addressing inequality, they would have supported the Roma people, who had long been marginalised. However, this is not what the Nazis did. They instead tortured, dehumanised and murdered them, just as they did Jews, gay men and people with disabilities.

A core element of the rise of Nazism in the early 20th century was to distort reality to turn societies against certain groups and build a pathological culture on a foundation of lies and propaganda. Though overt Nazism itself is much more marginal than it was, we can see the same themes in other far-right movements today, and in those slightly less extreme movements I would define as hard-right rather than far-right.

The plurality of extremism

The term far-right goes back to the era of the French Revolution, where those in favour of unrestrained powers of aristocracy and the conservation of old power structures sat on the far-right of the assembly. When I use the term, I refer to movements and ideologies steeped in nationalistic, racist and ultra-conservative sentiment. There is very often a strong authoritarian focus of such movements, despite claims leaders and adherents often make about being in favour of freedom. Anti-immigrant narratives are common among the far-right, as are attacks on civil rights, human rights and religious freedom.

Far-right movements in the UK range from registered political parties, such as the BNP, to volatile street movements, such as the EDL. Far-right groups are monitored, to an extent, but far-right individuals who are discreet are more difficult to monitor and can go under the radar. Dangerously extreme views, hate, fear and anger can be bubbling away under the surface, with those around them, let alone intelligence organisations or the police, oblivious.

In northern England on June 16, 2016, a week before the EU referendum, a man who had previously had communications with other white supremacists, but generally kept himself to himself, calmly left his house to assassinate a Member of Parliament. Jo Cox, a pro-EU MP, was stabbed, shot and stabbed again by Mair, who had been researching her, as well as methods of murder, online. Mair, 52, also attacked 77-year-old passer-by Bernard Carter-Kenny, who bravely intervened. Mr Carter-Kenny was stabbed in the abdomen but fortunately survived.

Birstall, the village where the murder took place, is ordinarily a calm place, with a population of just over 16,000 people. Jo Cox was popular locally, having grown up in the area. After she won the Batley and Spen seat in 2015 for Labour, with a sizeable majority, Jo used her maiden speech in the House of Commons to celebrate her constituency's ethnic diversity. She was 41 when she died, and the mother of two small children.

Mair is a far-right nationalist and appears to have regarded Mrs Cox as an 'enemy of society' for being positive about the EU, as well as a 'traitor' to white people for being positive about diversity. Prior to becoming an MP, she worked for Oxfam and was still, as a politician, very much concerned with the plight of those displaced and harmed by war.

Mair had experienced some mental health symptoms, as many people have, but his long-standing far-right political stance is what drove him to his brutal crimes. He, like many far-right individuals and groups, had (and almost certainly still does have) the belief that left-wing people, liberals and the media are responsible for the world not being how he feels it should be.

As a white supremacist, the way Mair would like the world to be is simply not how it is. He is not part of a master race but a pathetic embittered thug who will be locked up until the day he dies. In the meantime, countries like the UK will become more diverse and many of the innovations that help and give pleasure to citizens will be fruits of this diversity.

It is important to state that mental conditions, such as depression and obsessive-compulsive disorder (OCD), which have been linked to Mair, are quite common and sufferers are far more likely to diminish or take their own lives than kill others. A neighbour or colleague struggling with OCD and depression is incredibly unlikely to be hatching the sort of plans Mair was, and should be someone to show compassion for rather than fear.

It is also important to note that Mair's mental health experiences were not used in his defence case. Furthermore, a psychiatrist who examined him after the murder found no evidence that any mental health issues limited his responsibility for his crimes. Though his views about life are clearly wrong and dangerous, he does not therefore suffer from a condition like paranoid schizophrenia, which distorts reality and causes considerable confusion and distress for affected individuals.

It seems likely that Mair's far-right mentality, reinforced by other 'evidence' he found in reading extremist material over the decades, was the ultimate driver of his hate and violence. The far-right in many settings in the world have all too often demonstrated a willingness to use violence to attack a society or reality they disagree with. A rigid authoritarian personality is likely to struggle when they feel impotent, as Mair appears to have done for much of his life. Lashing out violently against a world changing in ways you hate and fear can be a weapon of the weak.

Unless Thomas Mair one day sits down and writes about what he was thinking in the weeks leading up to the murder, we may never know how much significance each element had on events. However, it seems unlikely that the proximity of the referendum to remain in or leave the EU and murder was a coincidence. His racist leanings can be traced back decades but, for a vehemently anti-EU nationalist, the referendum – which seemed quite likely at that point to favour the UK remaining in the EU – would have been a source of intense heat for Mair's already bubbling rage. The right's chance for pull down the steel gates of nationalism was fading because of the meddling of 'liberal do-gooders' and multiculturalism enthusiasts.

There is more to learn about how Mair came to have the perceptions and prejudices he has. We know that he was involved with white supremacist ideas many years before the murder and had Nazi memorabilia in his home. Aside from an outburst in his first court appearance, when he yelled: "Death to traitors, freedom for Britain", in response to simply being asked his name, Mair has not explained his specific actions. However, his internet search history, from visits to the local library, is revealing.

Subjects Mair searched for included far-right groups such as the BNP and Ku Klux Klan, and the South African apartheid. He was also revealed to have a fascination with the far-right Norwegian terrorist Anders Breivik, who murdered 77 people and injured 319 with a bomb and a shooting spree.

Several of Breivik's shooting victims were children, and most of those killed by the bomb were public servants. The bomb was placed in a van parked near the building that housed the office of Norway's prime minister and various government departments. The subsequent shooting massacre, at a left-wing youth camp, went on for an hour and a half, during which time Breivik, who was dressed as a policeman, repeatedly shouted: "You are going to die today, Marxists!"

Thomas Mair kept newspaper clippings about Breivik, who carried out his atrocities in 2011 and will be covered in more detail shortly. Police also found information about how to make bombs in Thomas Mair's house.

Mair received a full life sentence for his crimes and, unlike most murderers convicted in the UK, therefore has no possibility of parole. This suggests that the judge saw no remorse and recognised that his far-right extremism is fundamental to his character and not the product of an acute illness that can be treated. It is also a recognition that as well as a crime against one woman and a passer-by, Mair's attack was an attack on democracy itself and freedom.

Within his sentencing remarks, the judge, Mr Justice Wilkie, said:

> Because of her position as a Member of Parliament, her death was both a personal tragedy and a crime with great public significance. To her family, friends and colleagues Jo Cox was a wonderful mother, daughter, sister, partner and companion, her generosity of spirit evident in the selfless concern she had for others even when facing a violent death. Their loss, caused by your actions, is and will be, almost unbearable.
>
> But because she was a Member of Parliament, the reason you murdered her, your crime has an additional dimension which calls for particularly severe punishment. She was just 41. Before being elected as an MP she had already demonstrated herself to be a credit to herself, her community and her country in the work she performed for Oxfam and other organisations, devoting herself to seeking to better the lot of those less fortunate than her.
>
> She had only recently embarked on her role as an MP but had already shown herself to be passionate, open-hearted, inclusive and generous as well as highly effective. The tributes to her from across the political spectrum were spontaneous, sincere and fulsome. The fundamental importance

to our democracy for Members of Parliament to be able to perform their duties and meet their constituents safely and fearlessly is reflected in the fact that no respectable political party contested the by-election caused by her death.

In the true meaning of the word she was a patriot. You affect to be a patriot. The words you uttered repeatedly when you killed her give lip service to that concept. Those sentiments can be legitimate and can have resonance but, in your mouth, allied to your actions, they are tainted and made toxic. It is clear from your internet and other researches that your inspiration is not love of country or your fellow citizens, it is an admiration for Nazism, and similar anti-democratic white supremacist creeds where democracy and political persuasion are supplanted by violence towards and intimidation of opponents and those who, in whatever ways, are thought to be different and, for that reason, open to persecution.

The judge went on to say:

Our parents' generation made huge sacrifices to defeat those ideas and values in the Second World War. What you did, and your admiration for those views which informed your crime, betrays the sacrifices of that generation. You are no patriot. By your actions you have betrayed the quintessence of our country, its adherence to parliamentary democracy.

You have not even had the courage to admit and acknowledge what you did. You have, instead, forced the prosecution to prove this case in detail, withholding your agreement to anything which would have lessened that task, thereby adding, I have no doubt deliberately, to the anguish of Jo Cox's family and the witnesses to these awful events forced, as they have been, to relive them.

Despite all the evidence against Thomas Mair, and no discernible defence to his actions, there are those who believe that the whole thing was a conspiracy to stop Brexit. Ideas I have seen expressed include: Jo Cox wasn't really killed; Thomas Mair was a poor 'patsy' used by the intelligence service and government to cause outrage and stop Brexit; everyone involved was an actor; it was a 'false flag' attack to turn the public against Brexiteers, and it was a New World Order plot to stop people voting to leave the EU. For far-right extremists, the EU is often seen as a communist plot, a New World Order plot or a plot to fill countries with dark-skinned people and Muslims.

There was no shortage of people on Twitter and Facebook accosting users with these wild fantasies, and there have also been numerous blog posts on far-right and conspiracy theory sites disseminating these sorts of notions. The people spreading the ideas were frequently angered by people putting real facts on social media and took every opportunity to share their own 'insights' or alluring conspiracy webpages with those who were merely reporting established facts.

However, there were also far-right agitators on social media who recognised what had happened and were very happy about it, and some used it to encourage people to vote for Brexit. One of the Twitter accounts of the Nazi youth group National Action tweeted a photo of Mair with the words: "#VoteLeave, don't let this man's sacrifice go in vain. #JoCox would have filled Yorkshire with more subhumans!" In another National Action tweet, Mair's photo was made to resemble a comic character called Pepe the frog, which has been appropriated by the 'alt-right'. The tweet read: "Our thoughts go out to Thomas Mair. #BritainFirst JoCoxMP #WhiteJihad".

Numerous people reported these tweets to the police, Home Office and Twitter. The specific account, of several National Action accounts, was quite quickly suspended from Twitter but others remained. Following national media coverage of the fascist group publishing these tweets, the UK government took steps to designate it a terrorist organisation and ban it. The Twitter accounts of the organisation cannot therefore be easily viewed in the UK, though they can in many other countries.

The large social media platforms, such as Twitter, Facebook and YouTube, have received a lot of criticism for failing to get rid of extremist material and communications inciting hatred. However, it should be said that the UK authorities themselves were slow to deal with National Action, and it took Jo Cox's death and the aftermath to do so. It is, admittedly, more difficult for the intelligence service and police to infiltrate groups composed primarily of young people, especially when those groups are small enough for new members to stick out like a sore thumb.

For many people, its idiotic and vicious tweets would have looked little different from the malicious spite seen every day on social media. On the day that the National Action tweets about Thomas Mair appeared, a friend on Twitter said to me that he thought it was just "stupid kids". The fact is that many of them *are* stupid kids but they are also part of a dangerous fascist movement that at the very least incites hatred but quite possibly has trained members to commit serious crimes.

Which agency, of the police or MI5, investigates a specific group deemed to be 'domestic extremists' is not entirely clear. The MI5 website, as of the time of writing, states: "Domestic extremism mainly refers to individuals or groups that carry out criminal acts in pursuit of a larger agenda, such as 'right-wing extremists'. They may seek to change legislation or influence domestic policy and try to achieve this outside of the normal democratic process. For the most part, they pose a threat to public order but not to national security and are investigated by the police, not MI5."

I find this slightly strange, as it is known that home-grown suspected Islamist extremists are monitored by MI5. Given that some white supremacists would like there to be a race war, it would be concerning if they are not taken as seriously as ethnically Asian domestic extremists. Efforts to start a race war *are* about 'a larger agenda' but also a threat to national security. However, as explained below, the status of National Action and the level of scrutiny it is under *did* change significantly as a direct result of its communications about the killing of Jo Cox.

There is money behind National Action, which was formed in 2013, but the identity of any financial backers is not clear at this stage. What is known is that it has attempted to differentiate itself from groups like the BNP by recruiting university students. That is not to say that members are not ignorant thugs, but they appear to regard themselves as more intelligent than the average far-right thug.

The notion that undergraduate and graduate neo-Nazis, with minds full of hate and ludicrous ideas, would necessarily be brighter than neo-Nazis who didn't attend university is clearly flawed. Regardless of how long they stayed on in education, their understanding of our human reality is simply wrong. Furthermore, to get through a degree in the healthily multicultural university environment and *still* maintain white supremacist beliefs is quite a feat of stupidity.

National Action in the UK has held rallies and also celebrated the election of Donald Trump. Their leaflets, which have been distributed around the UK, included swastikas and a Nazi salute. In 2015 the group abandoned one rally, in Liverpool, after they were confronted by hundreds of protesters. The 'White Man March' as they billed it, was meant to pass through the city centre but the Nazis ended up cowering in a lost property office at Liverpool Lime Street train station.

It is easy to mock the above outcome for National Action, and it is always more fun to mock Nazis rather than fear them, when we can. However, some of their activities have been terrifying for people. They have targeted individuals and premises, and one member, 21-year-old Garron Helm, was jailed for four weeks in 2014 for sending a threatening anti-Semitic tweet to Luciana Berger, a Jewish MP. In the tweet, Helm used the hashtag #HitlerWasRight. The barrage of abuse the politician received increased dramatically when Helm, who was seen as a hero by other online far-right fanatics, was jailed.

In 2014, members of National Action, along with people linked to other far-right groups, attended an international training camp in the Brecon Beacons, Wales. The event, which included training to use knives and other martial arts, was called Sigurd Outlaw Camp, in 'honour' of far-right mass murderer Anders Breivik, who used Sigurd as a pseudonym. Sigurd, a medieval Norwegian crusader, has long been a preoccupation of Breivik.

This sort of nationalist youth camp attended by National Action members has been common in Russia for some time. The fascist

Eurasian Youth Union (ESM) is an accepted aspect of the Kremlin's policy of 'patriotic education' and receives extensive state funding, according to the Center of Economic and Political Reforms. Some ESM-spawned 'volunteers' fought with Russia-backed separatists in eastern Ukraine in 2014.

White supremacist training camps also have much in common with Jihadist training camps, which is not surprising as extremists on both 'sides' anticipate and wish to promote a race war.

In 2015, 26-year-old Zackery Davies, who has identified himself as a member of National Action, attempted to murder and behead young dentist Sarandev Bhambra in Mold, Flintshire. Dr Bhambra suffered life-changing injuries in the machete and claw hammer attack. Davies claimed that the attack was 'revenge' for the murder of Lee Rigby, a soldier murdered by terrorists in London. Ironically, given Davies' spurious claim to be on the side of the military, a former soldier, Peter Fuller, intervened to save Dr Bhambra's life. Davies fortunately responded to Mr Fuller's request to put his weapons down.

Davies singled out Dr Bhambra, who had simply walked into the supermarket at lunchtime, for the attack, which caused extensive wounds across his body and on his head. Dr Bhambra, a 24-year-old Sikh, had absolutely no connection with the killers of Lee Rigby. He was chosen because, in the words of Davies, he "looked Asian". In questioning, Davies told the police: "It was irrelevant what religion he was. It was his appearance, just the way he looked. It did not matter to me what religion he was, it was his racial appearance."

Zackery Davies, who shouted "WHITE POWER" during the attack, was jailed for a minimum of 14 years. In their investigation, the police found a large amount of white supremacist material at his home. He was also found to have a YouTube channel, which had enabled him to share neo-Nazi material.

Davies was found to have a preoccupation with the Daesh killer known at the time in the media as 'Jihadi John', who was subsequently named as Mohammed Emwazi. It is both interesting and troubling that Jihadi murderers could be a source of inspiration to far-right supremacists, while also reinforcing their hatred of

Muslims. Emwazi was filmed decapitating a number of hostages, before being killed in a drone strike in Syria in 2015.

Outside court, after the verdict, Dr Bhambra's family expressed concern that the crime was not being reported as an act of terrorism. Speaking to assembled journalists, his brother, Dr Tarlochan Singh Bhambra, stated: "We are in no doubt, given the racial and political motivations, that this should have been rightly defined as an act of terrorism. By his own admission the defendant, Zack Davies, had extreme neo-Nazi views and is a member of a white supremacist organisation. Sarandev was singled out because of the colour of his skin. The media have a responsibility and an obligation to report these aspects of the trial and bring to the fore the major implications of these.

"We are in no doubt that, had the racial disposition of this case been reversed, this would be reported as an act of terror, with a wider media coverage. All extremist groups, including white supremacists – as in this case – that advocate racially motivated hatred and violence on innocent people should be dealt with as terrorists."

He also said: "The display of ignorance has been evident throughout this trial. Ethnic minorities have and continue to contribute to the multicultural Britain of 2015. And indeed, Sikhs have sacrificed their lives in both world wars to facilitate the freedom that Britain enjoys today. Racial intolerance is a thing of the past and should not be accepted in any society."

National Action has denied any association with Zackery Davies and distanced themselves from his actions. This makes it extremely curious that they should praise Thomas Mair as they did. The group's denial also contrasts with Davies' own public communication of membership of the group. Hours before the attack, Davies uploaded a photo of himself in front of the distinctive flag of National Action. He was also brandishing a large knife.

National Action was proscribed as a terrorist organisation in December 2016. This means that it is a criminal offence to support or be a member of it. It is the first white supremacist organisation to be proscribed as a terrorist group in the UK. It is important to state that it has absolutely no connection with the National Action Network, which is one of the leading civil rights organisations in the United States. It seems very possible that the media-savvy neo-Nazi group chose a name that conflicts with an aspect of the ongoing civil rights movement, just as the Nazis undermined socialists by mislabelling themselves as socialists.

There have been several arrests of alleged members of National Action since the group was banned. In September 2017, four servicemen in the British Army were arrested under the Terrorism Act 2000 on suspicion of being members, and another man detained in Cyprus. The arrests led to two British soldiers being charged with terrorism offences and subsequently 11 further men were arrested in raids in the UK. In January 2018, six alleged members, five men and a woman from locations across England, were arrested on suspicion of being concerned in the commission, preparation and instigation of acts of terrorism.

There have been a number of charges related to some of those arrested over recent months and proceedings are active at the time of writing, which prevents me from going into detail about charges or individuals.

National Action members, just as Thomas Mair does, regard Anders Breivik as a hero and inspiration. In 2014, then leader of the group Benjamin Raymond wrote on his blog: "There are non-whites and Jews in my country who all need to be exterminated. As a teenager, *Mein Kampf* changed my life. I am not ashamed to say I love Hitler." He also said Breivik is "the hero Norway deserves".

Anders Breivik

When planning this book, I considered not saying much about Breivik. I felt that many readers would have had a stomach full of him when he committed mass murders of teenagers and during his trial. My reluctance was also because of his narcissism. He would no doubt like the idea of being in books, especially if he felt that presence supported his agenda. Given that he regards himself as on a mission to 'save' Norway and Europe and has said that the attacks were designed to enable him to market his manifesto, it could be argued that his views should be ignored.

However, this book from the start highlights insurmountable

weaknesses of the far-right position, and if a fellow fanatic wanted to access Breivik's warped ideas it is easy to do so. In writing a book, documenting ways in which the veneer of civilisation can be made to appear fragile by the actions of atrocious people, it would be remiss of me to ignore this aspect of far-right terrorism, especially since we know that he has already inspired other fanatical far-right racists, and could influence others.

It is therefore important in any writing about Breivik to explain why his ideology is so flawed and incompatible with anthropological reality. Unfortunately, the sort of perceptions and claims he puts forward can be read day after day on Twitter and Facebook and in some online publications. Breivik himself appears to have got many of his views and beliefs from the internet.

Breivik's childhood was not always happy and abnormalities in his response to life were flagged up very early on though these were not acted upon in the manner which the psychiatric team who assessed him recommended. The extent to which his behaviour and damaged relationship with the world can be blamed on his childhood experiences is debatable. Some personality disorder elements might be present from before birth, though how they manifest themselves can change over time and be influenced by external factors.

It could be that in different circumstances Breivik would have responded differently to life. Assessment and intervention by child psychiatry and social services may not cure fundamental problems, such as certain personality disorder characteristics, but by changing the circumstances around a child they *can* change the life trajectory and impact of an individual. A good diagnosis can also help any agencies that deal with the individual in the future to understand them and respond effectively. It is worth considering some elements of Breivik's background as they would have shaped, if not led to, the expression of his pathology.

Anders Breivik's father was a diplomat and his mother a nursing auxiliary, and they split up when he was a year old, in 1980. They had been living in London as a family, but after the relationship broke down his mother, Wenche Behring, returned to Oslo with Anders and his older sister. Behring had previously had a baby and was a lone mother in a vulnerable state when she met Breivik's father. Her own childhood had been traumatic and isolated.

His father, Jen Breivik, already had three children when he began his relationship with Behring. Jen Breivik quickly moved on from the relationship with Behring, though tried, subsequently, to gain custody of their son. Jen, who later moved to Paris and married another diplomat, received visits from Anders in school holidays. This appears to have stopped by the time he was 16, according to Anders Breivik, who put this down to his father becoming isolated. Breivik has said he tried to resume contact with his father five years before he carried out his atrocities but claims this was rejected because his father "was not mentally prepared".

Divorce was a far from unusual occurrence by the time Breivik was born, though this case was complicated because his parents lived in different countries. Regardless of the normality or otherwise of the circumstances, it certainly loomed large in Breivik's mind over the years. Claims of the importance of two-parent families, references to the apparent erosion of male power and a deep misogyny run through his 1,515-page manifesto, which came to light after the killings.

The manifesto, entitled *2083 – A European Declaration of Independence*, was written in English and published under the pseudonym Andrew Berwick, an anglicised version of his Norwegian name. The manifesto was sent to 1,003 email accounts, including numerous far-right agitators in the UK, just before he began his attacks. Quite a bit of the writing appears to have been copied and pasted from far-right web pages and also from the manifesto of Ted Kaczynski, a US terrorist known as the 'Unabomber'.

He spent considerable time building up a network of "likeminded" far-right contacts prior to the murders. By the time of the massacre he had built up 2,500 Facebook contacts. He wrote the manifesto in English as he thought this would give it maximum impact, proposing that: "The key to Western Europe's survival lies in the hands of German but especially French or UK conservatives."

His call for a war against those he regarded as enemies was clear and extremely specific, with three phases of a European civil war outlined to go on until 2083. In the document, he lists far-right groups across Europe, including the EDL, BNP and National Front, who he envisages as part of a network of militia which would rise up. He also suggests political parties, gun clubs, military and police organisations, boy scout movements and football supporters as recruits to far-right militia groups. There are some chilling parallels in his desire to create such a force and the planning before the Rwandan genocide. He was clearly quite familiar with the genocide as he made references to Rwanda in his document.

The manifesto attacks realities and ideas, as well as imagined enemies. Familiar far-right targets, such as multiculturalism, feminism and left-wingers, are incessantly barraged. Not only does he refer to his separation from his father, but there is a preoccupation with fatherhood and manhood. He expresses alarm about the state, supposedly taking on the role of father, and claims that manhood is being eroded by a conspiracy involving feminists, the media and universities.

One chapter, entitled: 'The name of the devil: cultural Marxism, multiculturalism, globalism, feminism, emotionalism, suicidal humanism, egalitarianism – a recipe for disaster', has a section called 'The Fatherless Civilisation'. The same chapter has sections called: 'The Failure of Western Feminism', 'How the Feminists' "War against Boys" Paved the Way for Islam' and 'Feminism Leads to the Oppression of Women'.

The following are a selection of passages about fathers, divorce and feminism from Breivik's manifesto, verbatim apart from some paragraph breaks added to make the reading experience less unpleasant.

Perhaps no aspect of Political Correctness is more prominent in Western European life today than feminist ideology. Is feminism, like the rest of Political Correctness, based on the cultural Marxism imported from Germany in the 1930s? While feminism's history in Western Europe certainly extends longer than sixty years, its flowering in recent decades has been interwoven with the unfolding social revolution carried forward by cultural Marxists.

Where do we see radical feminism ascendant? It is on

television, where nearly every major offering has a female "power figure" and the plots and characters emphasise inferiority of the male and superiority of the female. It is in the military, where expanding opportunity for women, even in combat positions, has been accompanied by double standards and then lowered standards, as well as by a decline in enlistment of young men, while "warriors" in the services are leaving in droves.

It is in government-mandated employment preferences and practices that benefit women and use "sexual harassment" charges to keep men in line. It is in colleges where women's gender studies proliferate and "affirmative action" is applied in admissions and employment. It is in other employment, public and private, where in addition to affirmative action, "sensitivity training" is given unprecedented time and attention. It is in public schools, where "self-awareness" and "self-esteem" are increasingly promoted while academic learning declines

Somehow, Breivik also links feminism with the immigration of Muslims, and an apparent attack on the "foundation" of European culture:

> Today, the feminisation of European culture, moving rapidly since the 1960s, continues to intensify. Indeed, the present-day radical feminist assault through support for mass Muslim immigration has a political parallel to their anti-colonial efforts. This current assault is in part a continuation of a century-old effort to destroy traditional European structures, the very foundation of European culture.
>
> Who will rise to challenge Political Correctness? The fate of European civilisation depends on European men steadfastly resisting Politically Correct feminism. Even more, they must resourcefully oppose the wider grip of Political Correctness, the cultural Marxism for which radical feminism is only one avenue of attack.

In a section called 'The Fatherless Civilisation', Breivik laments the apparent loss of male authority and, tellingly, uses an f-word: "Fathers have been turned into a caricature and there is a striking demonisation of traditional male values. Any person attempting to enforce rules and authority, a traditional male preserve, is seen as a Fascist and ridiculed."

He subsequently states: "The absence of fatherhood has created a society full of social pathologies, and the lack of male self-confidence has made us easy prey for our enemies. If the West is to survive, we need to reassert a healthy dose of male authority."

Somewhat astonishingly, in this already ludicrous manifesto, Breivik describes himself as "a laid-back type and quite tolerant on most issues" and makes a point of stating: "Due to the fact that I have been exposed to decades of multicultural indoctrination I feel a need to emphasise that I am not in fact a racist and never have been."

Despite turbulence in his childhood, Breivik says: "I haven't really had any negative experiences in my childhood in any way. I had way too much freedom though if anything ... We never had any economical troubles." He claims that he enjoyed good relationships with his siblings. However, some mental health professionals who assessed him as a child saw something different from his account.

Two reports, written when he was four, outline concerns about his development and the parenting he was receiving, and there was a recommendation that he be removed from the care of his mother. Claims about his mother sexualising him and telling him she wished that he was dead were documented in a report by Norway's national centre for child and adolescent psychiatry (SSBU).

Focusing on Wenche Behring's mental state and background, the report describes her as having "an extremely difficult upbringing, borderline personality structure and an all-encompassing if only partially visible depression". The report, authored by a psychologist, states that the mother "projects her primitive aggressive and sexual fantasies onto him". The psychologist who wrote the SSBU report was blocked by Behring from giving evidence in Breivik's trial after the massacre.

It is known that his mother had a difficulty pregnancy with him and had decided that he was a "difficult child" before he was born.

Reports from his early childhood state that Behring described the unborn Breivik as "a difficult, fidgety child that kicked her, almost consciously". By the time Anders was four, Behring is reported to have experienced him as "fundamentally nasty and evil and determined to destroy her".

Two years before this, Behring was at her wits end with parenting and applied for weekend respite care for the two-year-old. A medical record from this time documents that she wished Breivik and his older half-sister would "bugger off". The record indicates that Behring felt he needed to be watched continuously to avoid danger and slapped him in an attempt to curtail his behaviour. For respite care, he was placed with a young couple, but Behring quickly ended the arrangement.

In 1983 the mother and son, along with his older sister, were admitted into a family outpatient unit at the SSBU. Observations of the family took place in 'real-life' events such as meals at the unit, and Anders was also placed in the centre's therapeutic nursery. Interestingly, the team saw a different boy to that which his mother described. Rather than being chaotic and out of control, they observed a child lacking in enthusiasm in an environment that would normally be stimulating for young children.

The following was noted: "A striking absence of emotional engagement whilst playing. Joyless application of toys. Does not interact with other children in play. He has no concept of pretend play ... He also does not display the mood variations typical of children his age ... He does not initiate contact with other children. He participates in activities mechanically, displaying little or no joy or interest. He often seems sad and struggles to express himself emotionally, but when he does react, his reactions are excessively strong."

The SSBU period of assessment of the family led to the professional view that Behring's condition and behaviour were so problematic that Anders should be removed from the family. A report concluded: "Considering the profoundly pathological relationship between Anders and his mother it is crucial to make an early effort to ward off a severely skewed development in the boy."

The SSBU recommended that Breivik be put in a foster home but the child welfare service argued that this measure would be too dramatic for Behring and a compromise was reached whereby the child was placed in respite care at weekends initially. However, Jens Breivik ultimately prevented this plan from being followed. He applied for custody and this altered how Behring, who had initially accepted it, responded to the SSBU's and child welfare service's plan. Ultimately the father did not get custody and the boy was not placed in respite care or foster care.

It is known that in his teens Breivik was preoccupied with his appearance, going on to use steroids to bulk up and having a nose job. His preoccupation with how he looked to others, a core element of narcissistic personality disorder, continued into his 'working' life. After dropping out of school, Breivik set up a succession of enterprises, including one selling fake qualifications online, and claimed to have been earning millions. This was a lie and in 2006 he was declared bankrupt and returned to live with his mother.

Breivik's manifesto outlines how he moved back to his mother to live cheaply enough to set in place his violent plan. In 2009 he founded a farming company and two years later, after he had researched explosives thoroughly, he rented a farm. This gave him a cover to buy the large quantities of fertilizers he required for bomb making.

It is interesting that Breivik ignores his early experiences of psychiatric evaluation in his manifesto, except for the mention that his father tried to get custody. His references to psychology are primarily related to his own 'assessment' of the "psychology of cultural Marxists" and he is critical of Freudian psychology and Wilhelm's Reich, who I refer to near the start of this book. His only reference to psychiatry in the whole document relates to female mental health patients being more likely to self-harm than males, before managing to turn it into an attack on the "newly feminised" West and Islam.

There are so many concerning ideas related to ethnicity, nationalism and religion in Breivik's manifesto that it would take a book to unpick them all but I will include some that are commonly expressed by those in far-right groups and 'alt-right' commentators.

Some of those who followed the trial and recall him doing a Nazi salute in court might be surprised to hear that Breivik regards Hitler as "insane". In a section lamenting the apparent decline of white European nationalism, he wrote: "Hitler's insane, genocidal and imperialistic doctrines have resulted in the post-war situation where nationalist doctrines altogether were branded as evil. In other words, that man contributed to completely annihilate the legitimacy and future justification of nationalistic doctrines for several decades to come. Today, even using the word 'nationalist' will involve certain stigma thanks to five decades of anti-nationalist brainwashing campaigns."

He also wrote: "Europe is heading towards cultural and demographical suicide due to the absence of nationalistic doctrines ... Campaigns of psychological warfare (anti-nationalism) have been integrated into the school curriculums and all intellectual public frameworks."

Returning to the theme of Hitler, Breivik also stated:

> Whenever someone asks if I am a national socialist I am deeply offended. If there is one historical figure and past Germanic leader I hate it is Adolf Hitler. If I could travel in a time machine to Berlin in 1933, I would be the first person to go – with the purpose of killing him. Why? No person has ever committed a more horrible crime against his tribe than Hitler. Because of him, the Germanic tribes are dying and MAY be completely wiped out unless we manage to win within 20–70 years. Thanks to his insane campaign and the subsequent genocide of the 6 million Jews, multiculturalism, the anti-European hate ideology was created.

Troublingly, the key concern for Breivik seems to be that Hitler is bad because his atrocities encouraged people to lay the foundations of multiculturalism, not because of the genocide and war which cost many millions of lives.

Fascinatingly and chillingly, given what he did just after emailing the document, Breivik also wrote: "People like myself, who are trying to warn people of this extremist hate speech, are systematically ignored and demonised as, guess what; racist, fascist extremists ... It is nothing less than insane and it borders to an advanced level of psychopathic absurdity." In that context, Breivik is referring to anti-nationalist narratives when he uses the words "extremist hate speech".

Anyone who has observed far-right accounts on social media will have noticed people who are extremely keen to distinguish

Islamophobia from racism, as though if they hide behind that particular pillar of prejudice they cannot possibly have other prejudices. Breivik is quite open about this issue and reveals a fear of being seen as racist. He states: "When I first started on this compendium more than three years ago I had already decided to only cover issues relating to Islamisation and mass Muslim immigration out of the fear of being labelled as a racist.

"I have always been terrified of the prospect of being labelled as a racist, to such a degree that I have put significant restrictions on myself, not only verbally but concerning all aspects of my social image. And I know this is the case for a majority of Europeans. I would say I have allowed myself to be paralysed by this fear. I was inclined not to bring up WW2, the relevance of ethnicity or mention the word race at all."

Given that Breivik coldly shot dead 69 people and attempted to kill hundreds more at a Labour Party Youth League summer camp, having just murdered eight people with a van bomb, it might seem strange for him to be worried about being seen a racist. This could be because his violence was planned for years and he felt his manifesto, marketed by his atrocities, would lose impact if he was seen as a generic far-right racist.

It also appears to have been important to Breivik that he was not deemed mentally ill, perhaps as he felt this would undermine the 'legitimacy' of his message. This added to the bizarreness of legal proceedings against him, as he was initially deemed to have a psychotic illness, which he disputed, and ultimately a revaluation came to a different conclusion.

He has now been diagnosed with personality disorders, which can be distinguished from mental illnesses such as paranoid schizophrenia. The latter is a profound alteration in perception that can cause people to respond completely out of character due to being overwhelmed with a distorted reality. The former relates to how the personality forms and can be shaped by how the brain develops, by experiences, or a mixture of both. Psychopathy is a type of personality disorder whereas psychosis is a completely different condition. This is something the media is often poor at distinguishing and the public can be confused by.

If it can be proven that someone who killed was suffering from a psychotic illness when they carried it out, there would be an effective diminished responsibility defence and the individual could be convicted of manslaughter rather than murder. This is because intent cannot be proven as the person's illness hindered their understanding of what was happening and what they were doing.

Conversely, if a court, having heard expert statements from psychiatrists, finds that an individual's responsibility was not diminished, and intent to kill is proven, the conviction would be murder. This would be the case, as it very often is, when the assailant has an antisocial personality disorder (such as psychopathy or sociopathy). Even though they have a lifelong mental condition (rather than a mental illness), such assailants know what they are doing and their actions are therefore purposeful. Making this distinction is often critical in homicides and influences what sort of institution the person is placed in.

After he was arrested following the camp massacre, Breivik had two forensic psychiatry evaluations. The first concluded that he had a psychotic disorder, namely paranoid schizophrenia. The second evaluation disagreed with this and made the diagnosis of personality disorders.

There were extremely interesting public and political narratives in the background concerning these different positions. It seemed for a while that there was some political hope that Breivik would be deemed mentally ill, as how could anyone but someone who has a mental illness do such a thing? I can understand why some well-meaning people would take this view, but the fact is that people with certain personality disorders routinely commit violent and sadistic acts. It is important to stress, however, that several different personality disorders have been identified by psychiatry and they are not all linked to high levels of violent crime.

Rather than attempting, via a label of psychosis, to expunge from reality the views that Breivik has, many of which are shared by other far-right Islamophobes, it seems more valuable to conduct research into personality disorder traits in those with far-right views – and with those who favour authoritarian systems, whether they are extreme right or extreme left in their politics.

The reason the first psychiatrists decided Breivik was psychotic was not because of his abhorrent far-right views but because of his beliefs about his own role in an imagined war he thought he was a key part of. In interviews and in his manifesto, he talked of being part of an organisation called Knights Templar. The title he gave himself in his manifesto was 'Justiciar Knight Commander for Knights Templar Europe and one of several leaders of the National and pan-European Patriotic Resistance Movement'.

Breivik also told the psychiatrists he could be the new regent in Norway following a coup. He said that he would, if he were to become the new regent, take the name Sigurd the Crusader the Second. He expressed the belief that the events he was involved with could start World War Three.

The above beliefs were seen by the first psychiatrists as grandiose delusions, and evidence that he suffered from paranoid ideas that went beyond the Islamophobic conspiracy theories commonly regurgitated online. The claims about being part of the Knights Templar supported the first psychiatrists' diagnosis, as there is no evidence that anybody else is in the 'organisation'. He claims that the order was established as an anti-Jihad crusader organisation in London in April 2002, by nine men from across Europe, including himself. Intelligence services have found no evidence that the network exists or that the 2002 meeting occurred.

It is important to recognise, however, that having fantasies and making up stories is not the same thing as having paranoid schizophrenia. People with personality disorders, particularly narcissistic personality disorder, are no strangers to personal myth making and claims that depict them as important and special. Psychopaths lie routinely and deceit is a key part of their character. People with paranoid schizophrenia commonly are plagued by auditory hallucinations, which Breivik did not have, and his level of organisation and planning did not fit the profile of somebody suffering from psychotic phenomena, which tends to limit activities and focus considerably over time.

By the time he was assessed by the second pair of psychiatrists, supported by ongoing mental health assessment in prison, Breivik was not in isolation and he had modified some of his self-aggrandising claims. The second pair of psychiatrists noted that the social withdrawal Breivik experienced in the years before the attacks, which *could* be interpreted as symptomatic of schizophrenia, was more likely to be the consequence of the planning he had to do to achieve his violent end goal. The conclusion of these psychiatrists was that he has a narcissistic personality disorder and antisocial personality disorder.

On August 24, 2012, Breivik was sentenced to containment, which allows his prison sentence to be extended indefinitely. It was pointed out in court that although many people share Breivik's conspiracy theory notions about the Islamisation of Europe, few share his view that this should be fought with terror attacks.

Where is the thin end of the far-right wedge?

It is clear from Breivik's document that he regarded his actions as part of a bloody war against Muslims and also a war against internationalism. His manifesto includes diary entries from 2009 until the day of the attacks, in which he documents his preparation to take part in what he calls the European civil war. This diary, as well as other parts of the manifesto, encourages other people to take up arms and undertake terrorist acts in this civil war. As we have seen in the discussion of National Action and Thomas Mair, there are those who would follow this path.

As we can see from the extracts quoted above and throughout his manifesto, Breivik believes and expresses the sort of things that many others can be seen publishing on social media daily. In fact, before he carried out the mass murder, he was one of thousands of Islamophobes who help spread fear on social media.

The problem we have as concerned citizens observing this sort of material is not dissimilar to one of the problems faced by the police and intelligence services. They have finite resources and there are similar posts being made by people who could be budding Breiviks, attention-seeking trolls, people who have a need to belong and people who simply aren't very bright and just copy what they see and hear. It is hard to know who should be disregarded and who warrants investigation.

Ironically, those who are more controlled in what they say are likely to be the most dangerous. Breivik was very aware of the dangers of being noticed by intelligence services and consequently changed his output and deleted Facebook contacts as he got closer to the attacks.

Some key things have changed the way the far-right functions and is perceived. One is the rise of Jihadism, which – as has been outlined – must be understood in the context of other battles and quests for power and resources. The reality and, importantly, the very visible presence of Jihadism through the media, supports the rise of far-right movements and provides a legitimisation of cultural hatred that was not available to those who simply feared and disliked people for being black, Asian or Jewish.

A completely novel factor in the way in which the modern far-right operates is the use of the internet, especially social media. Since the 2016 US election we have become painfully aware of the ease with which people can be taken in by fake news, and how it can be amplified by social media. If you read Anders Breivik's manifesto you will see that he sourced a great deal of his information from Wikipedia. That is not to say that Wikipedia is an unreliable source, but, if a person has a very narrow interest, they can rapidly find information which supports their obsessive journey down a thematic rabbit hole.

Similarly, if someone is a far-right Islamophobe, or an extremist of any kind, they can find those with a similarly limited awareness online. Rather than broadening horizons, social media and the internet more generally can therefore act as an echo chamber that merely inflames the anger of those who have bigoted views, bringing them together in collective outrage.

One thing that has not changed in the contemporary world of the far-right (including elements of the alt-right) is the simplistic evolutionist thinking discussed early on in this book. There is something ironic in the fact that the fundamental ignorance driving what we now call far-right thinking has not changed much in hundreds of years. Those who claim an exalted place in an imaginary evolutionary scheme have not evolved in their thinking since the early days of scientific racism. New ways are found to legitimise racism, but the fundamental flawed understanding of human reality persists.

Ignorant evolutionist models often 'inform' the focus and support the racism of groups and individuals. These days, at least in public, members of such groups may manage to avoid talking in the way early scientific racism proponents did about 'racial' characteristics, but the old evolutionist model has not gone away. Modern far-right racists routinely dwell on spurious claims about the spread of intelligence to justify their tendency to discriminate and dehumanise.

A flawed book called *The Bell Curve: Intelligence and Class Structure in American Life* (1994), by conservative commentator Charles Murray and animal behaviourist Richard Herrnstein, has become a Bible for far-right/alt-right adherents. There are a number of problems in the analysis and narratives within the book, which numerous scientists have critiqued very well.

Claims about the relative intelligence of white and black people are particularly concerning and have helped reinforce the prejudices of white supremacists. Though the authors do acknowledge that environment can influence relative IQ scores of populations (a highly questionable measurement), they contend that genes play a role. This leads readers to the conclusion, many of whom would be overjoyed by, that black people are inherently intellectually inferior to white people.

Critiquing *The Bell Curve* in the 2003 edition of his book, *The Tangled Wing: Biological Constraints on the Human Spirit*, anthropologist and professor of psychiatry and neurology Melvin Konner wrote: "This book presented strong evidence that genes play a role in intelligence but linked it to the unsupported claim that genes explain the small but consistent black-white difference in IQ.

"The juxtaposition of good argument with a bad one seemed politically motivated, and persuasive refutations soon appeared. Actually, African Americans have excelled in virtually every enriched environment they have been placed in, most of which they were previously barred from, and this in only the first decade or two of improved but still not equal opportunity."

A great deal of the 'evidence' referenced in *The Bell Curve* was funded by the far-right Pioneer Fund, which has advanced scientific racism since before World War Two. It is an organisation that supports and pushes white supremacist narratives, and it has shown considerable interest in eugenics.

Just as skin colour has been, the religion a person was brought up with or has adopted has become, and remains, a key way of categorising and ranking people – and of speculating about their level of intelligence or worth. Certain far-right groups that focus their outrage on and relentlessly attack Islam claim that, because 'Islam is a religion, not a race', they cannot possibly be racist. However, when you look overall at what any individual or group associated with such a narrative says and does, there are frequently other things that give away their prejudices.

White supremacists are a key category of far-right agitators, but it is important – and troubling – to recognise that far-right ideologies are widely distributed in human communities. The group that calls itself Islamic State has many of the characteristics discussed above. It is ultra-conservative, authoritarian and dogmatic, and has an anti-liberalism and anti-rationalism focus. It also constructs otherness and dehumanises and kills those who will not or cannot adhere to its ludicrously narrow parameters of living. Like other far-right groups and many religions, Daesh mythologises about the past and peddles fantastical narratives about the future, when those who submit will triumph.

It is both interesting and disturbing that a symbiosis supports far-right groups who are sworn enemies. For example, anti-Islam groups can gain strength and legitimacy when far-right Islamist groups such as Daesh attract coverage for atrocities. The hate peddled by far-right street mobs like the EDL, who often drink before marches, supports ultra-conservative Islamist extremists in their narratives that Westerners are degenerates. Jihadists also benefit from far-right agitators who tar all Muslims with the same brush as it allows the extremists to present a false narrative that Westerners all hate them.

After terror attacks, before the ethnicity of attackers is known, the far-right on social media inevitably spew out the narrative that 'we' are at war with Islam. Jihadists spew out the very same narratives. Neither are correct but both camps seek to capitalise on anything that can create division and conflict. Innocent people get swept up in these narratives and drawn into flawed ways of thinking.

Far-right groups do not all have the same focus or agenda as one another and therefore can be at loggerheads. When they are competing for members this can have the effect of weakening one or both 'sides'. However, when movements are very different, the conflict can bolster the power of each side and have a detrimental impact on citizens caught between their battles and tugs of war.

When one 'side' is criticised, such as an Islamophobic mob that spreads fear, their response is often to list ways in which Islamist extremists are much worse. This enables thugs to present themselves as heroes when, in reality, far-right mobs are not defeating terror by getting drunk and ranting in town centres. They are fuelling the fire.

The race war fantasy driving some far-right agitators shapes certain activities, such as nationalist training camps that involve combat. This is another way in which white supremacists have much in common with ultra-conservative apocalyptic death cult Daesh. As ideas about identity, the nature of humanity and relished battles of the future are such a preoccupation, these sorts of far-right movements arguably have a zeal more characteristic of religious cults than rational political movements.

Charles Manson, whose California-based cult was behind nine murders that took place in 1969, was preoccupied with an impeding apocalyptic race war. The murders were designed to trigger that war, which he referred to as Helter Skelter, a reference to Beatles songs in which he had read (or projected) into all sorts of delusional ideas involving Jesus (with himself as the Messiah), conflict and biblical apocalypse. The idea was that black people would be blamed for the murders of prominent white figures and revenge would be taken on black people.

Manson's plan was as convoluted as it was bizarre, but it ultimately relied on the assumption that white people would be wiped out in a race war, except him and his 'family' of young white cult members. Prior to the 'war', he and his followers were to make an album full of messages about the impending conflict, just as he imagined there were in the Beatles songs. The songs were intended to lure young white female 'hippies', who had flocked to San Francisco in the late 60s, to his group. This would, Manson imagined, deprive black men of white women to have sex with, and fuel their frustration and anger.

During the race war Manson and his enlarged cult (so he

anticipated) would remain hidden under Death Valley, where he believed, thanks to the Book of Revelations, to be a city of gold found in a bottomless pit. He hoped to later emerge, with his cult expanded to 144,000 people, to enslave the black population. However, even the most modest part of the plan, making the album, did not work out as Manson anticipated and so the murder spree, to speed along the race war, was initiated.

Manson died in jail in 2017, despite numerous attempts at parole. He had a Swastika on the centre of his forehead, which, at the time of his sentencing hearing, seemed scratched on his skin but was subsequently tattooed. Manson and members of his cult made connections with other far-right supremacists, who make up powerful gangs in US prisons, over the years.

How alternative is the 'alt-right'?

The term 'alt-right' has gained some traction over recent years and become a catch-all for a variety of outpourings from media-hungry self-appointed cultural commentators and their followers who amplify their messages through social media. Much of the output is extremist and provocative, and also includes hate speech masquerading as journalism. It is a product of the digital and social media age, as few established publications would stoop to such levels.

The desperate malicious communication seen routinely on social media by those aligned with the 'movement' may be indicative of social impotence and not getting the attention they feel they deserve. However, though there is an immaturity in arguments and an absence of coherent philosophy, it would be mistaken to assume that all concerned are just attention-seeking brats who say vile things to get a reaction.

When you examine the origins of the alt-right and some of those who have driven the movement, you face the troubling realisation that it is but a flimsy mask in front of old-fashioned white supremacism, nationalism and bigotry. Therefore, while acknowledging the term and the preference some have for it, it is important to carefully remove this mask and show the true nature of this dangerous, if also ridiculous, movement.

An early reference to the 'alternative right' was made in 2008 by a paleo-conservative philosopher and commentator, Paul Gottfried. Paleo-conservatism is a strand of right-wing thought in the USA, in which there is a focus on tradition, national and Western identity and the aspiration of a small state. It regards itself as a backlash against immigration and multiculturalism.

In a 2008 address to the H.L. Mencken Club, named after a racist journalist and critic, Gottfried spoke about what he called the 'alternative right'. That speech was subsequently published in an article entitled 'The Decline and Rise of the Alternative Right' on the conservative online platform Taki's Magazine. The following year, on the same platform, two further articles discussed the alternative right. The white supremacist Richard Spencer, who was executive editor at Taki's from 2008 to 2009, popularised the term in 2010 via his Alternative Right website.

Spencer, who gained worldwide attention in 2016 when he shouted: "Hail Trump" at an event, where many of his supporters responded with Nazi salutes, considers the alt-right movement to be about white identity. He has called for "peaceful ethnic cleansing" of non-whites and a white homeland. He has also refused to condemn Hitler or the Ku Klux Klan.

Others associated with the alt-right have attempted to play down the overtly racist tone of the movement, but it is impossible to deny this origin. Spencer himself has done nothing to demonstrate that it is not, fundamentally, a white supremacist movement. In 2012, his website published an article, written by co-founder Colin Liddell, entitled 'Is Black Genocide Right?', which claimed that the "black race" has contributed almost nothing to civilisation.

This sort of output can seem like childish provocative trolling, but it is important to accept that some people do actually hold these views and such people have a stronger voice and more influence on politics than they have had in several decades. Racist narratives have characterised much of the alt-right, from online 'news' and comment sites to social media. Donald Trump's campaign and debate style owes much to the glib, prejudiced and vacuous alt-right media and social media output. Alt-right media and agitators helped put Trump in the White House. This was also assisted by fake news sites that rapidly churned out fraudulent and defamatory stories about Trump's political opponent, Hillary Clinton.

Many of these fake news sites have been tracked to Russia, Macedonia and Romania. Evidence from intelligence services shows that overt Russian propaganda to support Trump, seen by the Kremlin as a pliable candidate, took place though fraudulent news sites.

The more such lies appeal to the prejudice of the reader, the more likely they are to share it and social media followers with similar views are to respond. While the real media was raising concerns about the suitability of Trump, fake news sites were churning out a continuous stream of 'stories' smearing Hillary Clinton.

These fake news stories, whether published in the US, Russia or Macedonia, were eagerly tweeted and shared on Facebook by the far-right community in the US and beyond. Because of this sort of intervention, Trump went from being a complete outsider to the alt-right's favoured candidate, and then became the winner of the 2016 election.

Ironically, since the election, Trump has labelled genuine and professional news organisations that dare to suggest he is ineffective as 'fake news sites'. For some time, the alt-right 'news' and comment site Breitbart was Trump's only vaguely established media supporter. Breitbart is a site with vastly less journalistic integrity or experience than news organisations Trump routinely smears as purveyors of 'fake news'.

Over the years, to a large degree because of Trump's rise to power, the small and grubby alt-right umbrella has turned into a quite large but equally grubby tent. It has incorporated a range of different far-right causes but there is a core fundamental conspiracy theory running through it, namely the belief in an encroaching white genocide. Propagators of this notion blame everything from the 1960s, the media, feminism, Marxists and Muslims for this claimed occurrence.

Multiculturalism is as despised by this ragtag group of privileged hacks, wannabe politicians, racist social media trolls and wealthy backers as it is by Anders Breivik and Thomas Mair. As well as white supremacism, Islamophobia and anti-Semitism, there is a strong leaning towards misogyny in the alt-right. Such is the bitter hate directed at certain parts of our societies, many prominent figures in the movement give the impression that their partner recently ran away with a Muslim man, or a woman.

The alt-right has had some success in appearing jokey, rather than full-on Breivik, at times. However, this makes it all the more dangerous when you consider that, at heart, it is a far-right movement in a creepy clown mask. Sprinkling the glitter of laddish humour over the most odious piles of political and linguistic excrement has enabled one or two alt-right platforms and a handful of prominent commentators and political figures to gain a troubling amount of influence. The semblance of humour also allows alt-right agitators to claim they were joking after saying things that, if said by the likes of Mair or Breivik, would be regarded as symptoms of dangerous far-right extremism.

I can remember journalist friends and other observers regarding alt-right figures as a terrible joke – though a joke nonetheless – a few years before Trump was elected. In the UK, and no doubt for many in the US and elsewhere, that joke wore thin some time ago. Apart from for already existing far-right groups and rabid social media racists and Islamophobes, the alt-right hasn't been as significant in the UK as in the USA. In the US, where the politics is generally much further to the right than most of Europe, the far-right rebrand has been more effective.

In August 2017, a two-day rally in Charlottesville, Virginia, called Unite the Right brought together white supremacists, white nationalists, neo-Nazis and anti-Semites. Despite the name, it was a coming together of the far-right, not the right in general. So-called 'alt-right' students rubbed shoulders with Ku Klux Klan members and middle-aged white supremacist militias brandishing guns.

The stated aim of the rally was to protest the removal of a statue of confederate general Robert E. Lee from a park. The far-right were already outraged that the park had been renamed Emancipation Park from 'Lee Park' two months before. Lee's statue was one of several statues of pro-slavery figures facing removal by communities in the USA, much to the upset of white supremacists. The decision by communities to remove confederate monuments followed a racist terror attack in a Charleston church in 2015. In the massacre, by far-right extremist Dylann Roof, nine people were shot and murdered during prayers. Three others survived. Roof hoped that his crimes would ignite a race war.

The Unite the Right rally was met with great opposition from local people and protesters opposed to far-right ideologies. The rally was stopped from proceeding because of violence and a state of emergency was declared. Far-right agitators felt angry that the rally had been stopped and blamed anti-racism protesters rather than taking responsibility for rioting and violence by their number.

After the rally had been stopped, there were still many white supremacists and anti-racist protesters around, and a white supremacist drove a car at a group of counter-protesters. His action killed a young legal professional called Heather D. Heyer and injured 35 others. The 20-year-old driver, James Alex Fields, was at the event representing Vanguard America, a supremacist group that believes the USA should be exclusively white. He has been charged with first-degree murder, five counts of malicious wounding, three counts of aggravated malicious wounding, and failure to stop in event of injury or death. His trial is set for November 2018

After the rioting and what many would regard as a terror attack by an extremist, Donald Trump took the decision to repeatedly condemn the anti-racist and anti-Nazi protesters along with the white supremacists. Creating an equivalency between white supremacists and those who oppose Nazis led widespread criticism for Trump, though he might have calculated that supporting the more militant aspects of his base was a good idea. By then his approval ratings were low and so Trump might have decided it was better to keep those on the far-right happy rather than lose their support by appeasing people unlikely ever to trust him.

In the days after the violent rally, amid accusations of Trump being on the side of the far-right, his chief strategist, Steve Bannon, was out of a job in the administration. Bannon immediately returned to his far-right website Breitbart News to attack the more moderate people around the president. Trump getting into power was an important milestone for Bannon's ultra-conservative agenda. He had established the behavioural microtargeting site Cambridge Analytica, which used harvested data to target psychologically susceptible voters with an online bombardment of 'information', playing on their prejudices and fears.

Under normal circumstances, a president's apparent acceptance of the far-right as a legitimate political movement (Trump said there were "very fine people on both sides") might have been more shocking, but by August 2017 Trump's bizarre antics were so familiar that people almost expected him to say or do the worst thing imaginable.

Where the alt-right has had some effect in Europe has been to inject some potency into tired old far-right movements and, temporarily, to give a sparkly new veneer to dreary old far-right narratives. Much of the potency the movement has had is in mobilising people (primarily embittered men) on social media to attack those who criticise far-right narratives and groups.

These malicious trolls, along with the distorting term 'alt-right', can function as shields to deflect from the reality of what far-right groups and individuals really are. In this context, I am using the term trolls to refer to those who disseminate hate and communicate malice, as opposed to the 1990s chat room pranksters who mischievously drew people in with linguistic bait.

After several years of observing the output of the alt-right and attitudes of those associated with it, I think most people can now see it for what it is. Apart from the most poorly informed and confused person, there can be no claims to not understand how far to the right the politics of the alt-right are. Few people can support the movement at this stage who are not aware of its true nature. However, the troubling thing about this is, although the far-right rebrand as 'alt-right' is a transparent sham, those remaining to support the movement are publicly positioning themselves as far-right foot soldiers. This suggests that they truly believe they are on the correct side of a war about human culture.

In the years before the Brexit campaign and Trump's campaign, it was unusual for people, especially young people, to stick their necks out and express views associated with the far-right, but these political upheavals suddenly made that seem acceptable.

To a moderate person, these views still seem extreme, but once more people express extremist beliefs and prejudiced views, it appears easier for more to do so. It is perhaps akin to offensive language written on a toilet door. Once one or two people have scrawled some expletives, those who would not normally be brave or who might not have thought of it at all, will be more inclined to vandalise.

The confidence given by the rise of the alt-right and Trump, as well as Brexit debates and the mask of social media, could be a vulnerability for some of those who attached themselves to this neo-right bandwagon. The bandwagon may seem fun to some, especially those who have felt like unheard outsiders before, but the faster such vehicles go, the more out of control they are. Furthermore, it is important to understand who is steering the vehicle and who benefits from the inevitable collision further down the road.

Those alt-right adherents who are aware of links to white supremacism should not be surprised when authorities, researchers and commentators take them seriously as threats. Over recent years quite a few people who call themselves 'libertarians' have been convicted of malicious communication after making threats on social media. Just as these pseudo-libertarians, hiding behind an ideological veneer, came unstuck, alt-right trolls who disseminate hate speech face the same risk.

No doubt many alt-right cultists, openly or secretly, enjoy the association the movement has with Nazism, perhaps in the same way right-wing skinheads (which not all were) in the 1970s enjoyed being in an aggressive mob and intimidating people. However, just as with far-right youth movements of the past, older privileged people support the development and use it to their own advantage.

For instance, Donald Trump's chosen chief strategist was Steve Bannon, a 64-year-old former investment banker and founder member of the board of Breitbart News. Bannon has described the far-right online comment and 'news' site as "the platform for the alt-right". Established in 2005 as a conservative platform, Breitbart has shifted further and further to the right. By the time of Trump's political campaign, it was seen by my journalist friends as something of a sick joke, and it certainly lacked credibility. However, with the rise of Trump, the poison peddled by Breitbart and its provocative contributors has spread more widely and been regurgitated more on social media.

Breitbart and Bannon's other activities certainly helped Trump get elected. And, in some unpleasant symbiosis, Trump clawing and lying his way to power could have given credence to a website popular with far-right agitators and spreaders of political poison. There has been a lot of backlash against Trump's hollow, deceitful and dangerous approach from the public, the professional media, the intelligence services, the courts and experienced Republicans. His popularity rating has fallen and his team has repeatedly fractured.

At the time of writing, Trump and his associates are subject to an FBI investigation led by special counsel Robert Mueller. The investigation, which spans allegations of collusion with Russia, financial crimes and obstruction of justice, had already led to guilty pleas from Trump associates. The Mueller probe has, as of spring 2018, issued more than 100 criminal counts against 19 people and three companies. Five people have pleaded guilty. Thirteen people and two entities indicted are Russian. Trump has repeatedly called the investigation a "witch hunt" during his Twitter rants.

Many commentators think Trump would fire the head of the FBI in order to end the Mueller investigation if he could do so without being impeached. Such is the unpredictability of his administration, that he may have done so by the time this book is released. His recent strategy has been to smear and invalidate it.

Over the same period in which Trump has lost the trust of many people and bodies, Breitbart appears to have settled into the level of disdain in which it was held before Trump made his grab for power. There has been pressure on companies to stop advertising on the site, which – in lieu of effective regulation of online 'press' – is the most likely way of being able to curtail its extreme content.

One prominent Breitbart commentator, Milo Yiannopoulos, left suddenly under a cloud in early 2017, after a recording of him on the Drunken Peasants podcast surfaced, in which he appeared to justify men 'having sex with' boys. He lost a lucrative book deal because of the recording and was rapidly removed from the line-up of an American Conservative Union conference.

Even prior to this especially low point, Breitbart had not managed to gain much credibility in the UK, where we already have a wealth of established newspapers churning out xenophobic and sexist bile, the most popular of which, the Daily Mail, ran editorial supporting fascism prior to World War Two. That paper has been through many changes since then, though still churns out enough poison to be nicknamed the Hate Mail and the Daily Heil. However, unlike Breitbart, it emits its poison in such an insidious way that it is extremely popular among pensioners, many of whom appear to regard it as a quality newspaper.

The readers' comments below Daily Mail pieces are often more overtly bigoted than the articles themselves. Judging by the sort of terms used time and time again, there is some overlap between readers of the Daily Mail and of the 'alt-right' bastion of Breitbart.

It can be difficult to distinguish between mischief, satire and genuinely alarming content online. A few years ago, after years in print journalism and after writing my first book, I was invited to write comment articles for the online Huffington Post. I quickly found that, when I wrote about the hard-right (as opposed to far-right) UKIP, comments would appear on the site and be sent to me on Twitter that suggested a far-right perspective from some of the more rabid ranters. Some comments, however, were so ludicrous that it seemed incredible to think that someone could live in the modern world and think those things. I hoped, for the sake of the authors of such comments, that they were mischievously trolling rather than truly believing such patent nonsense.

One memorable torrent included the suggestion that a Huff Post politics editor and then Mayor of London Boris Johnson, as well as myself, 'must' be gay and "go to wine bars together" because we all recognise the value of immigration. The notion that Boris Johnson, myself and Mehdi Hasan go out drinking together, let alone whatever else the lady imagined we do together, would be funny to those who know us. I don't know if the woman was joking, but she accosted me from such a range of inconceivable directions that comedy trolling or angry provocation seem more plausible than those being her deeply held convictions.

However, in the build-up to the EU membership referendum in 2016 and in the aftermath of that, as well as in the build-up to

Trump's campaign and its aftermath, it became clear that there are quite a lot of people with serious extreme right-wing views. White supremacists crawled out of the woodwork in the US, with the Ku Klux Klan publicly supporting Trump and people at his rallies doing Nazi salutes.

After the UK referendum, there was a sharp rise in hate crime against not only citizens from continental Europe but brown-skinned people who have lived in the UK their whole lives. Victims included children. It was as though the apparent shift to the right in politics had made what would previously have been regarded as abhorrent views seem acceptable.

This emergence and amplification of far-right narratives was perhaps more shocking in the UK, which is generally more moderate than the USA, where the Ku Klux Klan has been allowed to simmer through the years despite numerous racist murders by the supremacist gang. Overtly far-right movements in the UK, such as the National Front, have weakened since the 1970s, and newer movements such as the BNP had become something of a pitiful joke.

Groups that share some characteristics of the National Front and BNP, though, deny racism and claim to be merely concerned with Islam. These include Britain First and the EDL, which have grabbed attention in rallies and on social media. Though they are often the object of ridicule, their rallies have been alarming to members of the public, especially when there has been violence. The incoherence of groups like the EDL and Britain First has prevented them from making any real impact on political life, except perhaps to make UKIP, which is often less than coherent itself, seem by contrast like a proper political movement.

Emerging in 2009 as a Luton-centric group, the EDL is mainly known for rallies of generally drunk men, who can look suspiciously like ageing football hooligans who can't get into matches, so much so that even founder and former leader, a former football hooligan who calls himself Tommy Robinson, relinquished his position because of concerns about far-right extremism combined with drunken menace and violence.

In the last few years, the EDL has receded and Robinson

attempted to help the far-right German group Pegida to spread in the UK. Their much-publicised UK 'launch rally', which took place in Birmingham in 2016, did not have an impressive turnout. Robinson hoped that Pegida would attract a more "middle-class" demographic than EDL events and he encouraged a solemn march to the venue, as opposed to the "loutish behaviour and alcohol-fuelled violence" that characterised EDL rallies.

Having also observed EDL rallies, it cannot be denied that the Pegida event was more subdued and less loutish. Perhaps it attracted people who had been at EDL events a few years before but who had become older and less energetic, or perhaps the most energetic and loutish of the EDL rallies did not like to be told how to conduct themselves and so stayed away. However, Robinson afterwards claimed it a success and spoke of regular such events in Birmingham. Nevertheless, Pegida UK appears to have fizzled out. By the end of 2016, Robinson seemed much more interested in tweeting his admiration for Donald Trump than standing in a cold car park on the edge of Birmingham.

After a terror attack in Westminster in March 2017, in which citizens were run over and a policeman stabbed to death, Tommy Robinson was quick to appear on the scene and keen to rant on camera about Muslims. This led to a sudden run on online sales of his autobiography, and he has since decided that he is a journalist.

Robinson's idea of journalism thus far appears to be to turn up with a video camera at the workplaces or homes of people who he feels have slighted him, or rant in a public place or at home. In April 2017, he trespassed in the South Wales Evening Post newsroom after online platform Wales Online referred to him as far-right. Robinson and his associates stormed into the office and he confronted young journalist Jack Pitts, demanding that he explain why he was characterised as far-right.

The irony of a man with a history of violence, who has led a far-right group which has violently attacked the police, bursting into an office and ranting at journalists about being portrayed negatively, appears lost on Robinson. Attempts to intimidate and silence the professional press is a common characteristic of the authoritarian far-right. Doing so while your associates hold a video camera does not lift this from intimidation to genuine journalism, even if it gets lots of hits online.

An attempt to distance herself from her long-standing far-right associations was also made in April 2017 by French National Front leader, Marine Le Pen. Having got through the first round of the French election, she claimed to have temporarily quit the National Front. This was clearly designed to get votes from a broader range of people and to distance herself from the toxicity of her own party, which had previously been led by her father.

Le Pen's attempt to rebrand herself proved ineffective. She lost the next round of the election to the pro-EU centrist Emmanuel Macron, but not before being widely ridiculed for the attempt to distance herself from the reality of her life. Like Tommy Robinson, she has exploited murders by terrorists for her own benefit and that of her movement, but it appears that most of the public sees through this manipulation. Nevertheless, in the first round of the election, she gained almost 22% of the national vote and 34% in the second round.

Two days before the second round of voting, thousands of emails from Macron's team were stolen by hacking and released online, along with numerous fake emails aimed at discrediting him. This came just months after Russia was accused of involvement in the hacking of US candidate Hillary Clinton and her staff in a similar fashion.

Vladimir Putin, who shares Le Pen's nationalistic outlook, has had a strong relationship with the far-right leader for many years. There are financial links between them and the National Front leader gets glowing coverage from Kremlin-backed media. She, in turn, has spoken highly of Putin, backing Russia's 2014 annexation of Crimea from Ukraine. The National Front has struggled financially because of an unwillingness of French banks to lend them money. However, it was kept afloat by a €9.4m loan from the Moscow-based First Czech-Russian Bank. Russian officials have described the loan's approval as a thank you to Le Pen for supporting Putin.

Few states in the world would benefit as much from the break-up of the EU as Putin's Russia, as, rather than a strong and unified block, there would be weakened and divided countries. There are also extreme ideological differences between Putin's Russia and the EU. Modern Russia is hard-right, whereas the EU institutions are much further to the left. Given Russia's history of 'communism' this may seem strange to some, but, as stated above, the authoritarian regime of communist-era Russia was a long way from the liberatory vision of Marx. The ease by which the most powerful Russians grab the fruits of global capitalism has not reduced the authoritarian political culture imposed on the masses. Quite the opposite.

There are some who hastily dismiss any suggestion that Russia interferes with democratic processes of other countries. There are various reasons people might employ denial in this way, including the belief that Russia is a defence against neoliberalism or a corrupt West. Some who retain a belief in communism might imagine that Russia being powerful gives hope that the dream of Marx will one day be realised. Such people are mistaking an authoritarian nationalistic state with a socialist fantasy, which is an easy mistake to make as the pseudo-Marxism seen in 'communist' Russia was but a fantasy of socialism.

Regardless of the reasons individuals dismiss the evidence of Russia undermining democratic processes, given the reality of all that has gone before it is a bizarre position to take. In this book, I have covered many of the CIA's efforts to undermine political movements in other countries, including ultimately the destruction of the Soviet Union. A key reason why countries have built up vast intelligence services is to defend themselves against meddling from other states – and indeed to meddle themselves. The notion that strongly nationalistic Russia, which borders so many countries and is led by a former senior KGB figure, does not use resources to influence the world around it is extremely naïve.

Chapter 10 – Paradoxes of technology

Just as specific political and economic systems can be part of the veneer of civilisation or something perceived as tearing it away, technology can be both pro-social and destructive. A technology or process that is received almost uniformly as fantastic can subsequently be regarded and experienced as damaging. This can be because new technologies and processes emerge that eclipse the former, or because there is something inherently wrong with the technology that was not identified before.

An example of this is the morning sickness drug thalidomide, which was only revealed as harmful after babies of women who took it were born with malformed limbs. Another pharmacological example is the opiate drug diamorphine, commonly known as heroin. First produced in 1874, at a time when opiate addiction was rising, heroin was viewed as a cure for addiction to existing opiates, such as morphine.

From the late 19th century until around 1910, diamorphine was marketed under the trade name Heroin (hence the capital H for the branded product) from the German word for hero (heroisch), as a non-addictive morphine substitute and cough suppressant. As we know now, it is more addictive than the older opium-based formulations for which it was hoped it would be a safer substitute.

Heroin is a drug that not only blighted and ended numerous lives directly but became a major factor in the spread of HIV, through the practice of sharing needles. It also had a dampening effect on the revolutionary zeal of the late 1960s, as discussed above, with the transformative euphoria of the psychedelic era fading into the more sedate early 1970s.

A very different and superficially simpler example of a technology perceived differently over time is coal, a combustible sedimentary rock formed from fossilised plants. Coal has been burned for thousands of years and used for everything from smelting metals, heating water, driving steam-powered machines, cooking and funeral pyres. In recent centuries, it drove the industrial revolution and has been fundamental to manufacturing, transportation and electricity generation.

However, coal was ultimately proven to be an enemy of human health and the environment. It has the highest carbon content of all the fossil fuels, and the combustion of coal has been a significant contributor to greenhouse gas emission. This not only endangers human health and communities but also the habitats and existence of other species.

I used the words "superficially simpler example" because those humble lumps of coal have been a critical part of the technological evolution that has got us to the stage where we are now. Without the power generated by it, the transportation and processes enabled by it and the warmth created by it, it is hard to imagine where we would be now as a species. Just as fire has been key to the development of human civilisation, coal has been a crucial link in the technological and social evolution that has led to the lives, infrastructure and minds we have.

Not many years ago in the UK, coal miners were literally fighting for their jobs. Between 1984 and 1985 they took industrial action in an attempt to stop mines being closed down. Strikebreakers ('scabs') were brought in by the National Coal Board, a government agency, and striking miners tried to stop them from entering collieries. Police responded to confrontations between striking miners and strikebreakers by bludgeoning the strikers, and sometimes charged at them on horseback. Newspapers and TV news broadcasts were filled with images of running battles between miners and the police.

Ultimately Margaret Thatcher, 'the iron lady', had her way and collieries were systematically closed. In less than 100 years, from 1920 to 2015, the number of people working in British coal mines went from more than a million to around 2,000 in 2015. Though we use a lot less coal than before, the drop in demand for coal is not as great as the reduction in UK jobs in the sector. The UK simply imports more, just as we now export many of our more dangerous and physically tough jobs.

I haven't spoken to anyone who remembers the 1984 to '85

miners' strike who did not have sympathy for the striking miners and their attempt to save their livelihoods. However, public perceptions of coal itself have changed greatly since then. This is a result of observed changes in the climate and ecosystems and a greater awareness of the impact of burning fossil fuel on these.

The use of coal in manufacturing and power generation is widely regarded as harmful to society. However, if there was no oil, gas or nuclear power, and wind power and other renewables had not progressed, I am sure that coal would be seen as valuable to anyone wishing to use electricity.

To a large extent, the history of human beings has been the history of power, whether physical energy harnessed, political power, religious authority, social upheaval or economic dominance. All aspects of these have fed into the awareness we have as individuals and as a species.

Many things in human history seem like folly now, just as there are things we are doing now that will seem like folly to human beings in the future. However, folly, trial and error, experimentation and conflict have all fuelled our human journey, just as combusting a product made from crude oil, produced by long-dead organisms, propels cars along roads and planes across the sky. I will focus more on oil now, as a key source of power, driver of technology and source of great wealth, inequality and conflict.

Battles for technology and 'superiority'

Embracing, mastering and owning technology has always been a way in which a person or community can distinguish themselves from others, who can then be regarded as unsophisticated, ignorant or 'backwards'. From clothing to modes of transport and systems of communication, the use and display of technology can, as well as being useful and interesting, be a means of distinguishing oneself from others or of a group from other groups.

One extremely interesting example from social anthropology illustrates how individuals can be quick to creatively use technologies to distinguish themselves from those around them. This example, from communities some might label 'primitive', is relevant for any of our societies and communities. In fact, the more technologically advanced a community believes itself to be or sophisticated a person imagines themselves to be, the greater the lesson this ethnographic example can offer. It is a story about the construction of status and differentiation of the self – key themes of this age.

The French anthropologist Claude Lévi-Strauss, in a piece called 'A Writing Lesson' in his book *Tristes Tropiques* (Sad Tropics) recounts an event in which an illiterate Amazonian chief in Brazil managed to distinguish himself from his community by appearing to rapidly embrace the novel technology of handwriting.

Lévi-Strauss, writing in 1955 and translated in 1961 by John Russell, recounts:

> That the Nambikwara could not write goes without saying. But they were also unable to draw, except for a few dots and zigzags on their calabashes. I distributed pencils and paper among them, none the less, as I had done with the Caduveo. At first they made no use of them. Then, one day, I saw that they were all busy drawing wavy horizontal lines on the paper.
>
> What were they trying to do? I could only conclude that they were writing or, more exactly, that they were trying to do as I did with my pencils. As I had never tried to amuse them with drawings, they could not conceive of any other use for this implement. With most of them, that was as far as they got: but their leader saw further into the problem. Doubtless he was the only one among them to have understood what writing was for.
>
> So he asked me for one of my notepads; and when we were working together he did not give me his answers in words, but traced a wavy line or two on the paper and gave it to me, as if I could read what he had to say. He himself was all but deceived by his own play-acting. Each time he drew a line he would examine it with great care, as if its meaning must suddenly leap to the eye; and every time a look of disappointment came over his face. But he would never give up trying,

208

and there was an unspoken agreement between us that his scribblings had a meaning that I did my best to decipher; his own verbal commentary was so prompt in coming that I had no need to ask him to explain what he had written.

And now, no sooner was everyone assembled than he drew forth from a basket a piece of paper covered with scribbled lines and pretended to read from it. With a show of hesitation he looked up and down his list for the objects to be given in exchange for his people's presents. So-and-so was to receive a machete in return for his bow and arrows, and another a string of beads in return for his necklaces and so on for two solid hours. What was he hoping for? To deceive himself perhaps: but, even more, to amaze his companions and persuade them that his intermediary was responsible for the exchanges. He had allied himself with the white man, as equal with equal, and could now share in his secrets.

Lévi-Strauss went on to state: "The symbol had been borrowed, but the reality remained quite foreign to them. Even the borrowing had had a sociological, rather than an intellectual object: for it was not a question of knowing specific things, or understanding them, or keeping them in mind, but merely of enhancing the prestige and authority of one individual or one function at the expense of the rest of the party. A native, still in the period of the stone age, had realized that even if he could not himself understand the great instrument of understanding he could at least make it serve other ends."

It could be argued that the tribal leader was deceitful, opportunistic, manipulative and not unlike the "humbug" Wizard of Oz, who gained power over people with the use of technology they did not understand. However, it could also be suggested that his demonstrated initiative and creativity helps explain why he was the leader of his community. Most people, in supportive conditions and given time, can learn to read and write, but far fewer people would have the insight and presence of mind to do what the Nambikwara leader managed to do in those circumstances.

There is a sting in Lévi-Strauss' tale, however. He wrote: "Shortly after my visit the leader lost the confidence of most of his people.

Those who moved away from him, after he had tried to play the civilized man, must have had a confused understanding of the fact that writing, on this its first appearance in their midst, had allied itself with falsehood; and so they had taken refuge, deeper in the bush, to win themselves a respite. And yet I could not but admire the genius of their leader, for he had divined in a flash that writing could redouble his hold upon the others and, in so doing, he had got, as it were, to the bottom of an institution which he did not as yet know how to work."

With so many forms of communication available to us now, the technology of leaving signs and symbols on paper, parchment, walls, stones, coins or other objects to create messages that can be deciphered by other people can seem basic. I would argue, however, that writing is the most important technological and cultural development our species has generated and it holds the human world together, including in the code that makes computers work. The first example of writing to have been discovered is on the Tărtăria tablets, found in Romania in 1961 but created more than 7,000 years ago.

Prior to the development of writing it was necessary to be in the presence of the person who wanted to impart information but writing allows asynchronous communication. This means that one person can communicate to another person without being with them, sometimes hundreds of years later. Around a quarter of the books I can see around me as I write this contain messages from beyond the grave, enabled by writing and by machinery that can reproduce written words.

Many readers would have been forced to write neatly, perhaps in italics, but later had to familiarise themselves with things like typewriters, computers, software, code, the strange jungle of the internet, social media, search engine optimisation and an ever-expanding world of communication apps. Even if they have managed to avoid this relentless wave of technology at work, a great many readers will have felt a need to keep up for social reasons and ensure that they remain living in roughly the same technological world as their relatives and friends.

I am sure that there will be readers for whom the above journey through communication technologies felt far from natural but, as their careers and lives have progressed, have experienced a greater compulsion to venture into the ever-expanding forest of technologies. To not do this would be to fall behind, and as tribal leaders of the office world, this might feel as shameful as if you didn't at least do what the Nambikwara leader did and blag an understanding of novel communication technologies.

With each new development in communication technology, we all have the potential to feel as perplexed and left behind as the Nambikwara community did when the leader apparently managed to rise to a new level that seemed beyond them. Communications technology, from handwriting to coding, to Photoshop to web design, can add to the veneer of civilisation while also making us feel primitive if we do not master whatever happens to be the technology of the moment.

Children tend to pick up new communication technologies rapidly and this has the potential to exacerbate generation gaps if adults do not keep up. While children endure parents and teachers telling them how they should write, older people often have to face children leaving them behind with other communications technologies. However, as we have seen with online grooming and abuse cases that have resulted from this, if parents (and police) do not keep up, children can be harmed.

When it comes to social media, young people will naturally seek spaces that are their own, just as they would rather play with friends than parents. New websites and apps open the possibility for segments of society to find their own spaces and define themselves. As well as developments in technology, online social spaces that appear to particular segments of society define themselves by language, which can attract certain age groups while attempting to shut others out. This is similar to how jargon and slang works in society, functioning as a key for the initiated and a locked door for those to be shut out.

From the printing press to the internet

For some people today, the printing press will seem like an obsolete and irrelevant invention, but it transformed the world and laid the foundations for more and more transformations, which are happening daily. It not only ultimately educated populations but it rapidly allowed power to be torn from the hands of religious 'authorities' and set in motion processes that would make humans see themselves and their world differently. It stripped away one veneer of civilisation but created a myriad of other veneers.

Technology of moveable type was established by the 11th century, having been developed in China. In the 15th century, the German blacksmith and goldsmith Johannes Gutenberg introduced mechanical moveable type printing to Europe and this quickly transformed human culture.

It is known that Gutenberg was working on the contraption in 1436 and that he was using it by 1439 as he received a lawsuit as a result of his activity. To put this in context, highly elitist universities had been in existence in Europe for hundreds of years and the Roman Catholic Church had colossal power across the continent.

Prior to Gutenberg's device, books were extremely expensive to produce, few people could read, and the church and related elite powers had great control over what information and ideas were shared – and with whom. Scholarship was inextricably linked to religiosity, and at that point religion dominated the universities. Even in older world-class research universities today, the shadows of religious domination remain.

The printing press started the era of mass communication and this mass dissemination of words opened the floodgates of revolutionary ideas and challenges to the established order. Books and pamphlets could be produced relatively cheaply and, as this literature was easily transported and shared, revolutionary ideas quickly spread like wildfire from place to place.

As a result, a rapid increase in literacy levels took place. This undermined the economic and cultural elite's ability to dominate through its monopoly on education. This in turn supported the shift from feudalism to capitalism as described above, with an educated middle class emerging.

Gutenberg's press was initially found in a single print shop in Mainz, Germany, but by 1480 there were printers in dozens of places in Germany and as far afield as Italy, Belgium, Switzerland, England and Poland. By the end of the 15th century, Gutenberg's press had spread to more than 250 European cities. Italy, the epicentre of the

Catholic empire, also became a centre for printing. By the turn of the 16th century, the output of printers in Western Europe was in the millions. This capacity quickly multiplied.

One extremely significant event enabled by the ease with which words could be reproduced and shared was the Protestant Reformation. However, the foundations of this were laid more than a century prior to this event, in a publication in 1517 by Martin Luther. The work, *The Ninety-Five Theses*, disseminated theological heresy and challenged elements of papal authority.

Martin Luther was Professor of Moral Theology at the University of Wittenberg in Germany and a town preacher. In his theses, he argued that preachers selling plenary indulgences, which were certificates claimed to reduce punishment for sins, was wrong. These indulgences could be for the person buying them or for loved ones believed to be in purgatory. Luther asserted that it is not possible to avoid true spiritual repentance for sins by buying your way out of it in such a manner.

As well as sending the theses to the Archbishop of Mainz, Luther posted on the door of churches in Wittenberg, as was the custom of the time at that university. The reason for disseminating theses in this way was designed to lead to debate. Thanks to the capacity of the Gutenberg printing press, Luther's Latin theses were then reprinted. In 1517 they could be found in locations across Germany and by early 1518 had been translated into German. By the following year they had reached Italy, France and England.

By 1520, 300,000 copies of Luther's theses had been printed and sold. They may not have spread as quickly as a photo of a sloth with a funny caption or a stupid remark from a politician does today on Twitter, but, by 16th century standards, Luther's theses went viral. Pamphlets containing Luther's words spread from town to town and once local printers were aware of the interest in them, it became lucrative for them to make their own prints.

Some might find the specific social media comparisons made ludicrous but they are to illustrate the relationship between what Luther and his supporters did and what we see nowadays. A better example than a sloth with a caption is the spread of the 'Arab Spring'. The rapid spread of information not only challenged the status quo but gave contemporary 'heretics' the confidence to add to the revolutionary culture. In Luther's case, pages printed without the church's sanction represented the radical new media. In the Arab Uprising, social media circumvented the control of the political establishment and traditional media organisations.

For the Catholic Church, the process of Luther's theses being printed and spreading around European states was a bit like novel computer software altering how a machine works and then being sent to other machines. For those who had most to lose from the Reformation, the change was comparable to a virus infecting culture rather than a useful programme, though this parallel would be completely alien to them.

What happened was ultimately dramatic and changed the face of Christendom, but Luther does not appear to have intended his academic theological theses to lead to a schism in the church. It was the technology rather than an intention to make trouble on the part of the professor that made the theses so powerful.

Nevertheless, elements of the communication directly challenged the Pope's decisions. For example, in Thesis 86, Luther asked: "Why does the Pope, whose wealth today is greater than the wealth of the richest Crassus, build the basilica of St Peter with the money of poor believers rather than with his own money?" This was a reference to the sale of indulgences to raise money to fund the reconstruction of St Peter's Basilica in Rome, a pet project of Pope Leo X.

A punitive response to Luther from the Catholic establishment and unwillingness to consider reforms backfired and he continued to challenge it. However, Luther ultimately found himself contending with the extremes of the radicalism he spawned as well as the Catholic establishment.

The Gutenberg press continued to be used to challenge orthodoxy and religion itself. Radical religious ideas could be spread without the heretic having to actively preach to new audiences. Pamphlets were key to this written cacophony of new and 'dangerous' ideas but newssheets swelled into newspapers and satirical novels became a new way of challenging and mocking the political and religious establishment.

Novels, as well as printed poetry, encouraged readers to think more abstractly and creatively. It is reasonable to wonder if this wave of literature requiring abstract thought altered how the brains of readers worked over time, just as the development of symbolic thought altered the evolutionary path of our hominid species. Gutenberg's press was also invaluable to the scientific revolution, which moved the universities from being the cloisters of religiosity to bastions of rationality and research.

Propaganda became easier with the spread of the printing press, but so did the ability of individuals and radical movements to challenge assumptions and beliefs, and doing that challenged established powers. The written word, quickly reproduced and disseminated, became ammunition in the culture war we are still fighting today. If you need evidence of this, look at the trending list on Twitter right now, choose a politically contentious subject and look at how conservative traditional media are discussing it compared to what individuals free of the confines of those old media tribes are tweeting about the topic.

Much of the culture war has moved to social media but the printed newspaper still has a great deal of power, especially over older generations. Though there is a great plurality of views on social media, there are a small number of billionaires controlling the news empires. Their minions do manipulatively produce copy which appeals to the masses, but there is little else in the actions of these powerful new popes of the mass media that demonstrates a concern with the average person – far from it. The masses are cannon fodder in political and economic land-grabs.

New technologies often elicit sharply contrasting public perceptions and consequently lead to fierce debate. They are also sometimes perceived as a threat to prevailing social orders and a source of chaos. The internet was no exception. Despite the many horrors it reveals about human beings and sometimes brings to the surface, I rarely hear people these days speak about the internet as anything but invaluable. This wasn't always the case.

I can recall some alarmed responses to the internet once it had become widely used in the late-1990s. As a student at the time who saw massive potential in the internet, I found such negativity and alarm dreary. However, I must acknowledge now that some of these fears heard from older people have proved reasonable, especially those concerning personal security, hacking, deceit and distancing people from one another. The latter is a paradox as the internet can bring like-minded people from around the world together, while at the same time reducing how much face-to-face contact people have.

Considering how it has entered almost all areas of our lives, from how people start relationships to how beliefs are spread, how markets and hospitals function and even the memorials people have when they die, it is amazing to think that the internet is as young as it is. It would have been impossible for pioneers of the internet to envisage all its potential, but its emergence was a visionary development.

Prior to a mass journey into cyberspace around two decades ago, a few innovative technophiles used modems to send information along phone lines and created networks, though the technology was primarily used by academic and military institutions. In 1969, the US Department of Defence pioneered a computer network that transmitted information between different locations. The ambition at that stage was to create a communication network resistant to military assault.

If information and systems were in many places rather than a small number of places or a single place, they and the organisations and nations they served would have more protection. It was akin to going from having one or two baskets to put eggs in to hundreds, then thousands and so on.

With the supply of more affordable computers in the 1980s, some organisations and individuals created networks. The idea of a World Wide Web was conceived in 1989 and internet use was popularised in the second half of the 1990s.

One of the paradoxes of the technology became apparent quite early on. Though the web opened up the possibility for us to learn, find new contacts in our own professional fields and essentially evolve culturally, it became clear quite quickly that sex was a major preoccupation for web users. This demand was rapidly fed as, along with the mushrooming of websites for businesses of all types, there was a mushrooming of porn of all varieties.

It is quite comical and humbling that, given the most advanced technology humans had got hold of, they quickly used it to explore what some would say is our more primitive impulses. Sigmund Freud and Wilhelm Reich would, no doubt, have been pleased but not surprised by evidence of the enduring human preoccupation with and curiosity about sex. The use of the internet in this way was not just novelty or to do with the geekiness of the online community early on, as not only does porn continue to mushroom online but searches related to sex remain a preoccupation of our nimble-fingered and curious ape species.

The internet has been the key development that has normalised porn, habitual dating, polyamorousness, and a whole range of activities, impulses and perceptions that were more buried and disapproved of in the past.

On my way home from school when I was around nine, my friends and I used to a pass a 'Private Shop' advertising the sale of magazines and videos. We would find humour in the furtive-looking characters entering and leaving. The consensus seemed to be that these were disgusting and pathetic losers, little different to flashers or the sort of 'perverts', as we called them, who might try to lure children into a car with sweets.

I am sure we never saw a woman enter or leave that shop as, if we had, it would have been so notable as to lead to a conversation about the strangeness of the event – and of the woman. The demographic we noticed was entirely men, over 40, whom I assumed to be single. It didn't occur to me that some of these men could have been viewing porn with or buying porn for a female partner. However, with what we know about porn consumption levels today, this could have been a reality – though it seems at least as likely that culture has shifted to create a much broader market for porn.

In 2015, a survey by Typeform for Marie Claire found that more than a third of women surveyed watched online porn at least once a week. Contrasting sharply with the men seen leaving the 'Private Shop' on my route home from school, 70% of the women surveyed were aged between 18 and 34 and half were in relationships.

While the capacity for the internet to host sexual content has been liberating for many, some aspects are much darker and have a detrimental impact on individuals directly affected and, I would suggest, our culture itself.

There is an awful irony in the fact that the evolution of information technology has created pockets of the most brutal, savage and violent activity. People exchanging images of child abuse and sometimes murder represent one of the most revolting and shocking aspects of this technological evolution. Many of those involved are supposedly 'civilised' people in responsible jobs, but their impulses are far from civilised. Whether these people are abusing children themselves or are downloading or sharing such images, they are part of the abuse network.

Those convicted of downloading abuse material are often found to have thousands of images, and their demand obviously fuels the production of images and film. Additionally, consumption (for want of a more graphic term) of the images can be a step on the way towards these offenders acting out their fantasies and harming children in person.

The online trading of child abuse imagery, which many would have once called 'child porn', has been a problem since the internet became popularised, but it rapidly multiplied. Though improved efforts are being made to take down pages and convict those who create websites and trade images, it remains a massive problem. Though people who view and download images of child abuse might like to distinguish themselves from child rapists, they are vicariously abusing children and babies. In 2015, the Internet Watch Foundation identified almost 70,000 web pages containing images and footage of child sexual abuse.

Over the years, the way in which paedophiles (and I am using the term to mean 'a person who is sexually attracted to children' and not just to refer to someone who actively abuses children) share and gain access to such images has changed. Password-protected sites frequented by child abusers and people who get gratification from watching children be raped have existed for decades, and still exist in the dark corners of the web. However, preying on children on social media and manipulating them into sharing indecent images of themselves has become more common.

A related online problem, now recognised as a crime in many countries, is 'revenge porn', in which footage or images are uploaded onto the web by an embittered former partner or controlling and vindictive current partner. It is a form of psychological abuse and is recognised as a form of sexual abuse in some legal systems. When victims are minors, it is not accurate to describe the content as 'porn' as what has actually happened is that images of child abuse or indecent images of children have been shared. In some case the perpetrator has also been underage.

Mainstream social media sites have enabled and still enable images of child abuse to be in public view. In 2017, with the leak of Facebook's 'rule book' for site moderators, it became apparent that footage of physical child abuse was allowed to stay in public view as long as the footage does not contain nudity of sexual abuse.

The rule book also allowed images of violent death and animal cruelty. While most people would be appalled and disgusted by such footage and imagery, the reality is that sadists gain pleasure from watching people or animals be harmed. Violent threats were also deemed acceptable by the social media giant, unless these are threats about a prominent person, such as Donald Trump.

The sharing of images of murders online, such as beheadings by Jihadists, assists terrorists. As terrorism is about terrorising, sharing videos of people being decapitated or bomb or vehicle attacks is exactly what the terror groups want. It enables extremist material to reach more people, which amplifies its capacity to alarm, corrupt and radicalise citizens.

Those sharing such images and footage prolifically in the UK are often far-right agitators trying to spread hate of Muslims. Some people doing this might be genuinely alarmed and well-meaning people but they are unwittingly complicit with the terror groups in doing so. In 2014, as footage of US journalist James Foley's beheading in Syria was being spread online, the UK's Metropolitan Police announced that viewing, downloading or disseminating extremist material, such as beheading footage, could lead to convictions under terrorism legislation.

Much more common than convictions for sharing footage of extremist material are convictions for malicious communication. Such is the nature of the problem that the term 'trolling' has changed meaning over the decades. Rather than, as some people seem to believe, being linked to the fairy tale archetype who hangs around bridges and accosts people, the origin of the term troll is fishing. The fishing technique of trolling involves dragging a lure or baited hook from a boat. This connotation of trolling was used before the World Wide Web was available and early internet users communicated on Usenet, a discussion service.

The earliest references to the practice of online trolling were not about vitriolic personal attacks but more skilled and gentle efforts to trick new users of online communities. In 1992 the Oxford English Dictionary referred to people "trolling for newbies" on Usenet. It appears that this sort of behaviour was, at worst, a playful way of demonstrating the insider status of the troll and poking fun at the outsider or initiate. By the late 1990s, with an explosion of people online and on message boards and chat rooms, this playful baiting continued but a more malicious means of interaction, which also became known as trolling, became common.

Interestingly, tabloid newspapers, which themselves put a great deal of efforts into maliciously smearing people and baiting and toying with the emotions of the public, have been instrumental in the redefinition of trolling from non-malicious mischievous baiting to malicious communication. Even more interestingly, the traditional media, their representatives and the political parties they are aligned to sometimes label web users who ask awkward questions and criticise politicians as trolls.

The more gentle 'traditional' online trolling continues and is especially well-developed in parody accounts on social media, which sometimes manage to trick people into thinking they are the real politicians they are mocking. The darker connotation of trolling, malicious communication, has become a crime in many countries, though in media coverage of convictions the headlines routinely refer to trolls. This conflation makes it very easy for media and others to attack any dissenters, just as Donald Trump has made a habit of labelling any media that questions his integrity or actions 'fake news'.

Most malicious communication, along with online defamation, appears to be laughed off. I see it almost every time I am on Twitter and no more than a tiny fraction of cases lead to a conviction on libel action. Many victims may not realise that they can take legal action.

As many such people are just seeking a response, the best action is to ignore, mute or block them, but some communications are so malicious that action is necessary. One example is how the far-right group National Action responded to MP Jo Cox's assassination. Others include MPs and feminists being threatened with rape and murder. As we saw starkly in Anders Breivik's manifesto, far-right views and misogyny often go hand in hand. This is apparent in many malicious communication cases and in situations where people have been banned from social media platforms.

Some go beyond sporadic messages aimed at upsetting or intimidating people they take a dislike to, want attention off the back of or are envious of, becoming preoccupied with individuals to the point of obsession. Such harassment can lead to injunctions and jail sentences, but punishments do not yet reflect the impact on victims and their relationships.

Relentless harassment and abuse of this kind can have a physiological effect on victims. It can affect the functioning of the brain and therefore mood and behaviour, as well as increase blood pressure and other health threats. However, sentences are not what they would be if the perpetrator overtly wounded a person they followed around the streets.

From what I have seen of the statements of those who have subjected people online to malicious communication and harassment, many do not understand the impact they have. It is likely that some have disorders that prevent them from empathising, and therefore understanding the victim's distress, but it seems that the sense of remoteness makes it feel unreal and benign to many perpetrators. Just as they hide behind an online mask, they can assume that the victim feels equally distant. For a public figure, the remoteness the 'troll' experiences is absent, especially when threatened with murder or rape.

As a result of the nature of their work, people can find out where celebrities will be and therefore are trapped between the need to be seen and the threat of being harmed if they are located.

In a slightly different way, children being bullied and harassed online, perhaps by those they know using a variety of accounts, are equally trapped. Online bullying and harassment can spill over into the playground and beyond, and have a toxic impact on relationships between groups of children. It can lead to and exacerbate violent altercations. Just as adults who are stalked online often live in fear of violence and confrontations in the street or at their homes or workplaces, children, who are bound to a community which they cannot escape, can have their world shattered by this sort of vindictiveness.

Children who grow up with social media get information about life from it and can also develop a sense of identity and validity from it. We can argue that this is a sad state of affairs, but it is the reality. To be bullied off social media can be akin to being forced into social isolation for a child. Yet to stay, under such circumstances, can be damaging to mental health, family life, schoolwork, exams, opportunities, identity and friendships. To find themselves not knowing who to trust and under attack from a network of cruelty could have long-term impacts on a person's development, mind and ability to form relationships.

Nevertheless, there are also benefits to social media for young people. It can help them learn how to articulate their thoughts and build confidence in communicating and identity, as well as enabling them to get information rapidly, develop political awareness and make a broader network of friends. Also, it is obviously entertaining and fun.

Over the years I have been struck by how politically aware young people on Twitter are compared to how most people were when I was a teenager. Whereas in the past young people only had the people around them and those they saw on the television to shape their political views, which can lead to narrow-mindedness, young people now can explore a much broader range of political perspectives and ideological outlooks.

It is akin to people once only having a small number of books to read and albums to listen to compared to today, where they can read and hear almost anything. It makes for more open-minded young people and a greater capacity for them to transform politics, literature and music in the future. The shift in my life from three or four television channels to everything imaginable in the world is beyond going from a monochrome world to a technicolour world.

The apparently simple technology of the printing press is the foundation of this revolution of reproduction and creativity, which has transformed everything from science to the construction of identity.

There are some potentially catastrophic pitfalls in the power of the online world to shape how children and adults develop, and the ease with which information is spread. While it is extremely valuable that scientific, inspirational, technical and social information can be harnessed so easily, and that we are more open to new ideas, there is toxic pollution in this sea of data and ideas.

As well as having the ability to draw nurturing communities of faith together, communication technology enables every belief imaginable to be articulated and circulated in ways that would have been unimaginable to the radical reformers and religious visionaries of the past. The website of any movement or profile page or blog of any individual can compete on equal terms with those of ancient institutions. Furthermore, the interactive nature of the internet enables individuals to offer insights that help shape reality, rather than being passive recipients of ideas. This contrasts extremely sharply with traditional hierarchical religions where leaders and dogma retain ultimate authority.

While the general anarchic capacity of this is exciting, it also opens the possibility of people with malicious intent, or who are deeply disturbed though convincing to others, having a damaging impact on both the individuals they manipulate and societies. If we think about Charles Manson and the impact he had just from face-to-face contact, it seems fortunate that he didn't grow up in the internet age, where he and his attractive cult members could have used technology to draw in more followers and potentially do even greater harm.

Religious ideas have been spread online since the World Wide Web was launched. This was a key aspect of my postgraduate anthropological research into new religious movements. I was interested especially in apocalyptic cults, and at the time ideas pertaining to the Mayan calendar were spreading increasingly rapidly and with more and more fanciful notions.

For anyone who knew about Mayan cultures and their calendrical systems, this could be irritating, as so much nonsense was being peddled. However, it was also funny in its ridiculousness, at least to begin with. The Maya never said the world would end, and they have much larger cycles than the one that was apparently closing in 2012 (though continuing, like a turning cog), yet this is what many alarmist people projected into it. Others projected aliens, Jesus, orbs, the destruction of the financial system and a myriad of other things. The 'end-date' functioned as a massive blank screen, on which people projected their hopes, fears and elaborate fantasies.

In the year or so I was carrying out my research in the UK, the 2012 apocalypse bandwagon was akin to a clown car full of people making funny noises. However, within a few years, by 2011, things had got much darker. This was especially so in the USA, where it was not just a flaky new-age movement but fed into extremist political ideas that had been bubbling away on the fringes of society for some time.

In addition to self-proclaimed 'visionaries' sitting in marquees or teepees at festivals sharing their 'wisdom' with anyone who would listen, or too intoxicated to move, there were people peddling sinister conspiracies online and selling apocalypse bunkers. The doomsday 'prepper' market was booming and children were growing up with alarmed parents stockpiling guns and food ready for the big date in December 2012.

Conspiracies often centred around the mythical 'Illuminati' and their apparent drive for a 'New World Order' (NWO). I will not say too much about the so-called Illuminati in this book as went into some detail about the myth in my last book, *Psychopathic Cultures and Toxic Empires*, although it is worth mentioning that there is no evidence that they exist. This is despite the real existence of the Bilderberg Group, a network of wealthy and influential people that meets for private conferences, and the existence hundreds of years ago of a Bavarian Illuminati, which was concerned with equality.

The elite Bilderberg Group and the group that appeared in Bavaria in the 18th century couldn't be more different. This hasn't stopped those keen to find or peddle a conspiracy from fabricating a connection. Some believers imagine that the secret society wants global communism, while others believe that it is an elitist ultra-right cabal shoring up the wealth of the world. The fact that people on both political wings bought (and still buy) into it is significant. Whether the fear was big business or an oppressive state, NWO ideas offered explanations and confirmation. Fear of a police state obsessed, and still obsesses, both 'sides'.

Many, perhaps most, of the conspiracy theories around the Illuminati and the NWO can be boiled down to anti-Semitism. At the most basic level of the myth, a network of rich Jewish people or freemasons are controlling economies and politics. But, in some narratives, these are actually shape-shifting reptilian aliens.

The dissemination of these sorts of ideas online fuelled alarm as we headed to and through 2012. The internet and the Mayan cycle end date fuelled the fire but the foundation of the fire involved older ideas and conspiracies and prejudices. Paleo-conservatives in the US were preoccupied with fears of a globalist cabal since at the least the 'red scare' in the 1940s. Ideas of a Judeo-Masonic conspiracy are older.

As is generally the case with the spread of dangerous and divisive conspiracy theories, the vulnerable are most engrossed and most damaged. In the run up to the Mayan 'end date', NASA included on its website an area to debunk the doomsday ideas. The space agency fielded more than 5,000 questions from people, some of whom had asked if they should commit suicide or kill their families and pets.

The intoxicating ingredients of long-standing fears about the powerful, fantasies about mystical events and a date to fix upon proved mind-altering for many. Unfortunately, fundamental concerns about abuses of power, conspiracies and the reality of great inequality means that the core foundation of these beliefs has not gone away, even though we are beyond 2012.

In fact, billionaire power-grabber Donald Trump, hardly a man of the people, has played on the same sort of fears underpinning apocalyptic cults. In many ways, Trump has acted like a cult leader, who uses fears about elite groups as a way of manipulating his followers. He often ranted at rallies about "draining the swamp" of Washington but many people saw him as much more dangerous than any professional politicians or indeed real swamp creatures.

As we have seen, the Trump cult quickly began to break apart. This is the nature of charismatic cults, as charisma is a notoriously unstable quality and prophecy routinely fails. When this happens, the cult leader will often blame external forces, rather than take responsibility for their failures. This not only gives them an excuse, but also helps keep followers who will fight for the cult leader.

The failure of prophecies, if linked by the cult leader to external events or supernatural intervention, can ultimately bring the faithful more tightly together in their battle against the outside world. In the case of Trump, this has been limited by the checks and balances of those pesky things called democracy and the rule of law. In his period of ideological and administrative disintegration, which started as soon as he was elected, Trump has often used Twitter, as well as rallies, to mobilise his followers against anyone who would criticise him, including the media, intelligence services and other politicians. Though this made him look ever more disturbed and narcissistic to the wider world, it bolstered core support – for a while.

Another example of a dangerous cult that uses the internet to recruit and for propaganda is Daesh. Just as army recruiters do, ISIS uses glossy videos showing the life young men could have, driving around with weapons and killing the 'enemy'. For a geeky teenager living with his parents in the UK or France, feeling like his life is going nowhere and has no power or respect, such lures can be effective. The apocalyptic message that this is the time, this is the battle that must be fought, and if you die you will get to paradise quicker, proved alluring. The lure of being part of this final battle against 'non-believers' also attracted young women to places like Syria to support the cause and marry the 'fighters'.

As well as 'true believers' who followed the call to battle and to terrorist atrocities, some of those attracted to Daesh are likely to be psychopaths and sociopaths. Such people, attracted by power and sadistic drives, could just as easily have joined gangs or become career criminals. However, the ultra-conservative Wahhabism gives them an excuse to carry out depraved acts and become authoritarian leaders. While we cannot ignore the twisted take on Islam that Daesh leaders use to manipulate, it is also important to recognise the lunges for territory, power and money of many of those who use religion as way of raising armies of cultists.

Despite nothing dramatic and mystical appearing to happen at the end of 2012, or at the point of other 'end dates', apocalyptic movements persist, as do simplistic black and white ideas about who is good and bad. Once upon a time, aspiring cult leaders had to find people in their vicinity to convince to join the movement, and rely on their charisma and sense of authority. Then the printing press came and people spread religious ideas widely through pamphlets, which undermined some people's religious authority while also claiming it for new groups.

By the time the internet came, we were, apparently, living in a more enlightened and rational time. However, the speed with which it was used to disseminate radical religious ideas, conspiracy theories and even encourage young people to travel great distances to run around deserts and murder people, shows how powerful the need for meaning, camaraderie and a strong sense of identity is. The ease with which young people were sucked into being Daesh supporters and sympathisers is a tragic indicator of how marginalised and resentful towards societies many are. Pathological cultures, such as ISIS and gangs, are good at identifying those who are isolated and pliable enough to be manipulated into atrocities.

It is possible that as life seems more and more mechanical, dull and safe, the greater the need to find something that tells a different story and enables roles that feel more powerful. We cannot therefore assume, as dogmatic atheists often imagine, that we will follow a linear evolutionist path in which religion is cast away, like childhood fairy tale books. Many factors drive religious movements beyond hope of salvation. These include the need to feel part of something big, to challenge powers experienced as oppressive and corrupt, and to have something relatively exciting and transcendent to do.

Criticising people for having those drives doesn't help, any more than criticising someone who alters their consciousness with intoxicants, watches films, reads books or listens to music will make them stop doing those things. However, given that the internet allows toxic ideas masquerading as religion and spirituality to spread like wildfire, it would seem sensible that those who have a good understanding of different religions help prevent the vulnerable being exploited and manipulated.

Perhaps in the same way that advisers give good information about illegal drugs, to minimise harm, and fake news is flagged up online to protect people from malicious lies, support can be given to those looking for meaning in a way that protects them from manipulation. It would be better to do this without imposing ideologies on them. At the very least, more can be done to challenge dangerous ideas peddled by the malicious, the bigoted and the tragically deluded.

Weaponising data and hybrid warfare

Given that the human world has been held together by stories as far back as we can see, it has also been composed of contradictions – given that all narratives are not the same. From Martin Luther challenging papal authority, to the explosion of religious and political pamphlets enabled by the printing press, to the development and politicisation of newspapers, to online blogs and social media, the wave of 'information' flooding citizens has become both massive and incredibly diverse.

Due to the power of the internet, the skill of social scientists and data analysts, not to mention the greed of the exploitative and the manipulativeness of the power-hungry, this is not a one-way street. Over the past decade or so, the information given to Facebook by users of the 'free' site, is what has made the company and those who own it exceptionally wealthy. And Facebook is just one of many organisations benefiting from the valuable data which the public has been only too happy to share.

Given that we now understand that Facebook makes most of its money from harvesting data, which enables commercial advertisers and political propagandists alike to target site users with content likely to appeal to them, a point worth considering is if a site costs a lot of money to build and maintain and is free to use yet makes a fortune, then *you* are likely to be the product being sold. The adage, "There is no such thing as a free lunch" is pertinent when it comes to a situation where your valuable data is being plundered while social life is conducted online.

This trade of a bit of information from you for access to something web and app users want was something most people accepted until quite recently. The revelations about Cambridge Analytica, however, showed a far murkier aspect to this trade-off than many people were happy with. The organisation exploited work of academic psychologist and data scientist Aleksandr Kogan to plunder data from a vast number of people, with the aim of manipulating how they vote.

Dr Kogan, of the University of Cambridge, developed an app called thisisyourdigitallife, which he then sold to Cambridge Analytica. The company itself then arranged an informed consent process for research, after which hundreds of thousands of Facebook users completed a personality survey, the results of which were supposed to be for academic use only. That was not the case.

Due to what now seems like an astonishingly negligent breach of data on the part of Facebook, not only was the personality test able to harvest valuable data about those taking part, by both the survey itself and the expressions of opinion in the form of likes, shares and posts on the site, all their Facebook friends also had their data plundered in the process. Consequently, rather than just gaining politically valuable information on those who agreed to share data with the app, data of 87 million people was exposed. This information could then be used in the microtargeting of voters in the 2016 US election with a tsunami of material designed to play on recipient's prejudices, fears and desires.

As Trump won the election on wafer thin majorities in some areas, the number of people affected by the data plunder and ability to target individuals in specific areas would be a significant advantage. Trump has been known to boast that much of his electoral spending went on Facebook advertising.

By bringing together data about interests and opinions held by targets, they could then be served with bespoke messages they would be most likely to respond to. In the case of the 2016 election, the targets were not just right-wingers who would be encouraged to vote for Trump but also left-wing Bernie Sanders supporters who could be manipulated into not voting for Democrat candidate Hillary Clinton. The latter would have received very different messages to those identified as fearful, anti-immigration, gun obsessed right-wingers. One group was being triggered towards voting for a non-politician presented as an opponent to the establishment, the other group targeted to wipe out their vote.

Just before this book went to print, Cambridge Analytica was shut down, following investigations by The Guardian and Channel 4 News. In the latter and Channel 4's Dispatches programme, footage was shown of very senior people within the organisation meeting with what they believed were potential clients. In the covertly filmed footage, the Chief Executive Officer, Alexander Nix, talked of various ways the company smeared opponents and flooded an electorate with 'information' to get their own candidates into power. Sending prostitutes to candidates to discredit them and bribery were some of the methods mentioned. He also claimed that the firm ran Donald Trump's digital campaign, which would make sense as Steve Bannon was his campaign manager.

Other than Steve Bannon, key people connected to Cambridge Analytica were Robert Mercer and his daughter Rebekah. Robert Mercer is a billionaire computer scientist who has supported a variety of hard-right and far-right causes. As well as investing in Cambridge Analytica, has been a major stakeholder in Breitbart News and supported the Brexit campaign. He has some extremely controversial views about 'race', contending that the civil rights movement and the 1964 Civil Rights Act were mistakes and claiming that African Americans were better off before the civil rights moment.

Andy Wigmore, communications director of Leave EU, one of the groups pushing for Brexit, said Robert Mercer donated the services of Cambridge Analytica to Nigel Farage, who was then UKIP leader. As a result, voters could be targeted in the same way that US voters were in the subsequent US election. Clearly such a donation is invaluable in this era, as targeted messages could be sent to emotionally susceptible people, who would then spread it to those within their network. However, Leave EU did not tell the Electoral Commission about this donation. All donations more than £7,500 must be disclosed.

Cambridge Analytica was part of a larger data mining, analysis and political targeting firm called SLG Group, formerly called Strategic Communication Laboratories. SCL ceased operations in May

2018 as a result of the scandal surrounding Cambridge Analytica. Alexander Nix has been found to be director of nine related companies that share the same registered offices, including Emerdata and Firecrest technologies. It appears that SLG created a cluster of shell companies doing the same thing. As these operations just require motive, expertise and computers to do what they do, there are few barriers to reappearing in any number of guises and places.

As this book goes to print there are many unanswered questions about Cambridge Analytica and its allied companies. Before it closed down, I repeatedly asked Cambridge Analytica for a statement about links between Russian microtargeting and its own. I specifically wanted to know if the data it harvested from tens of millions of Facebook users was the very same data that Russian troll factories used when spreading fake news and social media disinformation. If it was the same data, I wanted to know how it got to the Russian propagandists. Despite several tweets to them, which got hundreds of retweets and therefore would be very apparent, I got no response.

Cambridge Analytica is being investigated by FBI special counsel Robert Mueller within the probe into Russian interference in the 2016 US election. Mueller has requested that the company turns over the emails of any of its employees who worked on the Trump campaign. However, in covert recordings of Nix and his colleague, it was said that the company uses an email system that automatically deletes messages after a short amount of time.

Another key issue that has not been resolved yet is what has happened to data Cambridge Analytica and its parent company had. Before the business was closed, the Information Commissioner took several days to get a warrant to search the offices and take computers. If the company did have anything to hide, it would appear to have a greater capacity than most organisations have to get rid of embarrassing or incriminating material. Nix has refused to attend a Parliamentary Committee about his comments and his company's activities, using the excuse of pending legal cases to avoid the scrutiny of MPs. At the time of writing new questions are coming to the fore about the relationship between the company and the Conservative Party itself.

Several other investigations are taking place about the firm's role is elections in numerous countries. The company has said that it has worked on more than 200 elections around the world.

Even if it can one day be proved that Cambridge Analytica and its many other guises swung the Brexit vote and 2016 US election, it seems unlikely at this stage that those would be overturned. To say to a large number of people, your psychological and emotional vulnerability was exploited and you were conned into making a bad decision, is likely to be counterproductive in efforts of shifting opinion. People feeling under attack and criticised are more likely to dig their heels in and reject any investigation as an assault on their freedom and insult to their intelligence. Perhaps the best that can come out of the Cambridge Analytica scandal is, therefore, a much greater focus by the public, journalists, regulators and the legal system on the actions of such companies.

The shift to this sort of tool in elections is highly significant. There is a substantial difference between political teams posting leaflets through doors and covertly getting a psychological assessment of you, coming into your home via phones and computers and subjecting you Clockwork Orange-style to propaganda images, film and words that trigger your fears and frustrations. I would say the latter is exploitation and mind control rather than democratic politics.

Plundering data and using that to target susceptible people with skilfully triggering messages and false news can only become more of an issue as people spend more and more time on social media. As well as alluring apps being used to lure citizens into giving away politically valuable data, suspiciously cheap or free mobile phone and sim deals have the potential to do the same thing. With many new providers appearing each year, consumers desperate for free connectivity might happily take attractive deals without knowing who or what is behind it.

In this book I have covered numerous ways in which superpowers have wrestled for the upper hand, with espionage and supporting (and undermining) populist uprisings being key methods in the 20th century. While the Cold War is meant to be over, we know of many incidences where the veneer of peace broke down and the public had a glimpse of ongoing battles.

Hybrid warfare is a term used to describe the myriad ways that states undermine and attack one another, often invisibly to most people and frequently done in such a way that it is extremely difficult to prove the source of the attack and therefore to get the public to back reprisals. As a result, retaliation will often be equally invisible to most citizens. The term hybrid warfare suggests the use of a combination of methods to weaken one's enemies, along with the recourse to traditional methods of military attack.

The media often portrays Russia as the key player in hybrid warfare, but as we have seen earlier on in this book, other global powers are rarely innocent. For its entire history the CIA has been involved with creatively finding ways to ensure the US maintained domination over other powers, more notably the former Soviet Union.

In modern definitions of hybrid warfare, cyber-attacks, such as on the websites of key institutions, terror attacks, the spread of fake news and attempts to rig elections of other countries are often mentioned. Unfortunately, the term fake news has been distorted by Trump to mean any news about him that he doesn't like. However, when used in relation to the mushrooming of 'news' websites linked to Russia and smearing Hillary Clinton, what was being referred to really was propaganda as part of a hybrid warfare attack on the US. Just as Putin would rather there is a hard Brexit and the EU then breaks further, it appears that he would rather have an individual like Trump in power who divides the USA.

There are two more key points about hybrid warfare I would like to get across. The first is that the concept of using a multitude of ways to outdo competing states and systems is not new, as has been seen in early material on espionage and counter insurgency. European invaders killing buffalo to starve indigenous Americans is an early example of American hybrid warfare, and I am sure military historians could tell us of examples from before the Roman Empire.

The second point I'd like to make is that our dependence on the online world has quickly made the rather geeky area of data harvesting one of the most powerful aspects of modern hybrid warfare – and has the potential to erode democracy as easily as termites can silently infest and destroy a home. As we have seen with Cambridge Analytica, those involved in it can be political extremists, such as

Steve Bannon, yet unelected rich fascists can have teams of little cyber termites eating away at democracy.

The industrial-scale plundering of data reservoirs to control votes cannot be seen as anything but an attack on democracy. When those who do it claim to be 'taking back control' for the masses or 'defending democracy', they are being extremely dishonest. Such is the power and value of data, it has been compared to oil, which has had huge implications for the distribution of power and wealth, as well as a myriad of other threats to our world.

Oil and ecology

The exploration of the murky and explosive subject of oil can help us illuminate ways in which technology can both support the veneer of civilisation and erode it. Many substances are found in nature that we describe as oils, including those produced by our own bodies. Natural oils come in a vast number of forms and have many different chemical properties and uses, including food and medicine. Oils may be vegetable or animal in origin but for the sake of this section I am specifically referring to what we call crude oil or petroleum.

Crude oil has historically sometimes been thought of as a mineral oil, but this is a misnomer resulting from a lack of understanding of its origins. Rather than the product of minerals, crude oil is the product of dead organisms subjected to heat and pressure under sedimentary rock.

Crude oil has been valued and used by human beings for thousands of years but has taken upon greater significance for our species and led to great economic and physical conflicts since the industrial revolution, especially since the invention of the internal combustion engine. Oil has enabled the production of a myriad of useful things, including those using plastics, and it has propelled cars and planes, heated buildings and generated electricity. However, in addition to these benefits, we must also acknowledge harmful aspects of our civilisation's crude oil and plastic addiction.

Given how many uses have been found for oil, and how it has

helped drive societies forwards technologically, it must have, like heroin, seemed like a wonder substance. Like heroin, however, the dangers of oil to society were not recognised until after the addictions had taken hold, though in this era we have much greater awareness of problematic aspects of this addiction.

For many years, supply, economic and international relations aspects of oil addiction were the chief concerns of politicians. In recent decades, attention slowly shifted to carbon emissions and climate change. Attention in recent years turned to the impact of plastics in our environment, and especially the sea, rivers and lakes. As well conspicuous products, which causes risks to marine life, the sea now contains trillions of microplastic particles under 5mm. We do not know yet what the impact of this will have on marine species that ingest or absorb the pollutants, or on species (including our own) that consume *them*.

Asphalt or bitumen, which is a form of petroleum sometimes found at the surface of the Earth, was used by Neanderthals around 40,000 years ago and has been found stuck to Neanderthal stone tools in Syria. It appears that they used it to stick handles to flint implements. Given that some believe Western countries and Russian interest in Syria today is related to oil, this continuity is both poetic and tragic.

Despite our species' claims to sophistication and all our 'advanced' tools and technologies, such as cruise missiles and planes, we arguably haven't moved too far from Neanderthals scrabbling around for decomposed dead gunk. I know of no evidence of Neanderthals killing one another over bitumen, and it is therefore possible to argue that they were more civilised than those who kill today for oil.

The above argument depends on your definition of 'civilisation', but personally I would question the notion that someone is necessary more civilised just because they have a gun or missile that can end many lives rapidly. I would also question the notion that primate groups that manage to use vast quantities of resources in a way that ultimately harms their habit can make too many grand claims to sophistication.

Bitumen was used by Homo sapiens in the building and waterproofing of boats. It was also used in preparing mummies in ancient

Egypt and is reputed to have been used in the construction of the walls of Babylon more than 4,000 years ago. There are many other references to oil being used in the ancient world, especially in regions in what is now referred to as the Middle East. Ancient Persian tablets suggest that petroleum was used there in both lighting and medicine.

At least 1,800 years ago in China, oil was extracted from the ground using bamboo-drilled wells. Gas was extracted with the same technology. The Chinese found many uses for oil, including lighting, weaponry, medicine, ink and lubricants. A 1088 CE book by Shen Kuo, called *Dream Pool Essays*, predicted that crude oil would be widely used globally.

Shen Kuo, a geologist, zoologist, mathematician, engineer, military general, meteorologist, botanist, pharmacologist, archaeologist, cartographer, diplomat, finance minister, poet and musician, offered a range of other visionary insights in his essays. He was the first person to refer to the magnetic compass, which would transform navigation and help change the face of the world. He also wrote about moveable type printing, a novel development in his era in China, which would lead to the social and religious revolution triggered by Gutenberg in Europe centuries later.

Shen Kuo coined the term "rock oil", which has been translated, via the Greek petra (rock) and oleum (oil), to give us the word petroleum. He appears to have understood the origin of petroleum as the product of ancient dead organisms. The following extract of his writing illustrates how far-seeing Shen Kuo was: "Petroleum is produced in the regions of Lu and Yan. In the past, it was called 'fat water.' It is normally found in a mixture with water and sand cobbles. The local people use pheasant tail feathers to collect it and then transfer it to a container. It looks like black paint. After it is burned, the residue looks like hemp. It burns with very thick smoke. When applied to curtains, draperies and tents, it dyes them black.

"Smoke collected from burned petroleum can be used to make ink, which appears as black and shiny as black paint and is even better than the ink made from the smoked pine resin." He also said: "This substance will certainly be used widely throughout the world." and "Petroleum is very abundant. It is produced beneath the earth in an almost endless supply."

Shen Kuo was undoubtedly an ingenious polymath, the like of which has not been identified in our era. However, even *he* could not have predicted how dependent the world would become on oil, how quickly deposits would be used and how much conflict there would be in the world because of 'rock oil'. Tragically, it could require another Shen Kuo to get us beyond this dependence and resolve the conflicts that it has helped fuel. Even more tragically, humanity is well aware of the many threats associated with our dependence on oil, but the dealers and those who support them have been able to undermine alternatives that could help us beat this addiction.

The oil addiction of our species currently runs to almost 100 million barrels a day. Variations in supply, and therefore price, can bring down economies. Therefore, governments will often see conflict and lost lives of military personnel – and perhaps civilians – as a price worth paying for maintaining our supply and keeping the economy reasonably stable.

Oil supply can be used as a way of manipulating countries to sell them arms or turn a blind eye to atrocities. Approximately 80% of the planet's accessible crude oil reserves are located in the Middle East. Most of that is within Saudi Arabia, the United Arab Emirates, Iraq, Qatar and Kuwait. Countries like Saudi Arabia, not known for their impressive human rights records, have the governments of other countries, which should be disgusted by their brutality, literally over a barrel – or millions of barrels.

As well as being used to encourage those who might otherwise criticise to gloss over things like capital punishment, institutionalised sexism, funding terror groups, lack of democracy and lack of justice, oil can be used as a weapon by countries that have it in an abundance.

A key example of this is the 1973 oil crisis, which resulted from the members of the Organization of Arab Petroleum Exporting Countries (OAPEC), made up of the Arab members of OPEC (Organization of the Petroleum Exporting Countries) as well as Egypt and Syria, announcing an oil embargo against the USA, Canada, the UK, Japan and the Netherlands. The embargo was a response to the USA's support for Israel during the Yom Kippur War. The USA had supplied Israel with arms less than a week into a conflict, which involved Egypt, Syria and Israel.

Though the war lasted for a matter of weeks, the oil embargo had a huge economic and political impact. The embargo ended in March 1974 and, by then, the price of crude oil had risen from $3 a barrel to four times that price. The impact of the embargo has been referred to as an 'oil shock'. Immediate international relations consequences included tensions within NATO, and some nations hit by the embargo tried to distance themselves from the USA's position.

The embargo was enacted at a time when it could exert maximum leverage for Arab countries, as there had been sharply rising demand for petrol by Western countries. The US was especially addicted to oil by then and had to import a great deal. The oil price shock led to a stock market crash lasting until 1974. With US life so tied up in consumerism and objects, recessions seem to really take their toll on the country's identity. This could explain, if not justify, subsequent extreme and violent measures to ensure supply of the USA's oil addiction.

Though it can easily be argued that aftershocks of the 1973 oil crisis are still being felt today, political and religious fault-lines between Middle Eastern countries existed long before oil became such an addiction for the world. The need of countries for oil enables politicians to cover these fault-lines, but when there is tension between certain countries, oil, rather than being used to lubricate relations, can be used as an explosive and devastating weapon.

Nevertheless, while it is certainly the case that ideological differences between certain countries are ancient, the existence of vast oil reserves enables more extreme political and religious ideologies to be fostered and protected. For example, the social stratification and divisions of a country like Saudi Arabia have been amplified by the vast oil wealth that the rulers have gained. The ultra-conservative form of Islam practised in the country, Wahhabism, resonates with and gives ideological sanction to the oppressiveness, misogyny and sadism of Saudi Arabia.

Since the oil crisis, Saudi Arabia has spent a vast amount of money to spread Wahhabism, to the detriment of moderate forms of Islam and religious plurality. With the backing of the wealth of

Saudi Arabia, Kuwait and Qatar, Wahhabism has been taken by Daesh across the Middle East and beyond. The puritanical cult, which started in the 18th century as a reaction against religious innovation, has been weaponised, just as crude oil was by the Saudis and other states that imposed the 1973 embargo.

The Saudis, even with the help of murderous Jihadists, have not been as successful as their investment of billions in the project of spreading their puritanical death cult might have hoped. However, the rise of Daesh and the many terror attacks inspired by the cult have enabled those behind the movement to make it seem as though they can take over the world.

Drafting this chapter days before the 2017 UK general election, and days after an attack on an Ariana Grande concert in Manchester attended by children and two attacks on London, I have heard three people today make the mistake of assuming that the death cult of Daesh is the same thing as Islam. It is no more typical of Islam than the far-right extremists of the Ku Klux Klan are representative of Christianity, or indeed representative of Scotland, where the foundations of the Klan emerged.

While every violent death is a tragedy, especially young lives destroyed by a suicide bomber, it is important to state that being killed by terrorists is one of the most unlikely ways in which we will die. We are much more likely to die at the age of 103 in our sleep than be stabbed or blown up by terrorists. US citizens are much more likely to be shot dead by an extremist raised Christian than by a Muslim, let alone a Jihadist. However, terrorism is about creating terror and division, and the sickening nature of terrorist attacks, coupled with repetition of news about it in both old media and social media, can aid this effort.

It cannot by denied that oil and our addiction to oil can be a driver of war and encourage apparently liberal states to collude with those that routinely torture and kill citizens for highly questionable reasons. However, many believe a greater danger than either terror attacks or the sort of Middle Eastern conflicts we have seen so far, in the long term, is found in environmental degradation and climate change. These endanger large numbers of animal species and plants and can also drive conflict.

As it becomes harder to make habitats feed populations, we see more food riots and greater migration activity. Many experts, including those within the United Nations, have made the point that climate change fuels wars. Competition for good land, water and food is significant for human beings, as for other animals, and it should come as no surprise that these are a factor influencing armed conflict.

Mass migrations can, as we know, be caused by war, but this can also lead not only to vulnerability of migrants but conflict in communities they venture into. The far-right plays on fears of citizens and we see domestic conflicts and hate crimes as a result.

There is strong evidence from the past five decades in particular that not only are GDP and population growth key causes of increases in greenhouse gas emissions but that this is the core driver of man-made climate change. As well as the earth heating up, consequences include polar ice melting, sea levels rising and some areas becoming unsustainable for farming and unsuitable for habitation, and more extreme weather has considerable impact. It hinders human beings' ability to ensure stable food supplies and maintain stable communities. Additionally, more extreme weather, including heatwaves, can be fatal, especially to older citizens.

Humans everywhere in the world are dependent on other animals. As well as providing food, animals play vital roles in many communities, including carrying loads. Communities most starkly dependent on livestock are often in parts of the world where global warming has its most unpredictable consequences. In addition to this vulnerability, climate change also increases the likelihood of zoonotic disease outbreaks. These diseases, which move between humans and other animals, can have devastating impacts and although they often have a more damaging impact on the 'developing' world, Western civilisations are also vulnerable. Examples of zoonotic diseases include Zika virus, toxoplasmosis, West Nile fever, tuberculosis, Lyme disease, rabies, Ebola and influenzas.

The greater proximity of humans and other animals, and animals with one another, increases the chances of transmission of zoonotic diseases. Climate change therefore has an impact on human and animal health in that way.

Global warming also increases the likelihood of pandemics of zoonoses and other diseases spread by insects and other organisms. This is because weather becoming warmer allows organisms that carry diseases (known as vectors) to survive in a greater number of places. Examples of vector-borne diseases include dengue fever, Rift Valley fever, Zika, Yellow fever, Malaria, Lymphatic filariasis, Leishmaniasis and Lyme disease.

Vector-borne diseases account for almost one in five cases of infectious diseases globally and cause more than a million human deaths directly each year. The impact of infectious disease outbreaks among livestock on human communities dependent on them also has devastating effects and increases the likelihood of famine, community breakdown and conflict.

The human population has multiplied in the past 100 years. In 1927 the global human population was around two billion and by 2027 it is predicted to be four times that. We reached the seven billion mark in 2011. Commenting on the rising human population, I pointed out in my first book, *Beyond the End of the World* (2010), that it is amazing that we are, as a species, able to feed, clothe and house so many individuals.

However, it is also important to recognise that the world and its resources are not infinite and changes to the climate have the potential to make it increasingly difficult to feed and house populations. Furthermore, it is likely that more regions will, whether because of war, climate change or drought, or a cruel mixture of the three, become unviable for communities. This makes for groups of displaced people, desperate for their basic needs to be met, rather than stable societies. It also makes for antagonistic, fearful and sometimes overwhelmed recipient populations.

Just as we cannot predict all the ecological impacts a two-degree increase in temperature would have on delicate ecosystems, it is impossible to predict the impact of environmental and linked economic changes on human populations. We are not the calmest or most rational of species at the best of times, and it can take very little to unsettle human societies. This, as we have all seen, can lead to catastrophes which tear away the veneer of civilisation.

As we have seen with the rise of Daesh and other fascist groups, human beings struggling to get by are vulnerable to manipulation, and, once primed for action against the claimed enemy, even formerly placid people can be turned into killers. The combination of this vulnerability we have as a species to be swept along by manipulators and conform to pathological human cultures and the potential chaos of future economic and ecological problems has the potential to be catastrophic. Technology is being used by government agencies to tackle Daesh and their supporters, but there has been resistance from some quarters, especially the US right-wing, to recognise the reality of climate change, let alone invest in tackling it.

Conclusion

We have seen and read of many points in history where the veneer of civilisation has become so eroded that primal drives that societies try to suppress have taken hold, with devastating consequences. Only by understanding as many of the complex circumstances surrounding these breakdowns and the historical contexts that helped fuel them can we have some chance of avoiding or at least reducing the impact of such tragedies.

To do this effectively and honestly, we need to do more than look at what other societies are doing while we ignore oppression, violence and inequality at the heart of our own systems. The CIA, for instance, was guilty of this in the past, as were many political leaders globally who were more concerned with power relations with the surrounding world than making their countries fairer and more democratic.

Unfortunately, politicians, especially those peculiar ones who feel they deserve to be 'world leaders', are commonly more concerned with their own power than empowering members of society. It is, therefore, as George Orwell outlined brilliantly in his dystopian novel *Nineteen Eighty-Four*, often easier to build and maintain power by focusing on 'enemies' abroad than the rot and inhumanity within one's own system.

In *Nineteen Eighty-Four*, different places overseas became the enemy, and the public was made to accept this through relentless, yet ever changing, propaganda. The process of focusing the public's attention on the apparent danger of foreigners does not just happen to justify war. The strategy is also used to whip up fear and loathing of migrants. It has been used by British Brexiteers to justify dragging the UK out of the EU. As I wrote this book, there was much TV debate about a 'divorce bill' the UK must agree to settle before leaving the EU.

This was presented by right-wing politicians and journalists as something that greedy and devious foreigners are unfairly imposing on the UK, rather than acknowledging that it is to pay for projects already signed and underway. They have been seemingly oblivious of the fact – or would like the public to be oblivious of the fact – that the reason the UK has to settle up is because *they* are attempting to take the country out of the EU.

The rise to power of Nazis and other fascists was the tragedy that led to Europe in the post-war decades building political and economic bridges and then, ultimately, a unified network of countries. The EU is the most democratic superpower the world has known, and it therefore represents an economic, ideological and political threat to countries like the US and Russia. Rather than deal with calls for improved democracy or greater equality in their own countries, Putin's Russia and Trump-era USA have been keen to undermine the EU. Trump not only treated nationalist Nigel Farage, who failed repeatedly to become a UK MP, as a visiting statesman, but aligned his own nationalistic campaign to the Brexit agenda.

Farage, Putin and Trump are all people who have worked for the disintegration of the EU. Putin's most recent transparent effort was to support the far-right National Front in France, led by Marine Le Pen. These are examples of hard-right leaders intent on the breakdown of a sophisticated civilisation built from the ashes of the defeat of fascism. It is also an attack on liberal values that emerged and were refined over many centuries.

Daesh, the apocalyptic death cult with strong ideological and financial links to Saudi Arabia and other oppressive regimes, is also concerned with breaking down European civilisations, as well as any settings in which social liberalism exists or is emerging. Interestingly, some of those who claim to be opposed to Islamist extremists, such as far-right groups like the EDL, are also often anti-EU. Rather than wanting peace in Europe, some far-right extremists talk of civil war. Extremist Anders Breivik murdered dozens of teenagers to get attention for his manifesto of terror, which he hoped would fuel civil wars across Europe. Searches on social media indicate that quite a few people share Breivik's anticipation – and relish – of civil wars and the killing of minorities.

There will be people who feel aggrieved by a section referring to

UKIP, Trump and Putin's efforts to break up the EU being linked to Jihadists, who are transparent in their contempt for contemporary civilisations. One reason for my doing this is to make the point that attacks on civilisations and democracies can take many forms. Some agitators will be in black with their face covered and holding a sword, some will be ranting in marches with far-right street mobs, and some will be quietly funding far-right or terror movements and undermining democratic processes of other countries. Readers will make up their own minds about which of these are the most dangerous and effective.

It is important to say that these are just some recent examples in which powerful people and violent agitators have attempted to undermine civilisation abroad. History is full of attempts by the powerful to undermine societies – and even continents – in order to impose a new order and plunder resources. In many, if not most, cases the 'other' being undermined, invaded and exploited was constructed as less than human, backwards, inferior, savage or in need of 'civilisation'. Examples of powerful invaders attempting to impose a new order while grabbing land and wealth include the Romans, European colonialists and the Nazis.

Few readers who have got this far in this book without ranting at me on Twitter would argue that the Nazis were offering a better civilisation than that which went before. However, there will be those who feel sure that colonialists 'brought' civilisation to the Americas, Africa and India. Ironically, the very same pseudo-Darwinian model the Nazis used to justify the Holocaust enabled imperialists to think they were 'giving' civilisation to plundered places.

The reality is, however, that humanity is *one* species and civilisation takes many forms. An island that feeds itself by fishing and growing produce is no less civilised than a country that spends billions of pounds on 'sophisticated' weaponry each year or one where there is vast economic, health and educational inequality. Many would argue that the 'simple' and peaceful society is more civilised than the weapon-hoarding nation where there is great wealth but also great poverty.

If we consider the murder rate in one of the countries 'civilised' by European colonialists, that nation's history of genocide and slavery, the state of politics in that country and the extreme inequality there, we must question assumptions that technology equates with 'civilisation'. The USA is built of the bones of indigenous people who lived more peaceful lives and with much less impact on the environment than the volatile money-worshipping cult of the individual that dominates currently.

Nevertheless, flawed old ideas about other societies being inherently savage and the West being civilised and sophisticated persist. Some of this persistence can be explained by racism and snobbery, but other factors are used to support the narrative and distract people from considering contextual factors. For example, a war that we have been party to, or a conflict caused by a vacuum of power that a retreating coloniser left, can provide 'evidence' to support the racist's narrative.

The above can be illustrated well by looking at a map of Africa. The viewer will see many straight lines. These were not there before the colonisation of the continent but created by colonial rulers shoring up other people's lands. These imposed borders divided communities, while also creating tension by enclosing different communities in more confined spaces.

Similarly, prior to India being granted independence in 1947, British powers appointed judge Cyril Radcliffe to draw the border between India and Pakistan. Radcliffe's border was not informed by substantial knowledge of ethnic, cultural or historical factors, nor infrastructure practicalities. In fact, he was chosen because his knowledge of India was limited and he was therefore deemed 'neutral'.

The partition divided communities and between 10 and 15 million people were displaced. Some seeking to get from one side or the other were able to travel by train, cars, planes, lorries or buses, but most were on foot. Up to two million deaths resulted from the frantic migration, with violence between ethnic factions, starvation, exhaustion or diseases such as cholera and dysentery being the main causes.

If we can imagine strange people coming and drawing lines, sometimes down the middle of our towns, villages and even houses, and saying we belong to one or other side of the line – and we must obey peculiar rules on different sides of the line – we can get a sense of how problematic this was when Africa was shored up by colonialists. Dividing established communities and causing tension between different tribal and ethnic groups was always likely to be problematic. This does not mean that those caught up in the resultant violence were inherently 'savage'. What *was* savage and primitive was the planning by the colonialists. This showed a real lack on insight into local people and their histories.

In considering the ridiculousness of the above situations, it might be tempting to think that this was some time ago and nobody would be so inept, foolish or culturally insensitive now. However, the truth is that the ineptness of detached dignitaries, the foolishness of political decisions and cultural insensitivity did not, unfortunately, vanish with the retreat of the British Empire.

As I worked on the technology section of this book, material used on thousands of tower blocks up and down the UK was being tested for how easily they burn, as the Grenfell Tower fire in summer 2017 demonstrated that cladding and other material used on some blocks is highly flammable. The leader of the Royal Borough of Kensington and Chelsea, which was responsible for Grenfell Tower, admitted after the tragedy that she had never set foot in a tower block. This reminded me of the aloofness of officials 'in charge of' the colonies, when many of those making important decisions about people in Africa or India had little or no direct experience with those communities or understanding of their needs.

One of the many linked tragedies that the tragedy of the Grenfell Tower fire has exposed is that the inequalities and cultural differences between those with influence and those with little or none is as vast as in previous centuries.

Although the British Empire is dead, the British class system limps on, enabling those with more wealth than insight to stumble into roles for which they are unsuited. This is something that would be familiar to anyone who attended university and listened to the more privileged students, as well as anyone who follows politics. Those who end up in powerful roles are often unburdened by a great deal of wisdom, compassion or empathy.

One of the ironies of the British class system is that those at the 'top' are supposed to be more sophisticated than everybody else, but, in reality, the system is a brutal and blunt tool of oppression, exploitation and social division. The British class system has all the sophistication of a cricket bat over the head.

The same could be said of the caste system in India and other systems of stratification, division and oppression that use the illusion of refinement and sophistication to perpetuate what could, reasonably, be described as a scam, or confidence trick, for those preferring fancier words. Just as black people, Asian people or indigenous Americans are not inferior to white people, those trampled under ludicrous class systems are not inferior to those who have, like oil or scum on water, risen to the top.

Once at the top of a system, inequality is perpetuated though expensive schooling and contacts, but these bought advantages often prove ineffectual at university level. There is an expression, "You can't make a silk purse out of a sow's ear". As we have seen in the UK with the 'elite' Bullingdon Club at the University of Oxford and in the US within elements of the fraternity system, the pretentious mask of sophistication can easily slip to reveal the brutality and cruelty exhibited by some of the boys in *Lord of the Flies*.

In certain industries dominated by people from 'elite' backgrounds, we have seen the savagery and callousness shown by Jack and Roger. In my last book, I covered the banking crisis and the weakness of the regulation of feral and self-serving financial industries. Since then we have seen some convictions for scams and scandals in the banking sector. This has cost the banks tens of billions of pounds in fines, compensation and legal fees, but has not led to the level of jail sentences we would expect from robberies in the thousands.

Just as news articles highlighting inequality of opportunities and justice can be read as profound stories with moral messages, fiction can raise truths that can be applied to many circumstances and over a long period of time. Moral lessons found in myths, poems, fairy tales and Shakespeare plays have been found relevant to generation after generation, despite the technological world we find ourselves in changing significantly. This could be because when you get to the heart of the stories, and strip away the particularities of our cultural context, we are left with human drives and nature.

The neurologist and psychiatrist Sigmund Freud made a sustained attempt at investigating the nature of human drives in the context of civilisation, but the great storytellers had got there first. That is not to say that Freud's theories are not valuable to us today. They still inform therapies used by mental health practitioners. Perhaps more significantly, Freud's ideas percolated into public discourse and had significant impacts on human culture.

Compared to late 19th-century and early 20th-century life, when Freud practised and theorised, people are more open, expressive, sexually unashamed and willing to listen to internal drives. Freud's ideas have also influenced a myriad of fields, including marketing, public relations, visual art and film making. Terms he used have become common parlance.

Though he is not as well-known as Freud, some of the insights of the psychoanalyst Wilhelm Reich could be as significant today as they were during the rise of the Nazis. His assertion in *The Mass Psychology of Fascism* that authoritarian movements are a symptom of sexual repression could be as relevant for ultra-conservative Islamist extremists and the contemporary far-right as they were for the far-right of Hitler's era.

Having observed quite a few far-right marches in the UK, I was struck by the disproportion of men involved – primarily men between the ages of 25 and 60. The overlap of misogyny and racism within the alt-right (which is a poorly rebranded far-right movement) lends weight to Reich's observations. My first response on hearing some of the 'journalists' at Breitbart News speak was to wonder if their partners had run off with Muslims or women, such was the relentless focus of their bile. The far-right terrorist Anders Breivik's misogyny and fury at feminism is as strong in his manifesto as his fury about cultural diversity.

Reich's theory of sexual repression and authoritarianism ringing true for ranty far-right movements and groups like Daesh is not the only thing they have in common. They share dogmatism, antagonism towards liberal values and a hatred of those who do not conform to their narrow conception of life. Each struggles to accept change and mythologises an imagined 'golden age' or idealised future.

To reach that idealised future, according to far-right dogma, there needs to be conflict. This, of course, provides a role for men who might otherwise feel quite small, powerless, insignificant and overwhelmed by an ever more complex world – a world of diversity, fun, openness and experimentation, where women have a stronger voice than previously.

If not conscious collusion between these disparate branches of far-right extremism, there is certainly symbiosis. Symbiosis is the close association between different organisms, often but not necessarily benefiting each other, and the concept can be applied to human groups. Just as different groups of football hooligans need one another to have an excuse to fight, far-right groups like the EDL use far-right extremists like Daesh as an excuse for their thuggish behaviour and hatred.

Anti-Islam and white supremacist groups can gain support and legitimacy after atrocities that are, rightly or wrongly, linked to Daesh. Similarly, hate peddled by far-right mobs and drunken aggression helps Jihadists to portray Westerners as dangerous and degenerate. Attacks, riots, footage of hate speech and social media vitriol helps extremists on both 'sides' to amplify their flawed narrative that all non-Muslim Westerners and all Muslims hate the other. It may be childlike black and white thinking, but, as Trump has demonstrated, many people respond well to simple political messages.

Both Daesh and white far-right extremists have deeply flawed ideas about human reality, and it is important to keep shedding light on this. If we believed the likes of Anders Breivik or Jihadist hate preachers, there would be civil wars across Europe – and this is exactly what they would like. Though the distortions such people try to impose on societies are wrong, their messages are alluring to the socially impotent, and their warped symbiosis is a danger to society.

Social media has been a key window through which we have been able to see how the symbiosis of these factions works, and social media is also an effective place to challenge it. As well as addressing the issue of fake news, we have to find ways of challenging distorted, manipulated views.

The Trump era, the resurgence of the far-right and the emergence of Jihadists who tell dishonest stories about reality emphasise how important and powerful narratives are. To take the view of certain dogmatic atheists like Richard Dawkins and vociferously attack religion – and therefore narratives that bind communities together – is of questionable value. In fact, it adds fuel to the fire. Most people on our planet believe in unknown forces in the universe, and no amount of patronising by people who lack insight into the complexity of human cultural and internal lives will stop that.

It does not demean us to say that human life is held together by stories – it is just anthropological fact. If human beings somehow lost our ability to think symbolically or to look into the sky, fire or our minds and come up with stories, we would not be the species we are. It is that symbolic thought and those stories that led us down the long and winding road to where we are now. Genes enabled information to be passed on through the ages as we evolved culturally, and so too did our stories.

The fact that human life is composed of narratives does not make any one of them true. Each story tells a partial truth, even if that truth is sometimes that the person telling the story is deluded or a liar. It is fascinating that Donald Trump has talked and tweeted so much about 'fake news', as he quickly proved to be one of the most dishonest politicians the world has known. His narcissism appears to prevent him from being honest with himself, let alone society.

"The Donald's" grand claims about his popularity were known to be false since his inauguration, but they have told an important story about Trump and this era. For instance, they tell us that an individualistic capitalist society has enabled someone with a remarkable level of narcissism and ignorance to be elected. With that in mind, every single ranting indignant tweet can be seen as a morality tale and lament of a system that has gone badly wrong. Long after Trump's term in office, we will have his tweets and rally speeches as evidence of a system going haywire. It should be a major lesson for voters everywhere.

There are billions of small stories that make up, explain and sustain human life. I visualise it as a vast number of bubbles in water. Just as no two human beings are the same, no two stories are exactly the same. Furthermore, the same story will be understood in different ways by different people. Or interpreted differently by the same person at different times in their lives.

As individual words have different meanings, this can put vastly different complexions on stories. For example, the term meta-narrative can mean "a narrative account that experiments with or explores the idea of storytelling, often by drawing attention to its own artificiality". A story can contain the truth that the story is not real, which is a quirky little paradox. However, another definition of meta-narrative is "an overarching account or interpretation of events and circumstances that provides a pattern or structure for people's beliefs and gives meaning to their experiences." Put more simply, a big story that gives meaning to human life and which is big enough to incorporate other smaller stories.

Examples of meta-narratives (or grand narratives) include religions, political ideologies or economic dogma. Grand narratives rely on the notion of universal truth. Even if people have never heard the term, they often live by assumptions that are meta-narratives. For example, the assumption that there will always be 'progress', the notion that suffering is worthy or the idea of the 'survival of the fittest' as justification for extreme power discrepancies.

Religions and other myths can be used to legitimise power discrepancies, including gender relations, the dehumanisation of ethnic groups or cruelty towards the less fortunate. I would argue that neoliberalism is so entrenched in the world we live in that it has the status of a meta-narrative. In the face of what can seem like an unstoppable trajectory towards the primacy of markets over community, those who express the idea that free market dominance is not inevitable or permanent can be made to look crazy. Somehow, a human invention given the status of an immortal god must be worshipped, or we deserve to be swallowed by it.

Curiously, the behaviour of the great god capitalism is more like a huge serpent swallowing things up around the world than the kind and compassionate god of the New Testament. As I have said, I value innovation, and capitalism does promote this and has many great benefits. However, the point about free market dogmatism is that, like all faiths, it can become so entrenched and all-consuming that it becomes heresy to question. It is as though a steamroller has run amok, but people just accept that this is what steamrollers do, rather than taking control of *our* invention to stop more people being crushed by it.

It is also curious that economic liberalism has been so accepted as an all-powerful meta-narrative, as there has been a great deal of scepticism about grand narratives for several decades. In the era in which neoliberalism has become powerful, other meta-narratives have come under sustained attack. Marxism is one such grand narrative, which is ironic as Marxist thought is a challenge to the meta-narrative of market dogmatism. Somehow, a meta-narrative that enables the powerful to retain and add to their power has been deemed acceptable and yet other meta-narratives, including those that challenge this, were deemed unacceptable.

This has been changing, however, and even those at the heart of the capitalist system have criticised neoliberalism. It has got to the stage where many question the assumption that free market dogmatism is inevitable, and there has been greater focus in recent years on the impact of globalisation on different communities around the world.

A decade ago it was easy for politicians, the media and politicians to portray anti-globalisation campaigners as deluded, dangerous anarchists. However, the counter-narratives they were putting forward to critique neoliberalism are now commonly expressed views. Hearing ideologies challenged by other ideologies is one thing, but experiencing the sharp end of globalisation and neoliberalism is more awakening. Despite what the hard-right media would claim, those campaigning in the global justice movement are not all middle-class students but often people hurt most severely by neoliberalism.

Karl Marx took an anthropological and historical perspective in his exploration of how capitalism came to be and how it would, he thought, give way to new economic and political systems. He was writing at a time when capitalism was in its youth, yet he could already see detrimental impacts on workers and societies. Just as he examined the vulnerabilities of feudalism that caused it to make way for capitalism, he scrutinised vulnerabilities of capitalism and suggested how it would give way to socialism and then, ultimately, global communism.

On one level, this is a mechanical way of looking at the world, in keeping with the mechanised industrial world Marx observed and critiqued. However, it was also a prophetic and apocalyptic way of looking, not so different from religions he characterised as "the opium of the people". When I use the term apocalyptic I do not refer to 'doomsday' or the end of the world but to the unveiling or uncovering of a different reality. Like other meta-narratives, Marx's model is a linear, evolutionary one.

It does not make Marx wrong because he introduced a meta-narrative to challenge a meta-narrative, or that he uses ideology to critique the use of religious ideologies. It is, however, interesting. Given how diverse human beings are and that meta-narratives have often led to disaster and oppression, if the only way to get rid of meta-narratives is to impose yet another, this would appear to be a recipe for ongoing conflict.

If the same thing happened in medicine, many more patients would die. While it is right that new treatments emerge and are trialled, not all medicines or techniques are right for all patients. Effective health services think systemically and include the perspectives of different clinical disciplines and researchers. Insights into genetics have proved the importance of individualised treatment and care.

To apply this to narratives, allowing a myriad of micro-narratives to exist at once seems preferable to the straitjacket of meta-narratives and battles inherent to one trying to depose another. However, this is challenging – for example, when advocates of one narrative want to roll out the free market and liberalism everywhere while adherents of another want to turn the clock back to an imagined golden age or kill those who do not conform to a puritanical ideal.

Postmodernity is fun at festivals, with a myriad of different musical styles from different decades played or fused creatively. It is not so entertaining when you have people who chop off heads and people who exploit resources for multinationals 'expressing' their own narratives, while citizens are displaced from their communities to avoid carnage and environmental catastrophe.

Despite assumptions in recent decades that meta-narratives are dead, influential narratives such as Jihadism and neoliberalism would not be happy to be relegated to micro-narratives. Consequently, given the finite nature of land and other resources, human groups remain at risk of falling prey to powerful narratives – not unlike neglected livestock at the mercy of different predators. The veneer of civilisation is often torn away when two powerful meta-narratives clash, or those dogmatically pushing them clash. It is always ordinary people who suffer.

It is important to say that meta-narratives need not be catastrophic, especially if they avoid rigid dogma. They may never do justice to the complexity and dynamism of the human world and our relationship with nature, but they can shed light on murky areas. Social models put forward by thinkers like Freud and Marx have helped us to consider vulnerabilities in our own civilisations.

However, it has sometimes been the case that good insights become distorted, weaponised by others and made into something damaging. Or models are misapplied, like a potentially beneficial medicine being given to the wrong patient. Marx's ideas are a good example of this. Marx and Engels anticipated that the proletarian revolution and socialism would start in a country with a large industrial working class, prosperity and relatively advanced technology and infrastructure. The strength of those economies would, it was hoped, allow it to successfully make the transition before supporting other countries through their own.

Germany and Britain met the conditions Marx felt were necessary for socialism to emerge with strength and gain momentum. Russia lacked those conditions, and what happened there and in China was a long way from what Marx and Engels envisaged. What was seen was a different form of oppression, coupled with an apparatus of state 'security' that made dissent suicidal.

As part of that machinery of oppression, Putin has maintained it, while also enabling the most powerful to enjoy the fruits of capitalism. Modern Russia combines the unfairness of both capitalism and feudalism, with those who had power in the Soviet era, such as KGB figures, becoming the neo-feudal leaders in a rigged system that favours a tiny elite. For these reasons, it is often referred as a kleptocracy rather than a true democracy. Power and wealth reinforces power and wealth, freedom of speech is curtailed, and any opposition can easily be smeared with the help of state-controlled media or destroyed in other ways.

There is no doubt that Marx's insights about shifts from one economic system to another were valuable and his related concerns about capitalism are still valid. The fact that power-hungry and sadistic people quickly exploited the situation was not down to him. Disciplines that would have explained the risk of the model being subverted by the power-hungry had not developed. From modern research into psychopathy, we know that empathetic people often have a blind spot when it comes to predicting the behaviour of those who lack a conscience. Marx appears to have had the best of intentions, but perhaps overestimated human nature and underestimated the corrupting nature of power.

Visionary people often struggle with the fact that many people are more concrete in their thinking and find abstract ideas difficult. Our species is often at our worst when following simplistic interpretations of complex, visionary or abstract ideas, such as those put forward by Marx and religious figures. It seems highly unlikely, given the value Jesus put on children and his antagonism towards greed, that he would respect the vast church empires built in his name, or his 'representatives' who abuse children or cover up abuse.

As well as challenging the narratives that still exist, such as scientific racism and warped religious interpretations, our experience as a species with brutal religiosity, fascism, economic dogma and the distortion of visionary ideas should make us wary of any more created. It seems more likely, at this stage, that a more pressing threat than an all-encompassing new grand narrative is that the power-hungry continue to take narratives from a variety of old sources to assist their power grabs.

This process is a bit like the way the Harry Potter books borrow powerful themes from other successful stories and the way musicians appropriate chords or sequences that have proved successful. We have seen with Trump, for example, a cacophony of narratives and ways of presenting himself that have struck a chord with a large number of people. It is so simple that it's akin to 'demagoguery by numbers' but it somehow got enough votes to take power.

Trump could be out of office by the time you read this book, and no doubt during his demise politicians will agree that nothing so dangerous to politics will be able to happen again. To that I would point out that when George Bush junior was in power, people commented daily on how inept, foolish and dangerous he was. Trump's rise would suggest that succinct and attractive messages – even if untrue — are more appealing to a disturbingly large number of voters than cleverness and detailed explanation.

In any age where experts are despised, we are vulnerable to politicians and agitators who are good at telling the desperate what they want to hear. When such inequality exists and many people feel they have little or no power, the snake oil salesman can clean up. The ironic and exasperating thing is that, in Trump's case, the snake oil salesman is part of the elite with which his devotees are angry.

In terms of his own life, Trump has been far from conservative. He has behaved more like a debauched aristocrat or entitled film star. To gain power, he aligned himself with the conservative Republican Party. We have seen Republicans try to distance themselves from his toxicity but we have also seen him demonstrate a leech-like capacity to cling to power, with little regard for the party, the population or the reputation of the US.

The price of Trump's political parasitism is yet to be calculated, but the veneer has already been torn from his inept regime and, regardless of how long he manages to cling on, the time when Trump was in power will do long-term damage to the veneer of US politics. Perhaps being taken beyond the edge of reason will show the US how dangerous a system dependent primarily on money and soundbites, as opposed to integrity and substance, is. I'm not holding my breath.

Wars, oppression by tyrants, violent revolutions, terror attacks, famines and racist attacks by other citizens are vivid examples of where the veneer of civilisation can be dramatically eroded or torn away. Technology and the encroachment of new economic models might not sound so dramatic but, ultimately, can be as much a challenge to our sense of safety as some of the above.

Neoliberalism was tested on Chile, a country ruled by a sadistic dictator, and so this obviously amplifies how dramatic and callous it could seem to those 'recipients'. The UK was an early recipient of the experimental economic medicine but, even though not under a dictatorship, many found the new regime and 'values' disturbing. Others, however, were delighted by the attack on the welfare state, the erosion of the unions and the acceptability of greed.

Despite the fact that the Conservative Party was in power for half of the 1970s, many Brits today speak as though somehow the Labour Party were responsible for the 1970s not being as bright and vibrant as the 1980s. That this was even the case is questionable – punk was pretty vibrant, and many of the big musical trends of the 1980s, from synth-pop, ska, indie rock, rave and grunge, were influenced by punk or had roots in the 1970s and before. An energised, if politically neglected youth, had split into distinctive tribes.

Even *if* the 1980s were more vibrant than the 1970s, in various areas of life, the rapid evolution of technology was more significant than Thatcher being elected in the UK – or Reagan in the USA. It was not as though technology only evolved the moment the neoliberal agenda was imposed. Computers had been evolving and becoming smaller and less expensive for decades, and the visionaries of the computer age were often the LSD-taking 'radicals' who had been in San Francisco in the late 1960s. Silicon Valley's relationship with psychedelics has continued, with micro-dosing of LSD believed by many today to improve performance.

The technological evolution that made the 1980s dynamic and colourful was not the result of Thatcher or Reagan but the fruit of experimentation and radicalism from earlier decades. It was also enabled by decades of investment in and expansion of university education, especially in the US. The anti-intellectual, anti-radicalism and anti-drug focus of Thatcher and Reagan was therefore at odds with the trends that created the decade in which they took so much pride.

I started this book by talking about being a child at time of great technological advancement and great novelty in music and other entertainments. To be balanced in our consideration of technology, however, we have to consider ways in which it can erode our sense of civilisation as well as help us and entertain us.

There is a brilliant story by Dr Seuss called *The Butter Battle Book*, published during the Cold War. The book is clearly about the arms race and the strategy of mutually assured nuclear destruction. However, I think it is also a good way of thinking about humanity's relationship with technology more generally. The more 'advanced' our technology gets, the more dangerous it can be for us and the less control humans can have over it.

In Dr Seuss' satirical parable, two communities, the Yooks and the Zooks, live on different sides of a wall. They look pretty much the same, except that Yooks favour blue clothes and Zooks prefer orange. Apart from the wall and fashion, the key thing that divides them is that one side eats bread butter-side up and the others butter-side down. This butter-related ideological disagreement leads to an arms race that threatens to wipe out both societies.

The technology of battle starts simply with catapults (or slingshots), then multiple catapults joined together, guns that fire nasty concoctions, a machine gun that fires explosives and something that covers the Zooks with "blue goo". The latter sounds suspiciously like Agent Orange, which the US dropped on Vietnam to deforest areas occupied by enemy forces and destroy crops, but it also killed, maimed and caused disease to civilians and combatants alike.

In *The Butter Battle Book*, the 'pinnacle' of the two sides' evolution in weapons technology was the creation of small red bombs which can cause mass destruction, just like nuclear bombs. The book finishes with generals from each side at the wall standing nose to nose, threatening to drop their bombs and annihilate the countries.

Since the Cold War ended, the nuclear fear has shifted towards 'unstable states' thought to be or actively producing nuclear weapons. In recent years in North Korea we have had Kim Jong-un, a man cartoonish enough to be in a Dr Seuss book, regularly firing missiles with huge glee, much to the concern of nearby countries. His threats to bomb the US were funnier to Americans a few years ago, when his missiles didn't reach as far as they can now.

To make matters more alarming, having someone as volatile as Trump in the White House is arguably the worst possible situation as North Korea makes progress in its nuclear ambitions. Trump has taken credit for getting the leaders of North and South Korea to meet but it seems more likely that it was his addition to global volatility rather than his diplomatic skills that brought about the meeting.

North Korean actions appear to have been designed to reduce sanctions and get US nuclear missiles removed from South Korea. Perhaps Kim Jong-un has been more rational than Western media gives him credit for if by ramping up tensions in an already tense time his leverage is increased.

Despite the revitalisation of nuclear threats and the great instability in the world – and of leaders – nuclear technology might not be our biggest threat. A number of technologies and processes related to technology are already wiping out vast numbers of species, while also creating conflict and hardship for human communities.

The burning of fossil fuels, for example, is likely to have been more destructive to our world than all the bombs ever dropped. However, without using the energy we have since the industrial revolution, it is highly unlikely we would have developed the complex societies we have. Not everyone would agree that it is a good thing we have.

Human beings have assumed dominion over nature, but in doing so we may be responsible for the loss of thousands of species and affecting the habitat to the extent that further extinctions are inevitable. According to the World Wide Fund for Nature, habitat loss poses the greatest threat to species. Human activity causes forests, swamps, plains and lakes to disappear, making way for agriculture, roads, housing, pipelines and other projects that serve our species almost exclusively.

Habitat loss has been identified as a key threat to 85% of all species deemed threatened or endangered. Climate change is also a major factor responsible for the loss of species. Scientists have been speaking for some years of a 'sixth great extinction' of animal species, and some claim that the rate of extinction of species in the 20th century was 100 times higher than it would have been without human influence.

Some might wonder what the extinction of other animal species, let alone plant species, has to do with the veneer of human civilisation being eroded. That sort of thinking makes neat distinctions between nature and human 'civilisation', but the truth is that what we call human civilisation has always been completely dependent on nature. Unless we are to live in domes cannibalising one other, we need other species and the ecosystem. The extraordinary civilisations we have constructed were also built on and by nature, even if some human habitats feel removed from nature.

Ironically, given how human beings often regard their civilisation as above and separate from nature and wildlife, the breakdown of nature and loss of species is eroding our civilisation. Lack of viable habitats for us and livestock, and the erosion of our ability to produce food, droughts and zoonotic disease outbreaks, can fuel more conflict and further genocides. The vulnerability of human communities to those spreading dangerous narratives, such as religious extremists or dishonest charismatic politicians, is heightened by lack of resources and unstable habitats.

What we call 'intelligence' and 'civilisation' could themselves ultimately be the biggest threats to humanity and the other species we share the planet with. As technology develops, it has a tendency to leverage up the risks. As with meta-narratives that become distorted, we cannot assume that the technological innovations of the most visionary people will be applied by others with a fraction of the intelligence that developed them.

In relation to some potentially dangerous technology, we are akin to children with access to a kitchen cupboard full of toxic substances. Many of us will remember that once something was marked dangerous, it became a matter of pride and adventure to remove the 'child-proof' lids. As a particularly curious, mischievous and arrogant species of ape, we have a tendency to push things to the limit. With some technologies, however, we have no idea what their limit is.

The best dystopian stories reflect a world we are already in or are about to enter. There has been a fear since the development of early computers that they might become more intelligent than and consequently dominate us. This idea sounded more far-fetched in the past, but, given how modern machines can actually learn and adapt accordingly, it is becoming less so. Also, they are already controlling us in quite subtle ways. At this stage technology is not consciously dominating us, but we have become captive to technologies designed to liberate.

Many people are already transfixed by gadgets, and a lot of power – and therefore future planetary vulnerability – goes into feeding our ever-present machines. That said, much of our gadget use now is about connecting with other humans, so arguably they bring us closer to our own nature, if not to the natural habitat. The vast number of online searches and posts related to cats, dogs and other species suggests both an estrangement from and ongoing fascination with animals.

Technological innovation is not inevitably valuable for our planet, even if it is beneficial to certain individuals and organisations. It is therefore important that we can moderate it and use innovations wisely. Perhaps for us to make great strides in innovation that benefit the planet, there needs to be a collective ideology to ensure that innovations that impact on our and other species are of value to the many not just the few. Without that, we could effectively end up with two distinct human species – one that suffers and goes without, and one that claims to be more civilised but is actually domineering, selfish and destructive. Just as in *Lord of the Flies*, the dominator may turn out to be the savage.

Technology can be democratising but also can exacerbate inequality. The concept of techno-feudalism is likely to become of more interest over time. Feudalism was about inequality enabled by one group owning the land that others worked on, while techno-feudalism is about the creation of a new elite who develop, own rights to and control new technology. Some people fear that this, coupled with robots taking many more jobs, would amplify the divide between the wealthy and others beyond anything that has been seen before. However, given that slavery has existed for much of human history, I suspect that this is a hyper-vigilant response. For there to be billionaire technological elites, billions of consumers with disposable incomes and leisure time need to exist.

In this book, I have discussed thousands of years of human life and given a broad spectrum of examples where it can be said that the veneer of civilisation was eroded or dramatically torn away. Building civilisations, holding them together and stopping them from destroying other human groups, species or habitats is not easy. It takes more than building fancy structures like castles, palaces or shiny golden towers.

There are many things that can erode or tear away the veneer of any civilisation. Human beings have a tendency – though this is not universal – to imagine that the society they are in and the era they live in has it right. Broken ancient civilisations are often looked upon as 'primitive' and consequently unsustainable, rather than warnings from the past.

It is perhaps good that we have the tendency to feel that the civilisation we live in is viable and sustainable. If many people questioned what was behind the veneer of their civilisation, then it could easily be torn away and this lead to unrest. However, once we really start to understand the factors that have caused other civilisations to fracture or disintegrate, we come to the realisation that breakdown was not because the people were 'primitive' or unintelligent but because of a variety of internal and external pressures.

The very process of building a civilisation is an acknowledgement of potential violence, destruction and chaos. Civilisations paper over the cracks of human nature and our impulsive ape tendencies. Consequently, it can be argued that the vulnerability of any civilisation was built into the foundations.

Some might even go so far as suggest that the whole concept of civilisation is flawed as the veneer tends to hide all sorts of power discrepancies, tensions, injustices and oppressions. And no civilisation exists in isolation, but, rather, civilisations are often aggressive and oppressive to other human groups, as well as feeding off and sometimes destroying nature.

When we look at civilisations that have broken down, we see that the splendour of buildings or novelty of artefacts did not manage to hold them together. We cannot therefore assume that our existing in a more prosperous and 'advanced' era will ensure that our civilisations last forever. There are many reasons why civilisations break down, including human frailties like arrogance, greed and oppression, and dehumanisation of parts of society or those outside. Disease and short life spans can also undermine society's ability to maintain stability.

External factors that cause societies to break down include invasions, climate impacts, loss of valuable habitat, the spread of new ideologies and outward migration of those who sustain key services and industries. Population growth without the skills, agricultural capacities and health services to sustain that life is a threat. So too is dependence on certain substances, such as oil and gas.

These are some of the threats to a great many societies over the coming decades. It is clear that the empires of previous centuries have as many vulnerabilities as civilisations with less grand histories. In fact, as is the case with towers, size can be a vulnerability to civilisations.

We do not know what the most successful civilisations of the future will be like, but we *can* understand threats to our current civilisations. Biblical battles that seemed the stuff of myth are played out on our screens every day. Above the grand structures and wealth of our civilisations, I would argue that stories, knowledge, handed-down skills, proven facts and insight into our species and others are our most valuable productions.

It is this, not the wealth of 'our' elites or the spectacular buildings they hide away in, that binds societies together and defines a civilisation. Amassed wisdom, unlike gold or money, is our shared heritage. It is this that has built all human societies and can help civilisations to function better, survive and respond to the needs of different human groups, other species and the planet with greater effectiveness and compassion.

References

Allen, Joe and Pilger, John (foreword) (2008) *Vietnam: The (Last) War the U.S. Lost*. Chicago: Haymarket Books

Boyd, William and Mackenzie, Muriel (1930) *Towards a New Education; a record and synthesis of the discussions on the new psychology and the curriculum at the fifth world conference on the New education fellowship held at Elsinore, Denmark, in August 1929*. London: A.A. Knopf

Burroughs, William (1959) *The Naked Lunch*. New York: Grove Press

Collins, Suzanne (2008) *The Hunger Games*. New York: Scholastic Press

Darwin, Charles (1858) *On the Origin of Species by Means of Natural Selection, or the Preservation of Favoured Races in the Struggle for Life*. London: John Murray

Darwin, Charles (1871) *Descent of Man, and Selection in Relation to Sex*. London: John Murray

Engels, Friedrich and based on notes left by Marx, Karl (1884) *The Origin of the Family, Private Property and the State in the Light of the Researches of Lewis H. Morgan*. New York: Pathfinder Press

Frank, Andre Gunder (1998) *ReOrient: Global Economy in the Asian Age*. Berkeley:

University of California Press

Freud, Sigmund (1930) *Civilization and Its Discontents*. London: Hogarth and the Institute of Psycho-Analysis

Freud, Sigmund (1922) *Beyond the Pleasure Principle*. Translation by C. J. M. Hubback. London: Vienna: International Psycho-Analytica

Friedman, Thomas (1999) *The Lexus and the Olive Tree*. New York: Farrar, Straus and Giroux

Friedman, Thomas (2005) The World Is Flat: *A Brief History of the Twenty-First Century*. New York: Farrar, Straus and Giroux

Geisel, Theodor Seuss ('Dr Seuss') (1984) *The Butter Battle Book*. New York: Random House

Golding, William (1954) *Lord of the Flies*. London: Faber and Faber

Herrnstein, Richard and Murray, Charles (1994) *The Bell Curve: Intelligence and Class Structure in American Life*. New York: Simon & Schuster

Konner, Melvin (2003) *The Tangled Wing: Biological Constraints on the Human Spirit* (2nd edition). New York: Henry Holt and Company

Kuo, Shen (1088) *Dream Pool Essays*.

Lévi-Strauss, Claude (1961) *Tristes Tropiques*. London: Hutchinson & Co

Malinowski, Bronisław (1929) *The Sexual Life of Savages in North-Western Melanesia; an ethnographic account of courtship, marriage and family life among the natives of the Trobriand Islands, British New Guinea*. New York: Eugenics Publishing Company

Marx, Karl and Engels, Friedrich (1932) The German Ideology. Moscow: Marx-Engels Institute

Mead, Margaret (1928) *Coming of Age in Samoa*. New York: William Morrow and Company

Morgan, Lewis (1877) *Ancient Society; or, Researches in the Lines of Human Progress from Savagery, Through Barbarism to Civilization*. New York: Henry Holt and Company

Orwell, George (1949) *Nineteen Eighty-Four*. London: Secker & Warburg

Reich, Wilhelm (1933) *The Mass Psychology of Fascism*. New York: Farrar, Straus and Giroux

Rowling, Joanne K (1997) *Harry Potter and the Philosopher's Stone*. London: Bloomsbury

Stiglitz, Joseph E (2002) *Globalization and Its Discontents*. New York: W.W. Norton

Also by Will Black

Psychopathic Cultures and Toxic Empires
Published by Frontline Noir 2015
ISBN 9781904684718